Thoughts Clothed in

Classical Rhetoric from a Biblical Worldview

Student Version

By Shaunna K. Howat and Tyler Howat

Second Edition

All that regards the study of eloquence and composition, merits the higher attention upon this account, that it is intimately connected with the improvement of our intellectual powers. For I must be allowed to say, that when we are employed, after a proper manner, in the study of composition, we are cultivating reason itself. True rhetoric and sound logic are very nearly allied. The study of arranging and expressing our thoughts with propriety, teaches to think as well as to speak accurately. By putting our sentiments into words, we always conceive them more distinctly. Every one who has the slightest acquaintance with composition knows, that when he expresses himself ill on any subject, when his arrangement is loose, and his sentences become feeble, the defects of his style can, almost on every occasion, be traced back to his indistinct conception of the subject: so close is the connexion between thoughts and the words in which they are clothed.[1]

– Hugh Blair

---

[1]   Hugh Blair, in Corbett, *The Rhetoric of Blair, Campbell and Whately*, 33

The challenge: Teach Rhetoric with a Biblical worldview to Southeast Asian students and prepare them to write a major thesis paper, and then deliver and defend it before peers, panel, and parents—in English, their second language! The resource you don't want to be without: Biblical Worldview Rhetoric by team Howat. The textbook is readable and replete with helpful exercises to guide your students on their journey.

Shaunna Howat *taught rhetoric, logic, apologetics, worldview, as well as journalism and drama in Christian schools, homeschool programs, and an online school for 24 years.*
She assisted in the development of Classical Christian programs, as well as conducting classical teacher-training workshops, in several educational settings.
She earned her Bachelor's Degrees in English Literature and Mass Communications. Shaunna and her husband live in Northern California and have three grown children, including her co-author.

Tyler Howat *holds Bachelor's Degrees in Literature and History, as well as a Master's in Literature.*
He also has over ten years of experience teaching writing, literature, worldview, logic, and rhetoric in online, international, and Classical Christian schools. He currently lives in central Washington where he writes both fiction and non-fiction, hosts a podcast, coaches Mock Trial, and teaches at a Classical Christian school.

Several authors from ancient to modern times have inspired and influenced the writing of this book, including Aristotle, Cicero, and Tertullian. George A. Kennedy collected and analyzed many of the ancient thinkers and writers in his *Classical Rhetoric and its Christian and Secular Tradition from Ancient to Modern Times*. Extremely helpful were Hugh Blair, George Campbell, and Richard Whately in their collected lectures edited by Edward PJ Corbett and James L. Golden. Corbett's *Classical Rhetoric for the Modern Student* (Third Edition), as well as Sharon Crowley and Debra Hawhee's *Ancient Rhetorics for Contemporary Students* (Second Edition) also played key roles in inspiring this writing.

This text differs from other "Classical Christian" Rhetoric texts in the respect that it received much help from Corbett, which is primarily a college text.

Thanks to Daniel Howat for his cover design.
Thanks to Kenna Howat Felix for bibliography assistance.

Shaunna K. Howat: howat.sk@gmail.com. Tyler Howat: howattp@gmail.com.

Please direct all questions, comments, and concerns to us at the above email addresses.

We highly recommend using the teacher text and the collection of discourses, called *The Art of Fitting Expression,* that accompany this book.

Table of Contents

Authors' notes:

[It] is true that copiousness and facility in expression bear abundant fruit, if controlled by proper knowledge and a strict discipline of the mind. (Cicero, *Ad Herennium*, Book 1)

The heavens declare the glory of God, and the sky above proclaims his handiwork. Day to day pours out speech, and night to night reveals knowledge. There is no speech, nor are there words, whose voice is not heard. Their voice goes out through all the earth, and their words to the end of the world. (*ESV* Psalm 19.1-4a)

The first edition of this text began in 1994, when I taught at a Christian school transitioning to Classical Christian (Tyler, the eldest of three Howat children, was eight years old at the time). An administrator asked me to design a rhetoric course. "What is rhetoric?" I asked. To which he replied, "I don't know. But I want you to research and design it." This has been a work in progress since then. Tyler caught the bug in high school, earned his Master's Degree in English Literature, and now teaches rhetoric and other courses in a Classical Christian school himself, and he has played a key role in enriching this text.

I do not claim to be the originator of the ideas herein; I have simply put a biblical worldview to this material and applied it to the teaching of Christian high school students. See our **Works Cited page** for other sources we have found valuable in assembling this text.

It must be acknowledged from the outset that this curriculum was not written by us alone. This was written with the daily inspiration of the Holy Spirit through God's word. I am bold enough to say this, because without submitting myself to His authorship, this could not have been completed. – *SKH*

It's strange to think about contributing to this edition, because I remember being in elementary school when my mother began writing what would eventually become this textbook.

Throughout this book, we hope that you'll see and feel our love for words, as that passion for words has steered our lives in myriad ways.

My own ardor for words may have come about through osmosis, or maybe from being read to at an early age, but it certainly accelerated as I picked up bigger and more difficult (and sometimes stranger) books, never being satiated, always looking for the next one. I have been enraptured by the impact of both the written and spoken word, not only in my life, but on the world as a whole, from the beginning of time, from the moment God *spoke* all things into existence.

What we have written here is an attempt to examine one of God's communicable attributes, not because mankind is impressive, impactful, or influential, but because he is. We want to worship him by reflecting those attributes and using them for His glory. – *TH*

How to Use this Text:

This text has been used by teachers in brick-and-mortar schools in classrooms around the world; in live, online courses; in homeschool extension programs; and one-on-one with parents or tutors sitting at the kitchen table. You can use this text as a standalone resource, assigning all or part of each week's work to your students. Supplement with discourses contained in the companion discourse collection *The Art of Fitting Expression (AFE)*. Where you have time, employ multimedia resources such as video, audio, photographic representations, etc.

The parent/teacher who decides to use this curriculum to teach his or her rhetoric course would be well-advised to prayerfully do the following:

- Submit himself to the inspiration of the Holy Spirit, through prayer and the reading of the Word, relying on Him to inspire where this curriculum may be lacking;

- Take part in some form of Classical Christian educational training, to be familiar with the methodology used (and if you don't have access to such training, become a consumer of classical education texts, some of which are listed in the next few pages and in our bibliography);

- Read as much as possible of primary sources: histories, essays, speeches, and letters (what we call discourses) written by historical figures and leaders;

- Learn as much as possible about the historical context in which these original documents were written;

- Take a course in formal syllogistic logic, including enthymemes, syllogisms, truth tables, the Laws of Thought, and fallacies.

Rhetoric is designed as a two-year course, for Juniors and Seniors (11th and 12th grades) in high school. Ideally a student entering rhetoric has had a complete grammar-school, junior high, and at least two years of high school education in English grammar and usage, a class in Logic, and (suggested) one year of Latin. A good understanding of world history is also important, as we study the background that leads up to, and gives the context for, the discourses we read. Students may consider taking a government class alongside, or at some point during, this two-year rhetoric course.

In order to prepare for university or post-high school, the student needs to **strengthen his or her writing ability**. A full background in English includes grammar, <u>academic</u> writing, and research techniques, with much reading of the classics all along. This course emphasizes academic writing skills while learning the Classical technique of rhetoric. If you take this course independently, without a writing instructor, please find a local or online writing tutor who will challenge your ability to write.

Wherever we have taught rhetoric, our students are required to take Logic before they complete the first quarter of rhetoric. They will either take it during summer school, or at home in a guided homeschool course, or in night-school sessions during the first quarter. They are also required to submit writing samples to prove their aptitude in English skills (if they come to us as new students who haven't gone through our English courses). These requirements may seem stiff, but the course of rhetoric is for those who are adequately prepared beforehand. Those not prepared will find it to be a difficult course.

We consider the first year of rhetoric to be consumed by learning Aristotle's Five Canons and applying what they learn to any of the discourses they study. The second year of rhetoric should be considered the "capstone" year. During that final year, students should study and practice public speaking and write/present/defend their large thesis project. (For more information on public speaking and thesis, SEE: Lesson 24 and following.)

Optional multimedia assignments have been included in this volume. Wherever possible, students should interact and argue with and about rhetorical concepts found in each lesson, related to the media they and their peers use. More than any other generation since Aristotle, our teenagers have the world at their fingertips via different types of media, and they should be given the tools with which/by which they should judge its use and application.

Parents of homeschooled students: Please check your student's notebook every few weeks to make sure he or she is taking notes from the weekly class, is highlighting important words or terms, and studying in advance of quizzes (available in the teacher version). ALSO make sure that you and your student review the graded assignments that come back from the teacher of this class. If your student is not making changes to future assignments based on teacher comments, he/she will not grow and progress as a student.

Homework Assignments: Some weeks will be too full to cover every assignment in every lesson. That's okay! Save some that look good, and reserve them for a lighter week.

Regarding our discourse book, *The Art of Fitting Expression* (hereafter known as *AFE*): Wherever we have not succeeded in obtaining reprint permission of a discourse (those not in public domain, or whose authors or estates refuse permission), we have provided some web addresses or hints you can use to find them online. We realize that links to documents may "die" or change over time, so we encourage you to "search smartly" and make sure that the discourse you find is reprinted in its entirety. That may mean you find two different sources and compare them.

Student Instructions

You are responsible for adhering to these instructions! Each lesson will be broken down into studies that will cover one week, unless otherwise noted. With the exception of the first week's lesson, one lesson usually covers a four- or five-day week. Students should spend at least one hour per day for four days each week.

1. **Take notes** as you study (this is called *Annotation*). When you come across new or difficult terms, stop to look them up. Therefore, keep a dictionary on hand as you study rhetoric (really, as you study anything at all). Keep a **vocabulary list** of the words you encounter, both in this textbook and in the discourses that you read for your assignments. Plan on being tested on some of those words each week or two.

   For further instruction on reading well and annotating books as you read them, look at *How to Read a Book* by Mortimer J. Adler, as well as his essay "How to Mark a Book," and *How to Read Slowly* by James W. Sire.

2. When instructed to write 2-3 **paragraphs** (or whatever length provided), this means you must write **in the form of an academic essay**. By "essay form" remember that we are talking about all the elements of well-constructed paragraphs, in which you explain the discourse, use a thesis, answer the questions, and provide examples (also known as *proofs*). "Proofs" include quotes with citations from the discourse we are studying. **Paragraphs** generally contain 5-12 well-written sentences. If a paragraph has more or less, you may well figure that it does not meet the requirements, and you must reevaluate and rewrite your paragraph. If you have never written an academic essay of less than the 5-paragraph model you learned sometime in early high school, then plan on having your paradigm challenged! You must still write an introductory sentence or two, a thesis, some support, and a concluding sentence or two.

3. When given just a **word count** (usually 250-500 words), you are not asked for a full academic essay format. This will be a quick (but meaty) argument that you will use to prepare for a classroom discussion. You will bring it with you to class to use in a debate or discussion.

4. Students are **graded** based on expressing complete thoughts (did you answer the question fully and accurately?) and use of the English language. By this point, students should not be locked in a constant struggle with punctuation or grammar rules: rhetoric is the stage beyond that, where we are taking those rules as assumptions and utilizing them stylistically and persuasively.

5. When this text refers to a **discourse**, that means a spoken or written body of work. This text could also refer to the piece as an oratory, an article, or an argument. A rhetorical piece could just as easily be called a discourse, an essay, a speech, etc.

6. Students must practice attentiveness as an audience to whoever is speaking. There is little understanding in a class whose students do not participate in the discussion. In other words, listen to the speaker, take notes, ask questions, and look for practical ways of applying what you are learning.

7. **Assignments written for this class must follow these requirements:** They must be typed in 12-point Times New Roman, with 1-inch margins all around. Your name, class name, teacher's name, and date must be in the upper left-hand side of the page (this is the heading). The title of the assignment (either by assignment number or by title of the discourse being analyzed) must be centered above the opening paragraph.

8. **Unless otherwise noted, assignments for this class must adhere to MLA (Modern Language Association) Guidelines.** (See Writing Tips–Introduction below.)

Discourses may not be the same in other collections. Please be aware that if you look for speeches elsewhere (online or in other books), the discourse titles we use in this book and in our companion book *The Art of Fitting Expression* (*AFE*) may not have been given the same titles in other collections. Similarly, some discourses may not appear to be the same. Some will be shortened, edited for length, or paragraphed differently. Some may not have been translated into English the same as what we have here. If you must use a different discourse format, be aware of these subtle differences.

Instructions for these lessons: When asked to read the material accompanying each lesson, read it more than once. The first time, read it just to become familiar with the language and tone. The second time, understand what is being said. In Edmund Burke's "Letter to a Noble Lord," for example, the language is complicated and rather difficult. Give yourself time to become accustomed to the high style of the diction. For each discourse, you will be given a small background of the author, including the times and the circumstances, wherever possible. After reading a discourse, there will be a brief discussion of how it applies to the type of discourse you are studying.

Abbreviations in this textbook:

Bibles:

ESV = English Standard Version

NASB = New American Standard

NIV = New International Version

Other frequently-used abbreviations:

TCW = *Thoughts Clothed in Words*, this textbook

AFE = *The Art of Fitting Expression*, the collection of discourses that accompanies this textbook

Why is this book subtitled Classical Rhetoric from a Biblical Worldview?

An essential aspect of this rhetoric text is <u>a study of worldview</u>. We will examine the worldviews behind the different discourses and their speakers or writers. Worldview is inextricable from rhetoric, for every man speaks from his worldview, even unconsciously. Once you begin to think in this manner, you will have a much more rich understanding of the use of rhetoric.

A "worldview" can be considered <u>the glasses through which we see the world–how we interpret and give context to what we see</u>. Everyone has a worldview, and every worldview is based on the philosophies to which we adhere. Matthew 6.22 says, "The eye is the lamp of the body. So if your eye is healthy, your whole body will be full of light, but if your eye is bad, your whole body will be full of darkness. If then the light in you is darkness, how great is the darkness!" (*ESV*). If our worldview, that window or glass through which we interpret the world, is clouded by deception, our thoughts will be polluted as well. That deception will affect everything about us.

A Biblical Worldview begins with the foundation–the understanding and the acknowledgment– that God is the author and creator of all things:

> He is the image of the invisible God, the firstborn of all creation. For by him all things were created, in heaven and on earth, visible and invisible, whether thrones or dominions or rulers or authorities–all things were created through him and for him. And he is before all things, and in him all things hold together. And he is the head of the body, the church. He is the beginning, the firstborn from the dead, that in everything he might be preeminent. For in him all the fullness of God was pleased to dwell, and through him to reconcile to himself all things, whether on earth or in heaven, making peace by the blood of his cross. And you, who once were alienated and hostile in mind, doing evil deeds, he has now reconciled in his body of flesh by his death, in order to present you holy and blameless and above reproach before him, if indeed you continue in the faith, stable and steadfast, not shifting from the hope of the gospel that you heard, which has been proclaimed in all creation under heaven, and of which I, Paul, became a minister. (*ESV*, Colossians 1.15-23)

Teaching with a biblical worldview does not just mean attaching a Bible verse to the week's lesson. It begins with the presupposition from Colossians, above. If God is the creator of all, and he holds all things together, does that affect the way we study the history, the people, the events? What drives men to do what they do? How do men react to the things that happen to them? How do they speak to and persuade one another? Take note of what sin does to the human mind, and how it drives people to act and react.

This kind of study means **thinking** *presuppositionally*–studying the underlying ideas that distort truth and deny biblical moral values. Everyone has a worldview, has presuppositions with which they think and act, whether or not they are consciously aware of those ideas. When we seek to persuade a person, we also must identify and address his set of presuppositions, his worldview. This kind of study will inform how best to address someone whose ideas differ from ours.

> For though we walk in the flesh, we are not waging war according to the flesh. For the weapons of our warfare are not of the flesh but have divine power to destroy strongholds. We destroy arguments and every lofty opinion raised against the knowledge of God, and take every thought captive to obey Christ, being ready to punish every disobedience, when your obedience is complete. (*ESV*, 2 Cor 10.3-6)

We must approach our neighbors–our audience–armed with the truth. And we must know the worldviews by which they operate. Nancy Pearcey regularly and fervently discusses the need for addressing people's worldviews before even discussing the Gospel:

Christians are called to tear down mental fortresses and liberate people from the power of false ideas. This process is sometimes called pre-evangelism because its purpose is to prepare people to hear and understand the gospel message. Once the walls are torn...down, then the message of salvation is the same for everyone–scientist or artist, educated or uneducated, urban or rural. (Pearcey, *Saving Leonardo* 15).

Ultimately, the goal of rhetoric is to bring people to the Lord, but it's not as simple as passing out tracts and reciting scripture at them. We must delve below the surface in order to get to the root of the problem, and as Dr. Michael Bauman of Hillsdale College says, "the problem of the human heart is at the heart of the human problem."[2] We know that the answers to all of humanity's deepest questions can be found in God's holy Word, by the inspiration of the Holy Spirit. In other words, *know the source of inspiration–the God of all Creation–and know your audience and how to address them.* Only then will we be able to engage with people on what ultimately matters most of all: the Gospel of Jesus Christ.

Suggested Readings on Worldview

- *How Should We Then Live?* by Francis Schaeffer
- *How Now Shall We Live?* by Charles Colson and Nancy Pearcey
- *Reading Between the Lines* by Gene Edward Veith
- *Saving Leonardo* by Nancy Pearcey
- *Total Truth* by Nancy Pearcey
- *Understanding the Times* by David Noebel
- *Battle for Truth* by David Noebel
- *Christianity and Liberalism* by J. Gresham Machen
- *Christ and Culture* by H. Richard Niebuhr
- *Art and the Bible* by Francis Schaeffer
- *Turning Point Christian Worldview Series*, ed. by Marvin Olasky:
  Turning Point: A Christian Worldview Declaration by Herbert Schlossberg
  Soul of Science by Nancy Pearcey and Charles B. Thaxton
  The Seductive Image by K.L. Billingsley
  State of the Arts by Gene Edward Veith
  Reading Between the Lines by Gene Edward Veith
  Beyond Good Intentions by Doug Bandow
  Freedom, Justice, and Hope by Marvin Olasky, Herbert Schlossberg, Pierre Berthoud, Clark H. Pinnock
  A World Without Tyranny: Christian Faith and International Politics by Dean C. Curry
  Recovering the Lost Tools of Learning by Doug Wilson
  All God's Children and Blue Suede Shoes by Gene Edward Veith
  Postmodern Times by Gene Edward Veith
- *Awakening Wonder: A Classical Guide to Truth, Goodness & Beauty* by Stephen R. Turley
- *The Universe Next Door* by James W. Sire

---

[2] "The Chronicle of an Undeception"–See *AFE*

Writing Tips Introduction

> Adopt the mindset of a careful student who observes and practices the requirements of his teachers. Precision is essential to good essay writing.

At the end of Lessons One through Fifteen, we have included a brief lesson devoted to your development as a writer. Take time to read and discuss, and most importantly, commit them to memory as you grow as a writer in this course.

Your teacher will provide you with an **Essay Checklist**. You must refer to this before submitting any essay to your teacher (in fact, your teacher may require that you turn in your essays along with the Checklist).

Using style guides

This text requires the use of Modern Language Association (MLA) as a style guide. We encourage you to *be aware of the style requirements on writing assignments in any course you take*. Be aware, too, that often two different teachers or professors may require two different style guides in the same semester, and it is up to you to know and adhere to those styles (other popular style guides include APA, Chicago, and Turabian, though many others exist). See Writing Tips Lesson One for more information on style guides.

For more information about MLA, purchase the newest version (new versions come out every four or five years). As of this edition of *TCW*, the best online source for MLA is Purdue's Online Writing Lab (OWL): https://owl.english.purdue.edu/. However, new sources and commentaries are always showing up, so please make sure to find a reputable resource (usually a university).

Correctly citing a quote:

Each time you provide a quote or use specific information from a source, you must also <u>provide a citation</u>. Include the source from your quote or specific information. MLA gives specific instructions on how this should look. A couple of examples are provided below.

When writing analyses for rhetoric, from a discourse your teacher has assigned, you only need to cite the paragraph number of the discourse: "They did not fight openly like soldiers. In all circumstances they were alone" (2). The parentheses contain the paragraph number from where the quote came. If the assignment solely concerns one discourse, all you need to provide is the paragraph number. Remember that the punctuation goes AFTER the citation.

When quoting from a source that is not the discourse assigned for homework, cite it correctly by providing the author's last name and page number, if from a book (Smith 24). If a website is your source, provide a shortened version of the website (www.fastweb.com). Note that the period is AFTER the citation in each of these examples. THEN at the end of your assignment, include the full bibliographical notation of the source on a separate page called "Works Cited."

Avoid dropping a citation into the middle of a sentence. To keep the sentence flowing smoothly, place the citation at the end of the sentence.

Lesson One

Introduction to Rhetoric

Between mediocrity and perfection, there is a very wide interval. There are many intermediate spaces, which may be filled up with honour; and the more rare and difficult that complete perfection is, the greater is the honour of approaching to it, though we do not fully attain it. (Hugh Blair qtd. in Corbett, *Rhetoric of Blair, Campbell, and Whately*, 128-129)

[It] is absurd to hold that a man ought to be ashamed of being unable to defend himself with his limbs, but not of being unable to defend himself with speech and reason, when the use of rational speech is more distinctive of a human being than the use of his limbs. And if it be objected that one who uses such power of speech unjustly might do great harm, that is a charge which may be made in common against all good things except virtue, and above all against the things that are most useful, as strength, health, wealth, generalship. A man can confer the greatest of benefits by a right use of these, and inflict the greatest of injuries by using them wrongly. (Aristotle, *The Rhetoric & The Poetics of Aristotle*)

Whether it's trying to convince others that something is more true, more virtuous, or more desirable–all communication is rhetoric in action. (Leonard Koren, *Arranging Things: A Rhetoric of Object Placement*)

Words—why do we study them? The word comes from God. He is the author of the spoken and written word. Read the following verses which include "word" in some way:

- In the beginning was the Word, and the Word was with God, and the Word was God. He was in the beginning with God. All things came into being through Him, and apart from Him nothing came into being that has come into being. In Him was life, and the life was the Light of men (*NASB*, John 1.1-4).

- And the Word became flesh, and dwelt among us, and we saw His glory, glory as of the only begotten from the Father, full of grace and truth (*NASB*, John 1.14).

- And he humbled you and let you hunger and fed you with manna, which you did not know, nor did your fathers know, that he might make you know that man does not live by bread alone, but man lives by every word that comes from the mouth of the Lord (*ESV*, Deuteronomy 8.3).

Read what God's word says about Samuel: "And Samuel grew, and the Lord was with him and let none of his words fall to the ground" (*ESV*, 1 Samuel 3.19). A commentary resource breaks down the verse into manageable chunks; see the emphasis on the value of words:

> **Samuel grew -** Increased to manhood.
>
> **The Lord was with him -** Teaching him, and filling him with grace and holiness.

None of his words fall - Whatever prediction he uttered, God fulfilled it; and his counsels were received as coming from the Lord.[3]

When God decides to use someone for his purposes, look at the value he places on words! Do you think he values Samuel's words as highly as His own? No! He values the words that he himself gave to Samuel to speak!

"WORD" occurs 651 times in the *NIV*; 323 times it comes in the phrase "the word of the Lord" or "the word of God." Obviously, the Lord placed great emphasis on "Word." He chose to communicate to us in the form of words—spoken and written. He chose to have his law recorded, and many times in the Bible His law was referred to as "word." So we choose to study the written word as well.

We know that the written word and the spoken word have power. They are the way in which God chose to communicate with us, so we know that they are important. Anyone who studies history can agree that words can be used to build up or tear down.

The Greek word is *logos*, indicating "first cause" in Greek philosophy. Before Plato begins his discussion of the tripartite soul in *Phaedrus*, he introduces an intriguing idea for a pagan:

> Now, the beginning is unbegotten, for that which is begotten has a beginning; but the beginning is begotten of nothing, for if it were begotten of something, then the begotten would not come from a beginning. But if unbegotten, it must also be indestructible; for if beginning were destroyed, there could be no beginning out of anything, nor anything out of a beginning; and all things must have a beginning.

> And therefore the self-moving is the beginning of motion; and this can neither be destroyed nor begotten, else the whole heavens and all creation would collapse and stand still, and never again have motion or birth.[4]

Here, Plato has reasoned himself–not to God, specifically–but to "an unbegotten beginning," or an "unmoved mover" whose name he did not know.[5] To Greeks, this indicated the great, unknown Intelligent Reason, Will, and Power behind the universe, which the pagans of that day, as well as ours, called "God." The beginning words of Genesis and John indicate that there was nothing before God Himself. In fact, God is infinite, meaning he has neither beginning nor end; he created the universe out of nothing (*ex nihilo*).

Moreover, Paul seems to agree with Plato's assertion that the Beginning (the first cause) is also responsible for the cohesion of the universe. By its very nature, whatever kickstarted the universe must be all-powerful and therefore responsible for holding everything together. "For by him all things were created, in heaven and on earth, visible and invisible, whether thrones or dominions or rulers or authorities—all things were created through him and for him. And he is before all things, and in him all things hold together."[6] In no way do we claim that Plato was a Christian, only that even the classical Greek philosophers–pagans, all–recognized the underlying *logos* at the heart of our universe and employed a fallen form of it in their writings. Paul knew of these philosophers, having

---

[3]   Clarke, Adam. "Commentary on 1 Samuel 3.4". "The Adam Clarke Commentary". https://www.studylight.org/commentaries/acc/1-samuel-3.html. 1832.

[4]   http://classics.mit.edu/Plato/phaedrus.html

[5]   Aristotle. *Metaphysics*. http://classics.mit.edu/Aristotle/metaphysics.12.xii.html, 12.7

[6]   *ESV*, Colossians 1.16-17

studied rhetoric himself. He exemplifies the way that a Christian must redeem and use these tools to the glory of God, for knowing these things, we "are without excuse."[7]

John used this reference of *logos*, infinite wisdom, which helped the Greeks understand the Hebrew concept of God. Here he also gave the Hebrews a way of understanding that God the Creator embodies infinite *wisdom,* as in Proverbs 8.22-31. Read what Wisdom says (and marvel at the beautiful choices of words and phrases to paint the picture!):

> The Lord possessed me [wisdom] at the beginning of his work, the first of his acts of old. Ages ago I was set up, at the first, before the beginning of the earth. When there were no depths I was brought forth, when there were no springs abounding with water. Before the mountains had been shaped, before the hills, I was brought forth, before he had made the earth with its fields, or the first of the dust of the world. When he established the heavens, I was there; when he drew a circle on the face of the deep, when he made firm the skies above, when he established the fountains of the deep, when he assigned to the sea its limit, so that the waters might not transgress his command, when he marked out the foundations of the earth, then I was beside him, like a master workman, and I was daily his delight, rejoicing before him always, rejoicing in his inhabited world and delighting in the children of man. (*ESV*)

Not only does WORD imply wisdom, it is also John's word for Jesus. And if you think about it for very long, you will be amazed at how perfect this is. For the Hebrew mind, knowing that WORD is the reference for God's wisdom and law, and that when God's WORD is spoken great things happen, to understand that Jesus is the WORD is to understand that JESUS IS GOD, the Christ.

In the beginning was the WORD. The WORD of the Lord came (255 times in the *NIV* –in reference to prophecy). The WORD of the Lord is the source of wisdom. "For the word of the LORD is upright, and all his work is done in faithfulness... For he spoke, and it came to be; he commanded, and it stood firm" (*ESV*, Ps 33.4, 9).

Now that we know and understand the Source of all WORDS, and the WORD Himself, let's begin a course that studies words and how they are put together to be understood, how they enlighten and encourage, and how they tear down and wage war.

---

[7]   *ESV*, Romans 1.20

What is Rhetoric?

Rhetoric covers a vast area of study, and therefore we find it necessary to break up its definition. Rhetoric is an ancient study of words and persuasive communication. As long ago as Aristotle, who lived from 384-322 BC, rhetoric has been studied as an art—taken apart, analyzed, and practiced. It has thrived since then, used in speech and in writing over the ages.

Aristotle stated that the purpose of rhetoric may be said "to discern the real and the apparent means of persuasion."[8] It is a partner with the Logic (Dialectic) stage of learning, both building upon and utilizing it. Furthermore, rhetoric is a universal aspect of the human condition, for "all men make use, more or less, of both" logic and rhetoric; even "[o]rdinary people do this either at random or through practice and an acquired habit."[9] All the more reason this should be studied and honed as an art, so that this daily practice of rhetorical engagement can be properly harnessed.

Plato, in perhaps a more whimsical–or at least a more artful–manner, says that rhetoric is the "art of enchanting the soul."[10] It isn't about beating someone with words until they submit with a cry of "uncle," but about convincing them through a balance of emotion, reason, and morality, using words to draw someone in to comfort them, reassuring an audience that their leader will protect them, leading a jury to proclaim someone's innocence or guilt, or honoring the lifetime achievement of a great person who has passed away. We enchant the soul with rhetoric. It is a mighty power, and when used correctly can be a great assent, but when abused it can lead to significant harm. We can see examples of both throughout this textbook.

Quintilian, another ancient rhetorician, commented that "The definition which best suits its real character is that which makes rhetoric the science of speaking well." Moreover, Quintilian spends a good amount of time, particularly in Book 12 of his *Institutes of Oratory*, expounding upon the need for ethics in a speaker. He refers to Cato the Elder's definition of an orator, which called for "a good man skilled in speaking."[11] However, he feels compelled to emphasize the *ethos* of Cato's definition, for "it is intrinsically more significant and important–let him at all events be 'a good man.'"[12] Therefore, we would characterize rhetoric as *the art and science of writing and speaking skillfully and virtuously*.

Notice that this definition contains all three appeals: the art (*pathos*) and science of speaking skillfully (*logos*) and virtuously (*ethos*). Rhetoric balances the application of the appeals in convincing others in the proper manner.

Today we need to take up this ancient art form and apply it not only in our education, but also in our lives, our careers, and most importantly in our effective witness to both believers and non-believers. We can take advantage of the practice from old days, and use it to advance God's kingdom. It is necessary to present the word—written or oral—in the best light and with the purest, most straightforward and logical structure.

---

[8] http://rhetoric.eserver.org/aristotle/rhet1-1.html

[9] *Rhetoric* 95

[10] http://www.americanrhetoric.com/rhetoricdefinitions.htm

[11] Quintilian 12.1, 197

[12] ibid.

Rhetoric and its uses

Rhetoric is also defined as <u>the study of written and oral communications and the art and science of persuasion</u>. The study of rhetoric contains the form of writing as well as the art. The following quotation from Hugh Blair says it quite well.

> All that regards the study of eloquence and composition, merits the higher attention upon this account, that it is intimately connected with the improvement of our intellectual powers. For I must be allowed to say, that when we are employed, after a proper manner, in the study of composition, we are cultivating reason itself. True rhetoric and sound logic are very nearly allied. The study of arranging and expressing our thoughts with propriety, teaches to think as well as to speak accurately. By putting our sentiments into words, we always conceive them more distinctly. Every one who has the slightest acquaintance with composition knows, that when he expresses himself ill on any subject, when his arrangement is loose, and his sentences become feeble, the defects of his style can, almost on every occasion, be traced back to his indistinct conception of the subject: so close is the connexion between thoughts and the words in which they are clothed.[13]

This extract was written long ago, when words and sentences were more complex and flowery than those with which we are familiar today. Students will find it difficult to read at first, but once someone's "ear" is accustomed to the language, the words will flow quite nicely. This is only the first of many such passages we use in this textbook.

Rhetoric is used to beautify truth and justice (style). It must communicate complex matters to the ignorant or uninformed (persuasion). Rhetoric teaches how to discover poor arguments in others and avoid them (reason). Rhetoric may be used for self-defense (persuasion). Aristotle reasoned that the inability to defend himself physically is disgraceful; how much more so is the inability to defend himself verbally, since speech is more natural to man than a strong body?

Rhetoric also makes use of the three major **appeals**: *logos, pathos,* and *ethos.* According to Aristotle, we persuade others by three means: 1. by appealing to their reason (*logos*); 2. by appealing to their emotions (*pathos*); 3. by appealing with our personality or character (*ethos*). One, two, or all three of these methods can and should be used in one discourse.

Quintilian's doctrine of virtue declares the necessity of *ethos.* Ethics, he reasoned, are inseparable from rhetoric: "Finally *ethos* in all its forms requires the speaker to be a man of good character and courtesy."[14] Thus according to him, an immoral man, no matter how eloquent, is not a true rhetorician.[15]

One question persistently arose from the time of the early Christian church and still begs to be answered today. Should Christians study something from a pagan source? Tertullian, one of the early Church Fathers, asked his persistent question:

"Quid ergo Athenis et Hierosolymis? quid academiae et ecclesiae? quid haereticis et christianis?"[16]

"What indeed has Athens to do with Jerusalem? What concord is there between the Academy and the Church? What between heretics and Christians?"[17]

---

[13]   Blair, in Corbett, *The Rhetoric of Blair, Campbell and Whately,* 33

[14]   http://penelope.uchicago.edu/Thayer/E/Roman/Texts/Quintilian/Institutio_Oratoria/6B*.html

[15]   See Quintilian's discussion on ethics and morality in Institutio Oratoria Book X11 Chapter 2

[16]   Tertullian, *De praescriptione haereticorum,* VII

[17]   Holmes, http://www.tertullian.org/anf/anf03/anf03-24.htm

St. Augustine, a student of rhetoric, defended its study. During his day, as well as today, critics have questioned why a Christian would study an art devised by pagans. "Should the Christian study pagan writing? Yes. 'We should not think that we ought not to learn literature because Mercury is said to be its inventor.'...The Christian has every right to take true ideas from the Platonists and transfer them as 'Egyptian gold.'"[18] Heathens, Augustine reasoned, discovered much of what is true. They discovered truth, but they did not always recognize God as the author of truth. As Moses was educated in Egypt, and Paul a Roman citizen trained as a pharisee, so might Christians profit from observing what wisdom could be found from heathens. Christian students of rhetoric must first be grounded in the truth in order to discern superstition from truth. As the Israelites plundered the Egyptians in the Exodus, Augustine implies, so must Christians appropriate for themselves the truths learned from heathens.

In much of modernity, however, rhetoric has come to mean exaggerated speaking for effect or political doubletalk. Even in centuries past, John Locke abjured it in Volume Two of *An Essay Concerning Human Understanding*: "It is evident how much men love to deceive and be deceived, since rhetoric, that powerful instrument of error and deceit, has its established professors, is publicly taught, and has always been had in great reputation."[19] Rhetoric is a tool for persuasion. Used unethically, it can be dangerous. Used correctly, it can bring about great good. In either case, it is important for students to be able to identify, analyze, and understand rhetoric in all its forms so that they will neither be caught unawares and swayed in an unfortunate direction, nor will they misuse it themselves and be guilty of unethical persuasion. As Christians, we must particularly be on our guard not to betray our *ethos*, for we are always ambassadors for Christ.

Why Study Rhetoric?

> Discourse ought always to be obvious, even to the most careless and negligent hearer: so that the sense shall strike his mind, as the light of the sun does our eyes, though they are not directed upwards to it. We must study not only that every hearer may understand us, but that it shall be impossible for him not to understand us.[20]

Rhetoric is everywhere, used by everyone. Everything contains rhetoric: from advertisements to t-shirts to music to movies and television and social media, as well as courtrooms, campaign speeches, and legislative assemblies. It is both vivid and obscure, in turns benign and insidious. Furthermore, it is no longer relegated to the verbal and written forms. Visual Rhetoric has exploded in the last century, surrounding us and drawing us in with neon lights and HD screens, and we must not sit idly by, letting ourselves be indoctrinated. We must take a stand, exercising our minds to recognize the things around us that are subtly attempting to convince us. This study will prepare us to perceive and respond critically to the rhetorical efforts of others in the oral, written, and visual forms. By dissecting and analyzing others' arguments and discourses, we can be better readers and discerners of truth. By imitating their art, we can become better rhetoricians.

---

[18]   Kennedy, quoting and paraphrasing Augustine's *De Doctrina Christiana*, *Classical Rhetoric and its Christian and Secular Tradition*, 154

[19]   Locke, http://www.gutenberg.org/cache/epub/10616/pg10616.html

[20]   Blair quoting Quintilian: Corbett, *The Rhetoric of Blair, Campbell, and Whately*, 67

First and foremost, the Christian speaker/writer must be solidly grounded in Christian doctrine. What are our basic beliefs? If we do not know, then we will fall prey to every manner of idea that comes our way.

The study of rhetoric will help us to respond critically and wisely to advertisements, commercials, pop culture, political messages, satires, irony, and doublespeak of all varieties. It will, in the end, assist us in becoming more effective writers and communicators.

The purpose of studying speech

During the course of Rhetoric, we will study the techniques of speech. The purpose of speech is always to rouse your audience, to secure a reaction. Some speakers do not seem to want any defined response from their audiences. Some speakers fail to elicit the response they desire. But behind nearly every discourse, unless it is given purely for entertainment, the speaker or writer intends to have his listener(s) follow a certain course of action.

In Summary, Lesson 1:

- Several descriptions of rhetoric, all culminating in one overarching definition: the art and science of writing and speaking skillfully and virtuously
- Three major appeals: *logos* (logic), *ethos* (ethics), and *pathos* (emotion)
- By studying the rhetoric of others, and thinking presuppositionally, we can become better readers and discerners of truth.
- This study will help us become more effective writers and communicators

Terms to Remember:[21]

- Virtuous
- *Ex nihilo*
- *Logos*
- *Ethos*
- *Pathos*
- Presupposition

---

[21] Avoid equivocation! **Remember** that any vocabulary word we cover in this text will <u>necessarily</u> be related to rhetoric. Some words we study will have different meanings in different contexts, but we will always concern ourselves with the context of rhetoric.

Lesson One Assignments

Assignment 1.1

What is the significance of the written word to the Christian? Talk about how God chose to communicate to us, and how He means for us to communicate as well. Use scripture. Three paragraphs. Include a thesis statement.

Assignment 1.2

Knowing just a very little bit about rhetoric, describe your goal for this school year in rhetoric (one to two paragraphs). Add two more paragraphs about yourself, your interests, and your educational background.

Assignment 1.3

What sorts of communications are acceptable today among contemporary audiences? Why/how can an immoral public figure get a wide audience today? Consider as an example certain politicians, actors or singers/rappers who have engaged in immoral acts. Three paragraphs with a thesis.

Assignment 1.4

Go to a major news network's website (ex: *BBC, New York Times, FOX News, CNN*) and look through the stories on the main page. Then write your first persuasive writing assignment of the Rhetoric year. Write a blog post (250-300 words) about something of a timely nature in the news today, using the site your teacher may have set up for this purpose (or the site you have chosen to use). Your teacher may also require you to turn in a copy for grading purposes.

Multimedia Focus 1.5

Take a walk or a drive around your town or city. Find the most noticeable piece of advertising (billboards, posters, viral marketing) you can, take a picture of it, and bring it into class.
<u>Before you come to class, answer the following</u>: What is the advertisement trying to say? Is it being subtle or overt? Which of the three appeals (*pathos, ethos, logos*) are used here? 250 words.

Writing Tips Lesson One

Standards and Styles

Every institute of higher learning uses a style manual. Every major employer requires its employees to adhere to certain styles when communicating with clients.

Thus the necessity of adhering to a style when writing and communicating. Make sure you follow a style manual for every writing assignment. Some commonly used style manuals include the Modern Language Association (www.mla.org), Chicago Style Manual (www.chicagomanualofstyle.org), Gregg's Reference Guide (www.gregg.com), and more. Each of them will tell the writer how to handle terms, punctuation, common phrases and titles, bibliography, citations, etc.

If you study this course independently and do not have a style manual, please find one right away. Use it. Get accustomed to its requirements.

The style manual for this course is based on MLA. Here are the very basic (not all-inclusive) expectations used by many teachers who use MLA.

Homework

- Typed in 12 pt. Times New Roman.

- Margins: 1 inch all around.

- Type: double space.

- Paragraphs: No extra space between paragraphs. Indent the first line of each paragraph ½ inch.

- Paragraphs: 5-12 sentences per paragraph.[22]

- Header: Top left corner of the page: Name, date, and assignment title, each on a separate line. Double space these as well.

- Assignment titles: Each homework lesson is titled with an Assignment Number, so title them accordingly. For example, the first assignment here is Assignment 1.1. Give it that title in the Header. There is no need to provide another title unless your teacher requires it.

- Use citations after a quotation. Refer to MLA for citation rules. This includes a "Works Cited" list at the end of your assignment.

- EXCEPTIONS to the MLA citation rule:
    - When quoting from a discourse we are all reading for an assignment, ALL you need to do is cite the PARAGRAPH NUMBER in parentheses after the quote.
    - There is no need for a "Works Cited" list if the discourse you're using is found in the accompanying *The Art of Fitting Expression* discourse book (*AFE*). Use full citation and Works Cited rules when you quote from any source OTHER THAN an assigned discourse. For example, if you quote from paragraph four of Winston Churchill's "Blood, Toil, Tears and Sweat" speech, your citation would look like this: (4).

---

[22]   If you see that the minimum number of sentences per paragraph is five, and you ONLY write the minimum every time, your writing ability will not improve much. If you only give your teacher five sentences, those five sentences should be the BEST you've ever written! You should write enough.

- Discourse titles are placed in "quotation marks." Book titles are *italicized*.

Miscellaneous Writing Tips

Make a habit of including the **discourse's author/speaker, the date of the discourse, and its title early in your first paragraph**.

How do we treat discourse titles? Since they are shorter bodies of written work, place them in quotation marks, NOT italics.

When writing an essay that answers a prompt you have been given, be sure to include at least one quote in every body paragraph. Get into the habit of **proving your thesis** by showing proof—that is, by showing how the discourse's author does what you say.

Lesson Two

The Objective and the Subjective

But though the method be not laid down in form, no discourse, of any length, should be without method; that is, every thing should be found in its proper place. Every one who speaks, will find it of the greatest advantage to himself to have previously arranged his thoughts, and classed under proper heads, in his own mind, what he is to deliver. This will assist his memory, and carry him through his discourse without that confusion to which one is every moment subject who has fixed no distinct plan of what he is to say. And with respect to the hearers, order in discourse is absolutely necessary for making any proper impression. It adds both force and light to what is said. It makes them accompany the speaker easily and readily, as he goes along; and makes them feel the full effect of every argument which he employs. Few things, therefore, deserve more to be attended to, than distinct arrangement; for eloquence, however great, can never produce entire conviction without it. (Hugh Blair, qtd in Corbett, *The Rhetoric of Blair, Campbell, and Whately*, 102)

Before delivering a speech (or writing a discourse), the speaker undertakes many considerations, two of which are the **Objective and the Subjective.**

The Objective is the Audience. Analyze your audience; know how it should be approached. View the topic through the eyes of the audience you propose to address (practical psychology). Who is your audience? What is their general makeup? Are they believers, non-believers, men, women, old, young, affluent, poor, uneducated? Will they be hostile to you or your subject? Are they judging your speech-giving abilities (as in a scholarship contest or speech-debate club)? Your discourse will obviously be aimed at your audience, so you must keep their needs and understandings in mind as you write.

<u>**Know your audience and address them in the way they will understand you.**</u>

Keep in mind that Christians often fall into the habit of using "*Christianese*" with one another—language that doesn't make much sense to people who don't attend church. For example, talking to non-believers (especially those unfamiliar with Christianity) about Christ rising from the dead without providing the proper, glorious context will make it sound like we worship a zombie, one of the undead. Consider the liturgy of the last supper:

> For I received from the Lord what I also delivered to you, that the Lord Jesus on the night when he was betrayed took bread, and when he had given thanks, he broke it, and said, "This is my body, which is for you. Do this in remembrance of me." In the same way also he took the cup, after supper, saying, "This cup is the new covenant in my blood. Do this, as often as you drink it, in remembrance of me." For as often as you eat this bread and drink the cup, you proclaim the Lord's death until he comes. (*ESV*, 1 Corinthians 11.23-26)

This ceremony that churches around the world practice regularly would sound cannibalistic to outsiders. We're habitually drinking the blood of the person we call our Saviour?

The hyperbole we have used here illustrates that language can be exclusive, and one who seeks to persuade must be aware of the terms he uses, must always know his audience so that he will not alienate them, losing his point in the vocabulary. This habitual use of what we call Christianese, while normal amongst Christians, will make unbelievers uncomfortable. Your discourse will need to use language that invites the audience to hear (read) your message and not immediately turn them off. Write in a compelling manner to those outside of the church. In the context of your academic classes, avoid using those words and phrases with which people outside the church will not be familiar. Understand us here: we are not telling you to be ashamed of the Gospel or your faith. However, do not let ambiguous or difficult vocabulary get in the way of the clarity of your message.

What words and phrases can you identify in your Christianese or in the "churchy" language other people use?

The Subjective is the Ability within yourself to achieve the desired result of arousing a response. It is what God has planted inside you that enables you to speak or write. Of course, the ancient world did not credit God for the gift of *any* ability. We understand, though, that we depend on God for those abilities. We believe that "in Him we live and move and have our being."[23] With that firmly in mind, we can see what some of the ancient rhetoricians say about the Subjective.

> [Isocrates'] views are that one must start with native ability, which training can sharpen, but not create. There are in fact three elements in successful oratory–and these remain permanent features of classical rhetorical theory–nature, training, and practice. It is the function of the teacher to explain the principles of rhetoric and also to set an example of oratory on which students can pattern themselves. Isocrates calls this training "philosophy" or pursuit of wisdom, by which he means chiefly a practical wisdom useful to men. A very important factor in it, in his judgment, is moral character; that cannot be taught, he says, but the study of speech and of politics can help to encourage and train moral consciousness.[24]

We know that we cannot boast of anything but what Christ has done in us and through us. With that said, we also know that we have been given gifts and talents that God will use for his glory. As you ponder on that, can you name some gifts and talents with which you have been blessed, that will enable you to speak or write well?

Be aware of the way you write! If you write how you talk, your audience may have much to criticize. Writing informally in the context of this rhetoric class will work against you. Academic writing demands a more formal voice. Imagine writing how you speak. Could you get by with so many uses of "like" and "um" you say in the course of a day? (We will get to that part of your speaking/delivering later in this book. For now, we would like you to focus on making your writing fit the occasion and the audience.)

You want to know your audience so that you can direct your writing or speeches to that audience. If you are speaking to a kindergarten class, you're not going to use high, florid language. Likewise, if you're speaking to an audience of university graduates, you don't want to use low diction.

---

[23] *ESV*, Acts 17.28

[24] Kennedy, 32

In Summary, Lesson 2:

- The Objective is the audience. Know your audience!
- The Subjective is the skills and knowledge you bring to your writing.

Terms to Remember:

- Eloquence
- Hyperbole

Lesson Two Assignments

Assignment 2.1

Refer to the quote by Hugh Blair at the beginning of this lesson. Rewrite it in your own words. Try to keep the syntax (sentence structure) the same as his. Use a dictionary or thesaurus, if you need to. This practice allows you to comprehend the meaning of discourses written in more formal language than we are accustomed to. Hugh Blair was an 18th century Scottish pastor and rhetorician. He taught at a university, commenting extensively on the study of rhetoric. You will encounter his words often during the course of this study; it is appropriate that we start here with an assignment in which you must interpret his words regarding rhetoric.

Assignment 2.2

Try to describe what relevance Blair's quote has on our own studies of rhetoric. Could this old guy from Scotland just be saying a lot of empty words? Why or why not? Two to three paragraphs. When developing your answer, consider this question: What is the proper use of rhetoric?

Assignment 2.3

Read Paul's delivery of testimony to the synagogue in Antioch from Acts 13:13-52, and his testimony to King Agrippa in Acts 26:1-31. Compare and contrast these two testimonies regarding a) Paul's understanding of his two different audiences, and b) his use of appeals (*ethos, pathos, logos*). (This will take 5-6 paragraphs. Answer this one carefully.)

Assignment 2.4

Respond to a recent news event your teacher brings up to you, or you have discovered in the news with your parents. Write a 500-word (plus or minus 50 words) opinion piece in response. Be persuasive. Use examples to support your point. As always, be polite. Turn it in or post it to the forum as your teacher directs.

Writing Tips Lesson Two

Passive Versus Active Voice

When writing, pay attention to the kinds of words used. Active verbs move the reader along. Passive verbs and phrases just sit still. A reader gets bored with passive word usage, so the writer must make his writing more interesting to his reader. That's his job.

We will first attack the dreaded "be-verb."

The "verb of being" consists of the following words: is, am, are, was, were, be, been, and (sometimes) being.

Limit yourself to just one be-verb per paragraph. If paragraphs contain 5-12 sentences each, then the writer is challenged to find a variety of words to say the same things. For example:

LACKADAISICAL
He was the first man to be elected president of the United States.
(contains two be-verbs)

BETTER:
He became the first president of the United States.
(no be-verbs, but "became" is still a passive verb)

BEST:
Americans elected him the first president of the United States.
(no be-verbs, more active verb)

This takes much more work and thought. When writing, a student may tend to get bogged down in avoiding be-verbs, and a writing project may take him a very long time. We advise our students to simply write, *then* go back over their work and rewrite or edit. The process of finally writing well will become part of their nature.

Pay attention to the words you use to replace be-verbs. Some students have decided that "exist" and "subsist" would make suitable replacements for verbs of being. In some cases we have forbidden these "inventive" students to use those replacement words! Their writing became as boring as before when they thought they had the ideal replacements (and they were surprised that we caught their "magical" formula!).

Overly Wordy Phrases

Become an expert at finding and removing phrases or sentences that are too wordy. If you said it in 15 words, why not try to say it in 10? Remember that when given a word limit in an assignment, it is bad practice to "fluff" your sentences by padding them with unnecessary words.

For Example:

Overly wordy: The reason why is because…

Better: Because

Overly wordy: I bring all of this up to say that people who care about their government should vote!

Better: People who care about their government should vote!

Integrating quotes

A very important part of supporting your own arguments in your discourse is bringing in outside sources: quotes. In order to smoothly integrate quotes in your essays, you must adhere to some standardized methods. Check out the resources here:

http://faculty.tamu-commerce.edu/scarter/integrating_quotes.ht
http://jerz.setonhill.edu/writing/academic/sources/integrating.ht

The websites above provide excellent advice on smoothly integrating quotes into your writing. Writers must walk a fine line between plagiarism, quoting, and rewording. Decide what you will do and when. If you want to reword information into your own words, make sure you don't get anywhere close to plagiarism.

If you decide to integrate a quote into your text, make a smooth move from your words to the quote. Introduce the quote well. Finish it well, also. NEVER begin or end a paragraph with a quote! Surround a quote with your own words. We call that "bookending" a quote—surrounding it with your own words.

Remember that a quote, a reference to a source, or borrowing/rewording information from a source needs to be correctly and consistently cited. Refer to MLA for citation information.

Briefly, after the quote include the author's name, title of the work and page number in parentheses. If it is a website, put the author and web address in parentheses. Follow the punctuation rules exactly. (SEE: "Citations" writing tip in Lesson 1.)

Please note that the above websites are provided only to give you advice and general help. Follow citation rules from MLA, and be aware that every few years MLA updates its manual. You should expect this and be prepared to purchase each new version as it comes out.

Lesson Three

The Five Canons of Rhetoric

And as I have been, as I say, considering all this for some time, reason itself especially induces me to think that wisdom without eloquence is but of little advantage to states, but that eloquence without wisdom is often most mischievous, and is never advantageous to them. (Cicero, *De Inventione*)

That since all the business and art of an orator is divided into five parts, he ought first to find out what he should say; next, to dispose and arrange his matter, not only in a certain order, but with a sort of power and judgment; then to clothe and deck his thoughts with language; then to secure them in his memory; and lastly, to deliver them with dignity and grace. (Cicero, *De Oratore* 1.31.142)

In class, look up the meaning of *canon*. Choose the one that is most pertinent to rhetoric. How could rhetoric have canons?

The Five Canons of Rhetoric are *Invention, Arrangement, Style, Memory,* and *Delivery*. We will refer to these canons throughout the rest of this textbook.

The First Canon: Invention *(inventio)* - Discovery, or invention, is a method for finding arguments.

The writer/speaker can talk about virtually anything, but he must first use research to find arguments to support his point of view. Invention, as it is used here, is a method for finding topics or arguments. Two means of persuasion are available to the speaker: *non-artistic* and *artistic*. The artistic proofs will be covered more in-depth later in rhetoric (SEE: Lessons 13-16 for the three methods of persuasion: *Logos, Ethos,* and *Pathos,* and Lesson 6 for Invention). We will just touch on them for right now.

Non-artistic or *non-technical arguments* (Aristotle called them proofs[25])—discover material to support your argument. These support your argument. They are primarily used in judicial arguments and presentations. They do not need to be invented; they already exist. They are:

- Laws
- Witnesses
- Contracts
- Tortures [26]

---

[25] Think of *proofs* in rhetoric just as you would think of them in math. Proofs are the means by which a rhetorician argues (proves) his point.

- Oaths

On the subject of proofs obtained through torture, Cicero says this:

> We shall speak in favour of the testimony given under torture when we show that it was in order to discover the truth that our ancestors wished investigations to make use of torture and the rack, and that men are compelled by violent pain to tell all they know. Moreover, such reasoning will have the greater force if we give the confessions elicited under torture an appearance of plausibility by the same argumentative procedure as is used in treating any question of fact. And this, too, we shall have to do with the evidence of witnesses. Against the testimony given under torture we shall speak as follows: In the first place, our ancestors wished inquisitions to be introduced only in connection with unambiguous matters, when the true statement in the inquisition could be recognized and the false reply refuted; for example, if they sought to learn in what place some object was put, or if there was in question something like that which could be seen, or be verified by means of footprints, or be perceived by some like sign. We then shall say that pain ought not to be relied upon, because one person is less exhausted by pain, or more resourceful in fabrication, than another, and also because it is often possible to know or divine what the presiding justice wishes to hear, and the witness knows that when he has said this his pain will be at an end. Such reasoning will find favour, if, by a plausible argument, we refute the statements made in the testimony given under torture…[27]

Aristotle notes that tortures are used, but he isn't convinced that they should be fully relied upon: "We must say that evidence under torture is not trustworthy, the fact being that many men whether thick-witted, tough-skinned, or stout of heart endure their ordeal nobly, while cowards and timid men are full of boldness till they see the ordeal of these others: so that no trust can be placed in evidence under torture."[28] It seems oddly barbaric to list torture as a means of obtaining proofs. The issue arises many times throughout history, and even in this century it is a topic of debate.

Artistic proofs persuade others by three means, which are covered by the category of rhetoric. We will cover these more in-depth. They are as follows:

- **Rational appeal** (*logos*)—appeal to reason. We learned in Logic that we can draw conclusions from affirmative or negative statements (syllogism), or by observing several pieces of data.

- **Emotional appeal** (*pathos*)—appeal to the audience's emotions to persuade. The rhetorician decides whether to use tears, or anger, or patriotism (or any other effective emotions) to sway his audience.

- **Ethical appeal** (*ethos*)—persuasion arises out of the speaker's character. The speaker or writer will communicate his virtue to the audience, thereby promoting good will toward himself. The speaker/writer could be the most skilled, but if he were not ethical (or did not appear to be ethical) his efforts to persuade would be fruitless.

---

[26]   Cicero's *Ad Herennium* describes the use of tortures as if they were a normal part of gathering evidence. Perhaps during those days, an extraction of evidence by means of torture was commonplace and was considered irrefutable. Testimony of a slave against his master was not allowed in court unless it was obtained through torture. (Kennedy, p. 27)

[27]   http://penelope.uchicago.edu/Thayer/E/Roman/Texts/Rhetorica_ad_Herennium/2*.html

[28]   http://rhetoric.eserver.org/aristotle/rhet1-15.html#1375b

Classical rhetoricians used the **Topics** to assist them in finding subjects for the three methods of appeal. Topics are the <u>methods of argumentation</u> used by a rhetorician. Aristotle spent quite a lot of time discussing different ways to search out a subject and then presenting and fleshing it out. There are two kinds of topics:

1. *The special topics*—those arguments used in certain types of discourse (such as closing arguments used exclusively in the law courts, or certain types of ceremonial speeches such as funerals or weddings).

2. *The common topics*—those used for any occasion or type of speech (such as graduation, political speeches, and so forth). For example, a politician or speaker who tours the country to speak to different audiences is not going to rewrite a new speech for each city he visits. He has a common topic—one we might call generic—that he (or his speech writer) pulls up on his computer screen, edits to fit his next audience, perhaps, and then presents his speech. Common topics can take one of the following forms:

   ◆ More or less (topic of degree)

   ◆ The possible and the impossible

   ◆ Past fact and future fact

   ◆ Greatness and smallness (the topic of size as distinguished from the topic of degree)

We will expand upon the topics later in this text.

The Second Canon: Arrangement—*(dispositio)*, **or organization,** is the systematic order or organization of the parts of a discourse (SEE: Lesson 7 for a more in-depth discussion of Arrangement). The traditional thesis-driven (persuasive) essay has three parts: Intro, Body, Conclusion. Aristotle's canon follows the same general format; it just expands the definition of the body by splitting it into three parts, giving a discourse five total parts, instead of three.

- Introduction (*exordium*)

- Statement of facts (*narratio*)

- Proof of the case (*confirmatio*)

- Refutation (*confutatio*)

- Conclusion (*peroratio*)

The Third Canon: Style *(elocutio)* is the adaptation of suitable words and sentences to the matter. This, therefore, involves both *diction* and *syntax*. Here we have mastered Invention and Arrangement, and now we are ready to make the words flow beautifully. This is where we examine a writer's use of language and ask ourselves, "Why did he choose the words he did?" "How did this communicate tone to the reader?"

Style usually falls into one of these three categories:

- <u>Low or plain style</u> (*attenuata*, *subtile*), for instructing–more often what rhetoricians declared to be fitting for uneducated audiences

- <u>Middle or forcible style</u> (*mediocris*) for moving the reader or listener, and often suitable for the average audience.

- <u>High or florid style</u> (*gravis, florida*) for charming; this would be used for higher classes, the intelligent and highly literate class.

At this point we will also look at figures of speech (SEE: Lesson 21) and observe how a writer or speaker employs them to effectively communicate and persuade.

The Fourth Canon: Memory (*memoria*) is a deep understanding and breadth of knowledge of a subject, including memorizing speeches, the constant practice of a virtue well-rehearsed and lauded in Antiquity. Once the most valued canon of rhetoric during that time, it has now fallen into disuse by most. We will concentrate on this in Lesson 23.

The Fifth Canon: Delivery (*pronuntiatio*) is the graceful regulation of voice, countenance, and gesture while speaking. Here, in the second year of Rhetoric, we will study the practice of speech and present our own oratories, in verse and in prose. This is the point at which we will also defend our Senior Thesis orally (SEE: Lesson 26).

In Summary, Lesson 3:

The Five Canons of Rhetoric:

- Invention
- Arrangement
- Style
- Memory
- Delivery

Terms to Remember:

- Canon
- Proofs
- Diction
- Syntax
- Florid

Lesson Three Assignments

Assignment 3.1

View your classmates' opinion pieces that have been posted and provide critique. Be kind: do not take this as an opportunity to tear someone down (remember that your classmates are going to do the same for you). Be constructive: look for ways the writer can improve. You will be graded on this assignment. Critique at least five pieces. Minimum two sentences each.

Worldview Focus 3.2

As Christians, what should be our attitude in addressing people? Why? Can you point out a verse or two that deals with your attitude toward others? Think in terms of you standing up to speak to a crowd about almost anything—it doesn't have to be your Christian witness. You might be instructing them in something or persuading them about something. Three paragraphs—avoid first/second person.

Writing Tips Lesson Three

Literary Present Tense

For most of a student's elementary and junior high years, he practices writing reports and essays in the past tense. Sometimes the "tense" of his essay skips randomly from past to present and back again. The awkwardness of the tenses confuses the reader, but in the younger years a student remains uncertain how to fix the problem. Perhaps he does not even recognize the awkwardness.

Generally it is only until he reaches his high school years that he must begin to learn "literary present tense" writing. In this method he abandons all that he has thought sensible about writing about authors and their literary works!

Instead of saying, "Churchill gave his speech in front of Parliament," a student will now write, "Churchill gives his speech in front of Parliament." This enables the student to discuss in present terms the elements of Churchill's speech, as well as the author himself ("Churchill faces opposition"). See the example we have provided below. You can fill in the blanks yourself.

Winston Churchill gives his speech in front of Parliament at a time when all of England, and most of the rest of the world, anxiously awaits a message of strength and sanity. This follows a time in which the former Prime Minister, Neville Chamberlain, has adamantly insisted that war would not reach their country, and that Hitler is genuinely interested in peace with the rest of Europe. Churchill's thesis appears in paragraph __, in which he calls forth _____. Britain needs his strong leadership in this anxious period, and his speech shows his dedication to the job at hand.

While this may seem difficult, as with any new technique this one will become easier with frequent use. From this point forward, any analytical writing must utilize the literary present tense. Ask for assistance if this seems too difficult.

Punctuation and Miscellaneous Writing Errors

Pay attention to the **punctuation of citations**. Use the MLA Style, which will show you how to place citations in your text and punctuate them correctly. How should you cite from discourses in this rhetoric course? When you quote from a source we all use (Churchill's "Blood, Toil, Tears, and Sweat," for example), just refer to the paragraph number. No need to name the author or the speech, unless your essay mentions more than one author or speech.

One or two spaces between sentences? Way back in the dark ages when one of these authors was in high school taking typing class with actual typewriters (manual, not electric), teachers instructed their students to add two spaces after the end mark of a sentence and before the next sentence. That was because visually there needed to be more separation between sentences. Today, though, that is being taken care of by the word processing software you use. Physically a tiny bit more space is added after the end punctuation and before the capital letter of the next sentence. So get into the habit NOW of just putting ONE space between sentences.

Lesson Four

Types of Persuasive Discourse

(I)n order to be persuasive speakers in a popular assembly, it is, in my opinion, a capital rule, that we be ourselves persuaded of whatever we recommend to others. Never, when it can be avoided, ought we to espouse any side of the argument, but what we believe to be the true and the right one. Seldom or never will a man be eloquent, but when he is in earnest, and uttering his own sentiments. They are only the unassumed language of the heart or head, that carry the force of conviction.

I know, that young people, on purpose to train themselves to the art of speaking, imagine it useful to adopt that side of the question under debate, which, to themselves, appears the weakest, and to try what figure they can make upon it. But, I am afraid, this is not the most improving education for public speaking; and that it tends to form them to a habit of flimsy and trivial discourse. Such a liberty they should, at no time, allow themselves, unless in meetings where no real business is carried on, but where declamation and improvement of speech is the sole aim. Nor even in such meetings, would I recommend it as the most useful exercise. They will improve themselves to more advantage, and acquit themselves with more honour, by choosing always that side of the debate to which, in their own judgment, they are most inclined, and supporting it by what seems to themselves most solid and persuasive. (Hugh Blair, Corbett, *The Rhetoric of Blair, Campbell, and Whately*, 100)

The earliest rhetoricians focused on a few types of discourses. Primarily, a discourse's purpose was to persuade. The speaker or writer wanted to convince his audience, or teach, or move, or simply demonstrate the skill of public speaking. This is still true today. Some of the earliest rhetoricians depended on their lessons in rhetoric to assist them in winning cases in a court of law. They used their skills to prosecute or to defend.

Additionally, as it grew in popularity and began to be taught in schools of rhetoric in Greece and Rome, style became a focus as well. The practical content mattered, and the manner of speaking (declamation) also became important.

Some of the oldest schools of rhetoric devised an enduring list of three types of discourse. We will add a fourth for our purposes in this textbook.

When trying to determine which type of persuasive discourse you are reading, always ask the following questions of the discourse:

- **Who is the audience?** Each writer or speaker is not addressing his audience *ex nihilo*, or out of nothing. He knows he has an audience: to whom is he speaking/writing? Does he have a physical audience (speaking from a podium), or has he sent a letter to someone? For example, Winston Churchill's "Blood, Toil, Tears, and Sweat" discourse (1940) is delivered to an audience in front of him, but he knows it will also be sent not only to all of Great Britain, but also to the rest of Europe and beyond.

- **What is its subject matter?** In other words, what does he want to say to his audience? What's his message? He makes an appeal of some sort, in order to persuade them of something. What's going on? What is happening in the world at the time–and, by the way, where in the world is he? Again, he speaks not from a void; events have precipitated this discourse. Does he want to change the course of events in his world? Or does he seek to impact the lives of the individuals who hear him?

- **What does it seek to prove?** Often we read a discourse in which a person tries to prove guilt or innocence, affirmative or negative, good or bad. What does the speaker want his audience to believe?

- **What is its nature?** This gets into the type of discourse you will study. What characterizes it? What are its attributes? It might be political in tone, legal or judicial, entertaining or accusatory.

I. Deliberative oratory

In this type of discourse, a writer or speaker attempts to persuade someone to take action or believe what is said. The audience of a deliberative oratory is generally lawmakers, usually taking place before a legislative body. It is therefore political in nature with an exhortative, dissuasive, or advisory subject matter. Often, someone seeks to persuade a body of lawmakers—a Congress or Parliament—to create or abolish a law, proclaim or end a war, or raise or lower taxes.

In his *Rhetoric* Book 1, Chapter 2, Aristotle declared that there are only a few purposes for deliberative oratory:

1. Ways and means
2. War and peace
3. National defense
4. Imports and exports
5. Legislation

As time went by, that list has seen much expansion, but the location of a deliberative discourse has remained the same: it is within a body of lawmakers.

The "deliberative" title will make sense if we read how Cicero described it:

> Deliberative speeches are either of the kind in which the question concerns a choice between two courses of action, or of the kind in which a choice among several is considered. An example of a choice between two courses of action: Does it seem better to destroy Carthage, or to leave her standing? An example of a choice among several: If Hannibal, when recalled to Carthage from Italy, should deliberate whether to remain in Italy, or return home, or invade Egypt and seize Alexandria.

> Again, a question under deliberation is sometimes to be examined on its own account; for example, if the Senate should deliberate whether or not to redeem the captives from the enemy. Or sometimes a question becomes one for deliberation and inquiry on account of some motive extraneous to the question itself; for example, if the Senate should deliberate whether to exempt Scipio from the law so as to permit him to become consul while under age.[29]

---

[29] http://penelope.uchicago.edu/Thayer/E/Roman/Texts/Rhetorica_ad_Herennium/3*.html

The speaker presents a situation to his audience, and he walks through the courses of action (he deliberates) in order to move his audience to a decision.

Deliberative oratories seek to prove the *expedient* and the *inexpedient*. They want to concentrate on or emphasize whether something is worthwhile or whether it should be rejected as worthless, whether a procedure is the best or the worst way to accomplish something. Consider an argument in Congress about a certain tax. One side will argue it is beneficial, while the other will attack it as a waste of taxpayers' hard-earned money. This type of discourse deals in the future, considering what will happen or should happen. Note that a deliberative oratory will also refer to the past in order to prove that a proposal is possible or impossible, but remember that the deliberative argues for or against a future event.

Note how Cicero explains one method of deliberation, and how he injects a purely ethical appeal:

> When we invoke as motive for a course of action steadfastness in Courage, we shall make it clear that men ought to follow and strive after noble and lofty actions, and that, by the same token, actions base and unworthy of the brave ought therefore to be despised by brave men and considered as beneath their dignity. Again, from an honourable act no peril or toil, however great, should divert us; death ought to be preferred to disgrace; no pain should force an abandonment of duty; no man's enmity should be feared in defence of truth; for country, for parents, guest-friends, intimates, and for the things justice commands us to respect, it behoves us to brave any peril and endure any toil.[30]

Effective deliberative oratory not only proves a case, it stands on the matter of right and wrong, honorable and dishonorable.

II. Forensic oratory

In this type of discourse, the speaker or writer seeks to persuade a judge and jury of the guilt or innocence of a certain person, or condemns or defends his own (or someone else's) actions. The audience of a forensic oratory is judges, juries, and others in a courtroom. It is legal or judicial in nature; its subject matter is accusation or defense. A forensic oratory seeks to prove justice or injustice. It deals in the past—what has happened (court trials) and whether it is fact or fiction. In this rhetoric course we will take very little time to cover this type of discourse.

It is interesting, however, to find closing and opening remarks of trials. This will demonstrate to us the kind of language and persuasive techniques attorneys utilize to win cases. For example, Johnnie Cochran's closing arguments in defense of OJ Simpson (1995, dubbed the trial of the century) are long and rambling, use much emotion, and cast doubt on evidence brought up during the trial. In the end, Cochran's defense proved victorious. Since the closing arguments are so long— his closing arguments took four days—we will not include it in this textbook, but students of forensic rhetoric should take a look at its highlights.

III. Epideictic oratory

Epideictic (pronounced eh-pee-dee-*ic*-tic) discourses are ceremonial, demonstrative, pleasing, and inspiring in nature, meant for broad-ranged and general audiences. This discourse's subject

---

[30]   Ibid

matter is praise or blame of a topic or a person, and it seeks to prove honor or dishonor of any subject or person.

Think of the occasions for a ceremonial discourse: presidential campaigns, graduation, marriage, funeral, dedication, inauguration, memorial, and other special events. Ronald Reagan's speech on the event of the space shuttle *Challenger's* explosion (1986) is epideictic. John F. Kennedy's inaugural address (1961) fits that category as well.

An epideictic oratory mostly takes place in the present time, although it will also deal with the past by referring to it in general terms and using it as example. It is by far the most popular and most-used type of persuasive discourse.

As stated earlier, these are the three common types of discourse on which early rhetoricians agreed. Moving on in history, deliberating bodies of lawmakers, as well as arguments in courts of law, fell into disuse for several centuries until the late Middle Ages. Rhetoric experienced a resurgence during the Renaissance. Then not only deliberative bodies of lawmakers, but also court trials were revived.

Students of history will recall that these types of oratory were revived in Europe when individual rights began to be recognized. It was a slow process that began with the Magna Carta in 1215, in which man's individual rights were declared, and continued growing through the development of parliamentary bodies in the West.

In Summary, Lesson 4:

Questions to answer when determining types of discourse:
- Who is the audience?
- What is the subject matter?
- What does it seek to prove?
- What is its nature?

Here is an easy way of remembering each of the different types of persuasive oratory.

	Deliberative	**Forensic**	**Epideictic**
Audience	Lawmakers and Politicians	Court: Judge and Jury	Broad or General
Subject Matter	Exhortative, dissuasive, advisory	Accusation or Defense	Praise or blame
Seeks to Prove	Expedient or Inexpedient	Justice or Injustice	Honor or dishonor
Nature	Political	Judicial or Legal	Ceremonial or demonstrative
Time Frame	Future	Past	Present

Terms to Remember:
- Declamation
- Deliberative
- Exhortative
- Dissuasive
- Extraneous
- Expedient
- Forensic
- Epideictic

Lesson Four Assignments

Assignment 4.1
Rewrite the above quote from Blair in your own words, keeping the syntax (sentence structure) the same.

Assignment 4.2
Read Winston Churchill's speech, "Blood, toil, tears, and sweat" in *AFE*. Select three passages in which he uses emotional language (*pathos*). Discuss how it might have affected his audience. Remember to consider his audience *at that time*, at the beginning of World War Two. Explain why this speech is considered deliberative, based on your understanding of deliberative discourses. Do all of this in two to three paragraphs. Complete the worksheet for this assignment and turn it in.

Assignment 4.3
Read Plato's "Apology of Socrates" in *AFE*. Answer the following questions in two to three paragraphs. Against what is Socrates defending himself? Against whom? What kind of defense is he using (describe his method of defending himself)? How does this fit into the criterion of a forensic oratory? Complete the worksheet for this assignment and turn it in.

Assignment 4.4
Read Lincoln's "Gettysburg Address" and answer the following questions. What makes this speech epideictic? What is the main point of his speech? What is most persuasive about his speech (in other words, what words does he use that are most persuasive)? Complete the worksheet for this assignment and turn it in.

Assignment 4.5
Read "I have the heart and stomach of a king" from Queen Elizabeth I. Answer the following questions. What makes this speech epideictic? What is the main point of his speech? What is most persuasive about his speech (in other words, what words does he use that are most persuasive?) Complete the worksheet for this assignment and turn it in.

Assignment 4.6
Read Winston Churchill's "This was their finest hour" speech. Answer the following questions. What makes this speech epideictic? What is the main point of his speech? What is most persuasive about his speech (in other words, what words does he use that are most persuasive?) Complete the worksheet for this assignment and turn it in.

Assignment 4.7
Find an online audio recording of Winston Churchill's "Blood, Toil, Tears, and Sweat" speech. You won't find a video of it, because it wasn't filmed. Follow along with the speech in print. Take note of what Churchill emphasized and where he paused for effect. How did the audio version of the speech differ from your first impressions as you read it? (In other words, if you read it first, what was your impression? Then, listening to it, how did it change for you?) For an excellent dramatization of the speech, watch the 2017 movie *Darkest Hour*.

Assignment 4.8

Read "They're Smiling in Heaven," by Don Lindman. Answer the following questions. Two to three paragraphs. What makes this column epideictic? What is persuasive about this essay? Point out words or phrases to support your answer. Complete the worksheet for this assignment and turn it in.

Writing Tips Lesson Four

Sentence variety: sentence openers

Variety makes more interesting writing. The reader may not notice it, but he won't be as bored! From here on out, watch your paragraphs. Make sure that <u>no two sentences begin the same way within one paragraph, and that no two paragraphs begin the same way within an assignment</u>.

As a writer I am constantly watching out for sentence variety. Did I begin my sentences the same way twice? Did I use a variety of words and sentences? Are my sentences all long or do I have a variety of short and long, compound and simple?

The key in better writing exists in my ability to vary my words and sentences, making my writing more interesting to the reader.

In-class exercise

Take your most recent writing homework and circle the first word of every sentence. Now look to see whether you have duplicated any of those words within the same paragraph as sentence beginners. If so, reword them.

Do any of your paragraphs begin the same way? Reword. From this point forward you must avoid this error in your assignments.

Types of Persuasive Discourse: Propaganda

Propaganda is to a democracy what the bludgeon is to a totalitarian state. (Noam Chomsky, *Media Control: The Spectacular Achievements of Propaganda*)

And if all others accepted the lie which the Party imposed—if all records told the same tale—then the lie passed into history and became truth. "Who controls the past" ran the Party slogan, "controls the future: who controls the present controls the past." (George Orwell, *1984*)

All art is propaganda. It is universally and inescapably propaganda; sometimes unconsciously, but often deliberately, propaganda. (Upton Sinclair)[31]

But the most brilliant propagandist technique will yield no success unless one fundamental principle is borne in mind constantly and with unflagging attention. It must confine itself to a few points and repeat them over and over. Here, as so often in this world, persistence is the first and most important requirement for success. (Adolf Hitler)[32]

Because of demagogues, rhetoric has a tainted reputation in our time. However, rhetoric is central to democratic governance. It can fuse passion and persuasion, moving free people to freely choose what is noble. (George F. Will, *One Man's America: The Pleasures and Provocations of Our Singular Nation*)

Propaganda is the negative side of Rhetoric. It is not generally considered the fourth type of oratory by rhetoricians, but we include it here so that you can see its use. **Propaganda** *is the expression of ideas in such a way that the speaker (or writer, etc.) gains or maintains power or influence.* Propaganda has two sides: beneficial and detrimental. We say it is negative because of its misuse of proper rhetoric, and though it may have good motivations, its employment does not follow a balance of *ethos, pathos,* and (especially) *logos.* It misuses the three appeals, not presenting a full argument, but using fragments of arguments to achieve its aims. It relies on *pathos,* often to the exclusion of the other two forms of persuasion.

It is often one-sided, lacking a complete, cohesive argument or the background or context needed to make a full, informed conclusion. It relies on manipulation, a swift means to an end. It is Aristotelian and Platonic in its *ethos* and Machiavellian in its methodology and pragmatism.

---

[31]   https://www.goodreads.com/quotes/160099-all-art-is-propaganda-it-is-universally-and-inescabably-propaganda

[32]   http://www.hitler.org/writings/Mein_Kampf/mkv1ch06.html

Advertising can be a form of propaganda, as it influences consumers' opinions so that a business can increase its wealth. Governments use propaganda to sway opinions about the country (in a positive way) or about its enemies (in a negative way). During wars, both sides use propaganda to influence the opinions of both enemies and allies.

In the 1930s Hitler appointed Joseph Goebbels as his Minister of Propaganda in Germany. As Hitler accelerated his plans for war, as well as for the annihilation of the Jewish people, Goebbels began his campaign of propaganda.

The fact that Goebbels had so much power is indicative of how important Hitler thought it was to ensure that the people were won over or intimidated into accepting Nazi rule.

> The essence of propaganda consists in winning people over to an idea so sincerely, so vitally, that in the end they succumb to it utterly and can never escape from it. Propaganda is not an end in itself, but a means to an end. If the means achieves the end then the means is good...the new Ministry has no other aim than to unite the nation behind the ideal of the national revolution. [33]

It can be chilling to realize that the rulers of Germany in that time were so purposeful in their use of lies and manipulation to achieve an end.

Demagoguery is considered a part of propaganda. Demagogues use lies, pointless or manipulative arguments, and emotional appeals to gain personal advantage while pretending to mean well.

In the 21st century War on Terror, both sides utilize prolific propaganda. Terrorist organizations use social media to distribute videos and images and make threats, and, horrifically, to showcase their barbarous murders. In the aftermath of an attack, they bolster their claims by boasting proudly to the world about their actions. Similarly, countries warring against terrorism also engage in propaganda of another kind, informing its citizens of the need for safety and awareness. Thus, it is easy to see how propaganda can be used for good or evil.

Propaganda is not always racism-filled demagoguery. Singapore, for example, is a small city-state in Southeast Asia that brought itself out of the rubble of World War II (they were invaded and decimated by the Empire of Japan the day after the attack on Pearl Harbor) and into a fully developed nation through the decisive, effective leadership of their first Prime Minister, Lee Kuan Yew. The Singaporean government used (and still uses) propaganda throughout the city to manage its people. There are signs throughout the Singapore mass transit system not only about being polite and kind to others, but also, at times, about having more children and growing the nation's population.

There is an assumption in propaganda that those who create it know more than the general populace who consume it, and that this supposed imbalance of knowledge means that the propagandist does not need to employ proper rhetorical appeals. They don't seek to persuade you; they merely seek to tell you what to think.

Characteristics of Propaganda

- Us vs. Them–This is one of the biggest characteristics of propaganda, for it is far-reaching. The propagandist seeks to create a divide between the speaker's side and the other side. The

---

[33] "Propaganda in Nazi Germany." HistoryLearningSite.co.uk. 2005. Web.

use of "We" will be prevalent, hoping that you, the audience, will innately side with the speaker. Anyone else who disagrees is obviously wrong, because we all agree, and if we all agree, we must be right (which fallacy is this?). The consensus is therefore the authority.

- ◆ Stereotyping or broad generalizations is a characteristic of Us vs. Them.
- ◆ Use of Fear–fear Them, love Us. What They say is wrong, but what We say is clearly right.

- Catchy phrases and repetition–this means that your audience will remember what you say and pass it along.

- Cult of Personality–often, a single leader is made into the object of the propaganda, held up as an example of what is right.

- Fallacy upon fallacy–remember, the information given in propaganda is not always wrong. Rather, it's the way that the information is relayed. There is usually a leap in reasoning. The process is skipped.

The important thing to remember about propaganda–and indeed all rhetoric–is that we must always remain steadfast and watchful, with our minds prepared to filter everything that we read, watch, and hear. Thus, too, the need to be immersed in God's word, in order to discern underlying presuppositions and worldviews. Christ implores us, "Behold, I send you out as sheep in the midst of wolves; so be shrewd as serpents and innocent as doves" (*NASB*, Matthew 10.16). He reminds us that we must not be doe-eyed and naive, but ready for anything. Peter expounds upon this: "Be sober-minded; be watchful. Your adversary the devil prowls around like a roaring lion, seeking someone to devour" (*ESV*, 1 Peter 5.8). Christians should stand ready, wary of being mauled by the world around us. We should never be taken unawares, but prepare our minds for action.

In Summary, Lesson 5:

Propaganda as a type of discourse:
- Us vs. Them
- Catchy phrases
- Cult of personality
- Fallacy upon fallacy

Terms to Remember:
- Propaganda
- Demagoguery (demagogue)
- Macchiavellian
- Discern

Lesson Five Assignments

Assignment 5.1

Given the definition of propaganda above, is all advertising therefore bad? Why or why not? Can you give examples of advertising you would consider propaganda or demagoguery? Two to three paragraphs.

Assignment 5.2

Read Hitler's speech to Germany on February 20, 1938 (called "Germany's Claims"), and his speech on May 4, 1941 (the "Reichstag Speech"). These are long speeches that require your attention. It's hard to make a definite statement about someone's character or work after having just read two discourses by him. But Hitler is one of those infamous people in history about whom we know or have heard much. From what you know, and from what you read, write 3 to 4 paragraphs describing how he uses *ethos*, *pathos*, and *logos* to influence opinion and gain power. Remember to cite the speech by citing the year of the speech (1938 or 1941). Complete the worksheet for this assignment and turn it in.

Multimedia Focus 5.3

Search for online examples of World War II propaganda. Look for American as well as Japanese and German propaganda. Note the use of symbolism, color, words, and images. Have three examples ready to show your classmates. Often images are stereotypes or exaggerations geared toward eliciting emotional reactions from the viewer. Take note of the underlying message of each piece of propaganda. What is the creator of propaganda saying to the viewer? What is he trying to get the audience to believe?

Multimedia Focus 5.4

Imagine you are creating an advertising (propaganda) campaign for your school or church or youth group.

You will create a piece of propaganda based on some of the values your school/church/youth group holds dear. You need to demonstrate the importance of those things and convince the audience (your fellow students) that they are essential and must be followed.

When communicating the meaning of your propaganda, remember that you seek to evoke emotion in your audience. You should emphasize symbolism and strong visuals when creating your poster. You should not need a lot of text to get your point across. A piece of propaganda should often get the meaning across to the observer before he or she gets a chance to read what it says. To make sure we understand the true meaning of your propaganda, you will also be presenting these to the class.

The best propaganda pieces use both words and pictures. You could use only words, but remember that the propaganda needs to be appealing to the eyes (and that sometimes a picture is worth a thousand words). Therefore, the propaganda needs to be visually appealing; otherwise nobody is going to support the things you're fighting for!

Your poster should include the following things:

1. Poster with design/artwork created or reworked by you—using a computer or drawn by hand. You should also have a catchy slogan or saying—something that people will

remember.
2. The posters should be in color.
3. 1-2 paragraphs submitted with one poster that explains what the images represent and what you want the piece of propaganda to do for your audience.
4. Presentation: You will present this in class. (5 minutes minimum)

Writing Tips Lesson Five

First/second person

Another writing challenge for the high school student includes avoiding first and second person. This means cutting out all references to **"I, me, my, mine, we, us, our, ours, you, and yours."** Some young writers have trouble moving to that new, more formal method. This IS more formal, and it aids the writer in attaining an expository tone.

From now on, <u>avoid</u> saying, **"I believe the thesis is in paragraph three."**

Just say, "The thesis presents itself in paragraph three" or "The thesis occurs in..."

Then, go on to tell the reader why. You don't have to tell me this is what you think or believe. Since the essay has your name on it, you are already communicating that you think/believe these things.

Similarly, <u>avoid</u> addressing the reader as **"you."**

Mature writers will steer clear of the <u>implied command</u>:

"Look at paragraph three."

"Consider the cross on which Christ died."

"Note that Paul finds himself at the mercy of his jailers."

Find other ways to write these things.

Avoid the Writing Rut!

Consider it a challenge to expand your vocabulary and usage. Don't rely on the same way to do things; you'll fall into a writing rut! This applies to many aspects of writing. (<u>Notice that</u> the way this section is written violates the very command to avoid second person! *Instructional writing—as opposed to expository writing—*will do that.)

Another rut that writers—especially Christian writers—fall into has to do with references to **groups** of people. "**We Christians** must…" "**As Americans, we**…" "**God tells us**…" All of these use the second person, and the writer must assiduously avoid this. The mature writer finds many different ways to get around this problem. He will notice that the first two examples are clichés anyway. Writers must diligently avoid cliché writing.

Lesson Six

The First Canon of Rhetoric: Invention
Formulating a Thesis

Invention is the devising of matter, true or plausible, that would make the case convincing. (Cicero, *Ad Herennium*, Book I)

[A] higher degree of eloquence, is, when the speaker aims not merely to please, but also to inform, to instruct, to convince: when his art is exerted, in removing prejudices against himself and his cause; in choosing the most proper arguments, stating them with the greatest force, arranging them in the best order, expressing and delivering them with propriety and beauty; and thereby disposing us to pass that judgment, or embrace that side of the cause, to which he seeks to bring us. Within this compass, chiefly, is employed the eloquence of the bar. (Blair, *Lectures on Belles Lettres*)

The process of Invention can be as simple as "brainstorming" or as complex as "the reasoning out of truth, or that which is like the truth, to make a case probable."[34] It does not mean that a rhetorician "invents" something to discuss (as in "I invented a new idea today!"). Rather, Invention is the process of discovering the means of discussing or arguing a topic.

Perhaps a student is handed an assignment to write a paper on the Just War theory. She does not know much about it, except for a classroom discussion of the theory. So she refers to her notes and sees that St. Augustine and Thomas Aquinas both wrote extensively about Just War, so she knows she can start there. Once she has skimmed through an overview of their writings, she lands upon a couple of aspects of Just War Theory that she believes will provide plenty of food for thought. At that point, then, she can begin asking herself questions about the topic and, digging into her research, narrowing in on what she will be able to write about.

As we progress through rhetoric, we will add skills to our repertoire for studying discourses. Already you are able to recognize types of discourses, from earlier lessons. Now you will be expected to find the thesis statement of any discourse. Some are easier to recognize than others, and there will always be room for discussion as to what the thesis statement actually is. We will spend time learning how to pick one out. It is also valuable to learn this, as the research paper you write in your first year must have a thesis statement.

Remember from your study of Logic that an argument is multiple premises leading to a conclusion: the thesis is the conclusion. However, in rhetoric the thesis will NOT be in the conclusion of discourses that we read or write.

---

[34] Kennedy, George A., *Classical Rhetoric and its Christian and Secular Tradition from Ancient to Modern Times.* University of North Carolina Press, 1980, p. 92.

Choosing the topic

Know your topic. Decide on the subject you want and what material to use in developing the topic. A good test for determining what is a good topic:

- The topic must fit your audience. Imagine giving a speech about the gift of tongues to a group of atheists. Not only would their frame of reference be zero, they would also be unwilling to sit and listen to your topic.

- The topic must fit the occasion. This is obvious. No one would expect to hear the dedication of a battleship at a funeral.

- The scope of the topic must be such that you may expect to discuss it reasonably well. Is the subject something you already know a little about? You would be better able to present a speech on that topic than, say, quantum physics (unless you are a physicist).

- Is this something you will find interesting to research and write, and also will your audience find it informative? A student once asked us to suggest a topic for his research paper. He perused a list of possibilities, and he literally closed his eyes and pointed. His finger landed on the subject of fascism. He wasn't interested in it, and therefore his paper was disappointingly dry, lacking cohesion. Note to self: find a topic that is interesting to you and your audience!

The beginning of all discourses is a topic, a question, a problem, or an issue. Once adequate research is done on a subject, work can begin on converting it into a thesis. A topic with a broad subject range will need to be broken down into sub-topics. The unnecessary sub-topics can then be discarded as you narrow down your topic.

The Thesis Statement

A thesis statement is stated in the form of a proposition: It is *a complete sentence or two that asserts or denies something about the subject*. A thesis statement is *not* a question, nor is it a summary of your discourse. It is not the *gist* of something. It *is* your **argument**. Your thesis directs where your discourse will go, stating your intentions. A thesis statement must be precise and specific about the position you're taking on a matter, not hinting at it.

> Failure to sharply define one's subject is the chief cause of fuzzy, disunified discourse. Vague beginnings invite chaotic endings. The audience for a discourse, whether written or spoken, can achieve no firmer grasp of the thesis than the writer or the speaker has. As a matter of fact, if we make allowance for what is inevitably lost in the process of transmission, the audience's grasp will always be less than the writer's or the speaker's.[35]

You do not want your audience to be confused about what you're getting at. Good rhetoric isn't about intimations or hazy insinuations, but about unambiguous, accurate language that convinces the audience to believe something. If you're unclear, your audience will be, too.

> For we may rest assured that whenever we express ourselves ill, there is, besides the mismanagement of language, for the most part, some mistake in our manner of conceiving the subject. Embarrassed, obscure, and feeble sentences are generally, if not always, the

---

[35]   Corbett, *Classical Rhetoric*, 31

result of embarrassed, obscure, and feeble thought. Thought and language act and re-act upon each other mutually.[36]

Finally, your thesis should pass the "So What?" test. To make sure that your thesis goes beyond a basic statement of fact, you must also make clear *why* your thesis matters. Just arguing that strawberry is the best flavor of ice cream may work when a grammar student is first learning how to compose the structure of an essay; however, when the student moves into persuasive discourse, this kind of topic is too trivial.

In order to make sure that your thesis statement is strong enough, ask yourself: "What am I arguing?" Moreover, check to see if your thesis statement contains the points you're going to use to prove your argument. If this is a longer essay, insert broader points into your thesis statement itself, then use the sentences following the thesis to expand on those broader points. You're laying out a road map for your reader in your introduction, and the thesis statement (your argument!) is the compass. It should direct *everything* that comes after it.

Some students of Ancient Literature, asked to write an essay comparing and contrasting the flood story in Genesis with the flood in the *Epic of Gilgamesh*, submitted thesis statements like this:

> There are many similarities and differences between Noah's flood in Genesis and the worldwide flood in *The Epic of Gilgamesh*.

Can you see the problem there? It's a statement comparing the two texts. Unfortunately, this statement doesn't say anything *about* the two floods. What is similar about them? What is different about them? So what? Why do those similarities and differences matter? This sentence may be an adequate opener to an essay (if still lacking creativity), but it's no thesis statement. How would you improve it? Try making a statement about those similarities and differences.

In-class Exercise

What's wrong with these thesis statements, and how would you improve it?

- The Greek gods are very different from the God of the Bible.
- Racism is wrong.
- Everyone should read *The Lion, the Witch, and the Wardrobe*.

Remember: Thesis Statement = Argument.

Cicero, in *De Inventione*, discusses the way of dealing with a controversial topic. He tells us to critique the subject in a four-question process of invention called Stasis Theory. "Every subject which contains in itself any controversy existing either in language or in disputation, contains a question either about a fact, or about a name, or about a class, or about an action."[37]

Note how he moves from general to particular. You can think about doing the same with the invention of your subject, as well as developing thesis statements.

- *an sit* (whether a thing is) - a question of fact. Was it done?

---

[36] Blair, *Lectures on Rhetoric and Belles Lettres* http://www.artsci.gmcc.ab.ca/people/einarssonb/blair.htm

[37] http://www.classicpersuasion.org/pw/cicero/dnv1-2.htm

- *quid sit* (what is it?) - a question of definition. What was done?
- *quale sit* (what kind is it?) - a question of quality. What was the nature of the act?
- (what should we do?) - a question of action.

Aristotle intended this line of questioning as preparation for debates and discussions on either side of the argument. This is where he wanted to begin, so that his students could effectively argue either side–not to prove what is wrong to actually be right, but to understand both sides of an issue.

Your thesis statement would then fall into one or more of the above categories. It would answer one or more of the above questions of fact, definition or quality, and then move ahead to the action that must be taken. The writer or speaker must also follow additional criteria:

1. **State the thesis in one or two declarative sentences.** It might be best to limit yourself to one sentence, especially in essays or speeches of three pages or less. Any more sentences may add too much, which eventually would muddle the argument.

2. **A thesis must assert or deny something about the subject.** In other words, it must say something in the positive or negative about a topic. For example, "John F. Kennedy was the victim of a vast government plot." Or "William Shakespeare was not the author of numerous plays and sonnets; several men authored those works attributed to him." It can be something simple or something controversial. The more exact, the better.

3. **The thesis statement can almost always be found in the first few paragraphs** of a discourse. Rarely is there any exception to this rule, though you may discover a few of those exceptions occasionally throughout this course.

The most common mistake of rhetoric students is that they cannot come up with the thesis (or that they hate writing introductions, but more on that later). If you have a hard time coming up with the right thesis statement, just verbalizing the topic will suggest lines of development; it may define terms used later in the discourse. One sentence helps to clarify whether you can narrow your topic.

Sometimes the thesis does not come to mind until midway through the discovery and writing process. But the thesis statement must occur before the first rough draft is completed. The thesis sentence is a good starting-point in the composition process, because it forces the writer to determine at the outset just what it is that he or she wants to say about his topic. It is the basis for a discourse that makes a point and hangs together well. It also suggests some of the topics that can be used to develop the subject. Your first thesis statement can be a bit rough, in terms of the actual wording. You can revise it later to make it sound better.

<u>When you read a discourse you will always (from here on out) be asked to find a thesis statement and usually defend or explain why you arrived at your answer.</u> Later in this course you may find discourses that do not have a clear thesis. The purpose here is to begin to understand the necessity for a clear, sharply defined thesis statement, both in what you read and what you write. When reading discourses from here on out in this course, the natural process of analysis must include finding the thesis and explaining reasons for arriving at this thesis. After you have read the discourse and are attempting to find the thesis statement, take a moment to write what you believe the thesis statement would be, if you were the author of the discourse. Make sure you've taken into account the main point of the text, including major supporting details. Then, use that as a road map as you reread the discourse; is there a sentence (or two) that is similar to the one you wrote?

Don't get discouraged along the way! Discovering the author's thesis statement is not always easy. You may land on one, and then your teacher may tell you to try again. If you can make a good argument defending your choice, perhaps you'll get partial credit. Sometimes a student will provide what he thinks is the answer, and his teacher may ask to find something similar to that idea a little earlier in the discourse. Deduction is a worthwhile exercise! Keep trying!

Could a discourse not have a thesis statement? Yes! What can you determine if one is very difficult to nail down? The writer/speaker did not make a good case. You will probably decide that the discourse, as a whole, was poorly conceived and inadequately argued.

One more note: Students might make the mistake of coming up with their own idea for a thesis statement in a discourse they have read. <u>Do not summarize what you believe is the main point of the discourse; that is not the thesis statement.</u> Provide the actual sentence (one or two at most) from the discourse that you believe serves as the author's thesis statement.

In Summary, Lesson 6:

Definition of Invention, with regard to rhetoric: The process of figuring out what to write about.

Know the topic:
- Must fit the audience
- Must fit the occasion
- Must be able to discuss it well
- Must be interesting to the audience

Definition of Thesis, with regard to Rhetoric: One or two sentences that assert or deny something about the subject

Stasis Theory—Four questions
- Was it done?
- What happened?
- What was the nature of the act?
- What should we do?

Essential criteria for developing a thesis:
- State in one or two declarative sentences
- Must assert or deny something
- Must be found in the first few paragraphs

Terms to Remember:
- Intimation
- Insinuation
- Stasis
- Declarative

Lesson Six Assignments

Assignment 6.1

List five topics on which you could realistically give a speech tomorrow, with minimal research and preparation. Only two can be how-to. The others must be persuasive. On those three, provide a thesis statement which you could reasonably support. This only needs to be a bulleted list, no more.

Assignment 6.2

Read the following articles (see if you can find them online): "This House is Not for Sale" by Andy Rooney, and "She Did Good" by Paul Harvey. Decide on the thesis for each one. Explain why you chose that thesis. Use short answers. Some discourses, especially contemporary ones, may not have a clearly defined thesis, but in these cases you should find one or two sentences in these texts which you could identify as the thesis.

Assignment 6.3

Read the following discourses, found in *AFE*, and decide on the thesis for each: "The Gettysburg Address" & "I Have the Heart and Stomach of a King." How did the speakers demonstrate that they know their audiences? 250 words (with support).

Assignment 6.4

Look at a reputable online news source or article in your local paper (if you don't subscribe to a paper, your local library does). Be ready to show it to your class or turn it in as part of your assignment (so print the article out or make a copy, as needed). Identify the thesis statement in the column and note, in 150 words, how the writer supports his thesis. If you cannot find a thesis statement and believe the author did not do an adequate job presenting and proving one, say so, and be ready to discuss that problem.

Writing Tips Lesson Six

Passive writing, continued.

As a writer becomes accustomed to eliminating be-verbs from his text, he then must look deeper and attack any other passive writing he encounters.

<u>Look for</u>: helper verbs, such as "will, had, have, would, could, should." For example:

"She has seen the river overflow its banks."
("has" as a passive helper)

"She watched the river overflow its banks."
("has seen" changed to "watched.")
OR:
"The evidence would seem to direct us to see the facts."
("would" helper verb is unnecessary)

"The evidence directs one to the facts."
(eliminate helper verb)

Find more active verb phrases that refuse to sit still. Use them. Change your sentences around to make your sentences more active and flow more smoothly.

Lesson Seven

The Second Canon of Rhetoric: Arrangement

Arrangement is the ordering and distribution of the matter, making clear the place to which each thing is to be assigned. (Cicero, *Ad Herennium*, Book I)

Arrangement: The Parts of a Discourse

Once we know what we should write about, we need to organize our thoughts. In developing the thesis, the writer has already determined the answer to the question: "What will I say?" As the thesis develops, the writer collects points (proofs) he will use to support his thesis. ("How will I prove my point?") This is what the writer will use, along with further research, to write his discourse.

Next the writer will ask some questions as he fleshes out his major points, or proofs: "How will I introduce my subject?" "Will I urge my audience to take action in some way?"

Without a clear arrangement, the discourse will frustrate the audience, and the speaker's points will be lost in the confusion. Any of us can point out a number of public speakers (politicians, pastors, etc.) who do not follow any semblance of an outline, and we express frustration at the murky mess the speakers have made of their main points.

Arrangement–a method of organization–has always been the key to an effective argument. Each part needs to build onto the previous one, so that from one section of a discourse to the next, there is a continuous, cohesive flow: every point is a "proof" of the thesis or main idea.

Not every detail is necessary; only include points that will support your thesis as precisely as possible. The act of proving a thesis using your most important points will be good training ground in concise writing and speaking. You have a main point–a thesis. You know you need to lay out your argument, proof by proof, to support your thesis. That's your first step toward organization!

When arranging a discourse, writers and speakers must choose words carefully; they must choose only the words necessary to make a point. They work to cut away (edit) those words that do not clearly communicate a point.

> On whatever subject any one intends to discourse, he will most commonly begin with some introduction, in order to prepare the minds of his hearers; he will then state his subject, and explain the facts connected with it; he will employ arguments for establishing his own opinion, and overthrowing that of his antagonist; he may, perhaps, if there be room for it, endeavour to touch the passions of his audience; and after having said all he thinks proper, he will bring his discourse to a close by some peroration or conclusion.[38]

Having a logical approach to a discourse is the most important element. It cannot persuade effectively if it is disorganized. When there is order, there is peace. By learning the order of historic discourses, you can grasp the importance of order in your own writing. Organization is vital when it comes time to write a thesis paper. <u>Always</u> take advantage of the opportunity to learn order, decide on the arrangement of your points, and use proper writing skills.

---

[38] Blair, in Corbett, *Belles Lettres*, 106

There is much reading in this section. On top of identifying the thesis in each piece (SEE: Lesson 6 regarding thesis), you will now begin to identify the different parts of the discourse.

Arrangement of a Discourse

The component parts of a discourse in Classical Rhetoric are as follows. We will elaborate on them more in the following lessons.

1. **Introduction**

   Obviously, this is the first element of a discourse. The Introduction should be proportionate to the length of the discourse. In other words, in a ten-paragraph discourse the writer will not take three paragraphs to introduce the subject. We will discuss the five types of Introduction in Lesson 8.

2. **Statement of Facts**

   Here, briefly, the writer or speaker will lay out the essence, the background, the context of his argument. There is no need to use much space and time for this element; that will be the job of the next part of arrangement.

3. **Proof of Case**

   As the name of this section implies, here is where the writer or speaker argues the point in its entirety. He has allowed the Statement of Facts to lay out the direction of his discourse, and now it is time for elaboration.

4. **Refutation**

   Now that he has made all of his points to prove his case, he can bring up any opposing arguments and proceed to disprove them.

5. **Conclusion**

   Aptly named, this section (obviously) closes the argument and leaves a favorable impression of his points in the minds of his audience.

All About the Audience

This is a good time to remind ourselves of the purpose of rhetoric: **persuasion**. When we read these discourses, and when we write our own, we focus on persuading an audience. Perhaps the writer/speaker wants to convince an audience to believe, or dissuade an audience from some action or belief.

So when we read OR write a discourse, we focus on the audience and look at:

1. WHO the audience is
2. WHAT the audience already believes
3. WHY they need to be convinced
4. HOW to go about persuading them.

In Summary, Lesson 7:

Arrangement consists of:

1. Introduction
2. Statement of Facts
3. Proof of Case
4. Refutation
5. Conclusion

When looking to persuade, we must answer:

1. Who...
2. What...
3. Why...
4. How...

Term to Remember:

Peroration

Lesson Seven Assignments

Assignment 7.1

Reread Churchill's "Blood, Toil, Tears, and Sweat." Now that you have identified the thesis, you should be able to outline his Arrangement. Does he follow the traditional structure? Where does each part of the discourse occur? This doesn't need to be written out, but labeled in your book or in your notes.

Assignment 7.2

We have read quite a few discourses that are short: many people believe that writing is about putting down as much as possible, cramming everything they can think of into a discourse. However, some of the most effective discourses are short and to the point: they are concise. Churchill declared a new government in "Blood, Toil, Tears, and Sweat." Lincoln commemorated the bloodiest battle in American history in "The Gettysburg Address." Queen Elizabeth I roused her troops to battle in "I have the heart and stomach of a king."

Try this task of trimming down a paragraph to make it more concise. Trim out unnecessary words, and re-word when you need to, but make it still effective.

Assignment 7.3

Choose one assignment you have written up until this point (it can be anything–something you're proud of and received a good grade on, or an assignment you feel you could improve). Trim the writing by 10%.

Start by rereading the entire essay, then go back through it and highlight the essential parts of what you've written–what *needs* to be there? What words and phrases *must* you have in order to get your point across? Is there anything unnecessary, even if it feels good to have it there? Cut out what is unnecessary. Now, things may feel slightly disjointed because you have taken out connecting words or phrases–fix it so that your words flow.

Writing Tips Lesson Seven

Agreement

Make sure your sentences have internal agreement: singular to singular, plural to plural, past to past, present to present.

Grammatical Agreement: When writing a formal essay, a writer must be aware of his words and the meanings he conveys. A writer should always make sure that his nouns, verbs, adjectives and pronouns agree in number. That is, if the noun is singular, the rest of the sentence must remain singular.

For example, the following sentence written by a student lacks agreement: "Many books that you will read within your lifetime will have a character change throughout it." The word "books" is plural, and the sentence works all the way through—until the very last word, "it." This makes no sense, due to the fact that "it" is singular. How would you reword this sentence?

Avoid mixing singular and plural words and phrases throughout your paragraphs.

Past and present tense: When writing in the past tense, stay in past tense. Do not begin a paragraph in the past and then move to the present. Keep each paragraph consistent. To be sure, some essays and research papers must transition from discussion of the past to relating to the present. Make certain those transitions are smooth, and keep them consistent.

For the purposes of Rhetoric, any analytical writing must remain in the literary present tense. (SEE: Writing Tips Lesson 3 for more information about this technique.)

Singular and Plural: For example, see the conflict in the following sentence: "When a person stands up to speak, they must be prepared to give reasons for their beliefs." See the conflict? A person is singular, but the pronoun does not agree, because it is plural. How would you fix this problem?

Lesson Eight

The Second Canon:
Arrangement–Introduction

> The Introduction is the beginning of the discourse, and by it the hearer's mind is prepared for attention. (Cicero, *Ad Herennium*, 1)
>
> This, then, is the most essential function and distinctive property of the introduction, to show what the aim of the speech is; and therefore no introduction ought to be employed where the subject is not long or intricate. (Aristotle, *The Rhetoric & The Poetics of Aristotle*, 3)

The purpose of an introduction is to tell the audience what our discourse is about and to ready them for what will come. Sometimes we do not have to generate interest in our subject; the subject itself will do that.

Often before writing an introduction, the following questions must be asked in order to clarify the introduction:

- What is our topic?

- Who is the audience? What adjustments do I need to make in order to get the audience ready?

- What is going on in the world/community that would affect the delivery or reception of this piece?

- What might be the audience's presuppositions?

- How much time or space may I take in delivering this? (It could be a 45-minute speech or a 500-word opinion piece.)

Though we will not take much time to learn Cicero's types of Introductions here, it is worthwhile to describe briefly what he says about them. According to Cicero, "there are two kinds of Introduction: the Direct Opening, in Greek called the *Proimion*, and the Subtle Approach, called the *Ephodos*. The Direct Opening straightaway prepares the hearer to attend to our speech. Its purpose is to enable us to have hearers who are attentive, receptive, and well-disposed."[39] In the Direct Opening the writer or speaker will lay out his arguments in a forthright manner and begin to honor or attack the subject of his discourse. There is not as much need to spend time laying out our case to our audience; we assume that our audience, or at least the majority of our audience, already agrees with us.

Cicero's "Subtle Approach" works best when we will be addressing an audience who has 1) favorably received a speaker whose argument is directly in opposition to our own, or 2) is generally predisposed to disagree with our argument, or 3) has already listened to plenty of arguments from the other side and are bored with–tired of–the entire subject. Perhaps you can identify with this last point if you recall hearing too much from political candidates right before an election. At least in the

---

[39] Ibid.

United States, when a presidential campaign can last as long as 18 months, the entire country is certainly worn-out!

Things to Avoid in an Introduction

- **Definitions** - An introduction is not the proper place for a definition. The Statement of Facts holds definitions, as it is intended to establish context for the argument.

- **Quotes** - Both definitions and quotes are clichés to avoid in the introduction. <u>The proper place for a quotation is proof for what you will say later on</u>. Obviously, this goes against a common method of introducing an essay that you may have been taught in the past, but you want to begin *your* essay with *your* words, rather than someone else's. You were probably taught that this is a creative, artful, or inspirational way to write an introduction, and you can see it at the start of each of our Lessons in this book. Thus you can see that there is a time and place for quotes, but not in a persuasive essay or speech.

- **Telling your audience what you're going to tell them -** "In this essay, I will explain why strawberry ice cream is the best kind of ice cream." This is redundant. Don't say that you're going to say something–just say it!

The Five Types of Introductions

Aristotle was careful to outline the important elements for writers of introduction. He emphasized that the length, style, and content of the introduction were vital considerations. He instructed the rhetorician to eliminate excessive introduction—a lengthy one was unnecessary.

The introduction should begin with the general topic, speaking broadly, perhaps with an anecdote, during which you set the stage for the argument to come. Introductions that capture the reader's interest are "hooks" that draw a reader in to the rest of the discourse. As you move toward the end of the introduction, proceed toward the particulars and the thesis. The closing lines of an introduction should transition smoothly into the next section, not seeming to end abruptly. Furthermore, your introduction should be concise and proportionate to the size of your discourse. If you're writing a two-page discourse, your introduction should not take up a whole page.

Following are the types of introductions found in formal rhetoric. These were coined by Richard Whately in his *Elements of Rhetoric*.[40] Each of these introduction types must ready your audience for your argument. These introduction types are not done in a vacuum, or without reason; each has a purpose. Everything is aimed at the thesis.

- **Introduction preparatory** – The point of an introduction is to set up for the argument and lead to the thesis statement, so each introduction should be preparatory in nature. It may announce how a subject will be dealt with, or it may try to forestall some misunderstanding. This is often a bland, "vanilla" introduction type, and it is the rare rhetorician who resorts to it, because the Third Canon of rhetoric calls for more style in a discourse than:

    > There are three choices for the best flavor of ice cream: strawberry, chocolate, and vanilla. Strawberry is clearly the best flavor of ice cream.

    You likely began an essay like this when you first started writing. It does the job of telling your audience what they're about to read, but little else. Think of this type as the basic

---

[40]   Corbett, *The Rhetoric of Blair, Whately and Campbell*

method of introduction–every introduction should prepare, but some do it with more flair than others, and those include the following types of introduction.

- **Introduction inquisitive** – The topic asks a question to draw interest from the audience and cause them to want to read or hear more. It rouses interest. The thesis statement answers this question. Questions in the introduction should provoke the audience to speculate as to how they might answer the question, or how that answer might make them rethink something they already know. This is often a problematic introduction, as it can lead to laziness:

> Ex: "Have you ever wondered which flavor of ice cream is best? Do you think chocolate is the most delicious? What about vanilla?"

This is lazy writing–or at least immature writing. Here, the writer asks questions that are too basic, too easily answered, even pandering to a mature audience. Also, in a mature discourse one should not directly ask a question of the audience with "you." (An exception will be in the case of the example below, in which Cicero attacks the offender, Cataline, for plotting to overthrow the Senate.) Instead, ask a rhetorical question or questions that inspire thought.

Consider Cicero's discourse against Cataline:

When, O Catiline, do you mean to cease abusing our patience? How long is that madness of yours still to mock us? When is there to be an end of that unbridled audacity of yours, swaggering about as it does now? Do not the nightly guards placed on the Palatine Hill—do not the watches posted throughout the city—does not the alarm of the people, and the union of all good men—does not the precaution taken of assembling the senate in this most defensible place—do not the looks and countenances of this venerable body here present, have any effect upon you? Do you not feel that your plans are detected? Do you not see that your conspiracy is already arrested and rendered powerless by the knowledge which every one here possesses of it? What is there that you did last night, what the night before— where is it that you were—who was there that you summoned to meet you—what design was there which was adopted by you, with which you think that any one of us is unacquainted?"[41]

Here, Cicero speaks against Catiline, asking whether or not he understands the situation he has created the the quandary in which he now finds himself. Cicero wants to cause Catiline to think upon his actions and then to elicit a response from him.

- **Introduction paradoxical** – We recall from Logic that a paradox is something which appears one way, but actually is another. This type of introduction should intrigue the reader, making him wonder if, although something may seem impossible, it may actually be possible. Furthermore, the world is often paradoxical, and we can learn from those apparent contradictions. The thesis is the clarifying response to the paradox. This is perhaps the most difficult of introduction types to compose, for it requires a nuance of style and forethought about what you intend to prove.

Frederick Douglass' Fourth of July speech at Rochester in 1852 makes use of this introduction type in order to point out the horrors of American slavery:

---

[41] M. Tullius Cicero. *The Orations of Marcus Tullius Cicero*, literally translated by C. D. Yonge, B. A. London. Henry G. Bohn, York Street, Covent Garden. 1856.

Your high independence only reveals the immeasurable distance between us. The blessings in which you this day rejoice are not enjoyed in common. The rich inheritance of justice, liberty, prosperity, and independence bequeathed by your fathers is shared by you, not by me. The sunlight that brought life and healing to you has brought stripes and death to me. This Fourth of July is yours, not mine. You may rejoice, I must mourn. To drag a man in fetters into the grand illuminated temple of liberty, and call upon him to join you in joyous anthems, were inhuman mockery and sacrilegious irony.[42]

The paradox comes as Douglass illuminates the simultaneous, different effects that sunlight brings: "life and healing" versus "stripes and death"; a chained man being brought into a "temple of liberty" with concurrent "joyous anthems" and "inhuman mockery and sacrilegious irony." Douglass argues that the liberty celebrated by Americans each Fourth of July is incompatible with the practice of slavery.

- **Introduction corrective** – In this type of introduction the speaker exposes a situation that has been neglected or misunderstood, and goes about preparing the audience for a solution. The thesis statement is the crux of the correction, the right viewpoint the audience is supposed to take.

  In 1873, when Susan B. Anthony spoke "On Women's Right to Vote," she begins:

  > Friends and fellow citizens: I stand before you tonight under indictment for the alleged crime of having voted at the last presidential election, without having a lawful right to vote. It shall be my work this evening to prove to you that in thus voting, I not only committed no crime, but, instead, simply exercised my citizen's rights, guaranteed to me and all United States citizens by the National Constitution, beyond the power of any state to deny.[43]

  Here, she corrects the notion that it is wrong for a woman to vote and that it is actually a right of every citizen.

- **Introduction narrative** – Tells a story, which often works well to excite interest in the subject. Again, this type of introduction may be weak if merely reduced to storytelling. Like all introduction types, we must point our audience toward the thesis. How will your story set up your argument? President Jawaharlal Nehru, in 1947, spoke before the Constituent Assembly of India in New Delhi about the independence they were about to gain. She desired to set up the gravity of the new step their nation would soon take in her speech "A Tryst with Destiny":

  > Long years ago we made a tryst with destiny, and now the time comes when we shall redeem our pledge, not wholly or in full measure, but very substantially.
  > At the stroke of the midnight hour, when the world sleeps, India will awake to life and freedom. A moment comes, which comes but rarely in history, when we step out from the old to the new, when an age ends, and when the soul of a nation, long suppressed, finds utterance.
  > It is fitting that at this solemn moment we take the pledge of dedication to the service of India and her people and to the still larger cause of humanity.
  > At the dawn of history India started on her unending quest, and trackless centuries are filled with her striving and the grandeur of her success and her failures. Through

---

[42]   http://www.historyplace.com/speeches/douglass.htm

[43]   http://www.historyplace.com/speeches/anthony.htm

good and ill fortune alike she has never lost sight of that quest or forgotten the ideals which gave her strength. We end today a period of ill fortune and India discovers herself again.[44]

Notice how she has briefly painted a picture for her audience: a nation has awakened to the need to move from darkness to light, and to step forth into self-determination, taking control of their own nation.

Ingratiating

In the Introduction, a speaker ingratiates himself with the audience. Corbett says, "The introduction seeks to render the audience *attentive, benevolent*—that is, well-disposed toward the writer and his or her cause, and *docile*—that is, ready to be instructed or persuaded."[45]

The writer seeking to establish himself as a credible source of information will do so subtly, not flaunting his credentials. Pastor and theologian RC Sproul, in a teaching series titled *Essential Truths of the Christian Faith*, notes something of importance about prophets in the Old Testament who need to convince their audience that God has sent them–has commissioned them as prophets. They give their credentials near the beginning of their prophecies. Why? Their audiences need to know that the Lord has sent them to declare an important word to His people. This gives them credibility with their audiences.

God has called Isaiah to deliver pronouncements of the terrible hand of judgment that would befall His people, as well as the promise of a deliverer, the Messiah who will save them. After he has delivered the first of God's judgments in Chapters 1 through 5, Isaiah then describes how he has been given the terrible and glorious mantle of authority that enables him to speak. "In the year that King Uzziah died I [Isaiah] saw the Lord sitting upon a throne, high and lifted up; and the train of his robe filled the temple" (*ESV*, Isaiah 6.1). He continues to describe how God had given this burden of prophecy. Isaiah protests that he is not worthy, but a seraphim touches his lips with a burning coal, and then God says, "Go..." (6.4-9). Given these credentials, now Isaiah can continue to speak the words that God had given him.

On the subject of making himself more credible, a speaker or writer must briefly forestall any damaging prejudices the audience might have of him. Corbett suggests **eight ways a speaker would counteract prejudices or misconceptions,** as listed below.[46] The *ninth* item was suggested by a former student who was concerned that a biblical worldview had not been included. The writer may need to take time to counteract prejudices or misconceptions about himself or his topic. Cicero talks about these ingratiations primarily in a legal sense–when accused, open your plea in these ways. As student rhetoricians, a legal defense is going to be a rarity. We should instead think: how do we want our audience to be disposed toward us? Ponder the following options in this light.

1. deny the charges that have created the prejudices against them
2. admit the charges but deny their alleged magnitude
3. cite a compensating virtue or action
4. attribute the discrediting action to an honest mistake on their part or to an accident or to an inescapable compulsion

---

44   https://www.wwnorton.com/college/english/nael/20century/topic_1/jawnehru.htm

45   Corbett, *Classical Rhetoric*, 267

46   Corbett, *Classical Rhetoric*, 266

5. cite others who were guilty of the same thing but were not so charged
6. substitute a different motive or cause for the one alleged
7. inveigh against calumny and malicious insinuation in general
8. cite the testimony of those who take a different view of the matter
9. repent and admit to error (not included by Cicero, but essential to a biblical worldview)

In the introduction, if it is appropriate, a writer may also arouse hostility against his opponent. When is it appropriate? Consider when a president or foreign leader wants to declare war. His task is to rally his people around the necessity and idea of a war.

Think of President Franklin Delano Roosevelt's address to the nation on December 8, 1941 after the Japanese attack on Pearl Harbor:

> Yesterday, December 7th, 1941–a date which will live in infamy–the United States of America was suddenly and deliberately attacked by naval and air forces of the Empire of Japan.[47]

Roosevelt uses the words "infamy," "deliberately," and "suddenly" to describe what happened. He is not softening the blow. He wants the American people to be outraged after the attack and Congress to feel compelled to approve his declaration of war on the Empire of Japan.

From here on, you should be able to decide the type of introduction in any discourse you read. This builds on the previous sections, in which you discover the type of discourse and the thesis statement of the discourse.

---

[47] http://www.americanrhetoric.com/speeches/fdrpearlharbor.htm

In Summary, Lesson 8:

Clarifying questions to ask

- What...
- Who...
- What is going on...
- What...presuppositions
- How much...

Five Types of Introductions

1. Preparatory
2. Inquisitive
3. Paradoxical
4. Corrective
5. Narrative

Terms to Remember:

- Forestall
- Paradox
- Crux
- Tryst
- Ingratiate
- Benevolent
- Docile
- Credentials
- Inveigh
- Calumny
- Malicious
- Insinuation

Lesson Eight Assignments

Assignment 8.1
Read an example of Introduction Inquisitive, Cicero's "Catiline" speech. Number the paragraphs. What makes this an inquisitive introduction? What purpose does that kind of introduction serve for this particular discourse? Find the thesis, and explain (briefly) why you think this is the thesis. Two paragraphs.

Assignment 8.2
Read Plato's "Apology of Socrates." Number the paragraphs, as always, and answer the following questions in two to three paragraphs. What type of discourse is this? What type of introduction is this? Why? How does he ingratiate himself/counteract prejudice? Complete the worksheet for this assignment and turn it in.

Assignment 8.4
Read William Pitt, "On the Stamp Act." How does he *prepare* his audience here, and for what is he preparing them? How does he ingratiate himself? One paragraph.

Assignment 8.5
Re-read Winston Churchill's "Blood, Toil, Tears and Sweat" and answer the following questions in two to three paragraphs. Be sure to give examples. What kind of introduction does he employ? Why? What is his thesis? Why? Complete the worksheet for this assignment and turn it in.

Assignment 8.6
Read George W. Bush's "Freedom in Iraq and Middle East." In two to three pages answer the following questions. Complete the worksheet for this assignment and turn it in.

- Tell what kind of speech this is, and why.

- Tell what you believe the thesis is, and why. Where is it found? How does he support it?

- Tell what kind of introduction you find, and why. There could be more than one answer here. Explain which paragraphs cover the introduction (paragraphs one through…?). Remember that since this is a longer speech, the intro may be more than just a couple of paragraphs. It must be, like a statement of facts, proportionate to the length of the discourse.

- Discuss the importance of this speech given the time (era) in which it is delivered. In other words, here is the time for you to do a little content analysis. Why is it important to discuss the topic at hand, at that time? Does it have relevance? Tell briefly the essence of what he says (perhaps by telling me how he supports his thesis).

Assignment 8.7
Using the last essay you wrote for class, take out any introduction you may have had, and write three different introductions, using three different introduction types we have learned in this lesson. Make it a full paragraph that will lead smoothly into the rest of your essay.

Assignment 8.8

Read Vaclav Havel's "A Contaminated Moral Environment" and examine how he ingratiates himself to his audience. He's a newly inaugurated president of a country just coming out of Soviet oppression, so he has a lot of people who are wary of new leadership. How does he begin to bridge that gap of trust?

Multimedia Focus 8.9

Search online for a video of Winston Churchill speaking. (There are many in which he stands in Parliament to speak.) Make note of how he addresses his audience: he uses both his body language and his words. What are his gestures, and how does he hold his audience's attention? Search online for a video of a recent US President. What do you notice that is unique to Churchill? What is the difference in body language between the two speakers? Compare Churchill with the president you chose. Be ready to discuss.

Multimedia Focus 8.10

Look at a TED Talk online–find one that interests you–and do the same thing as in Assignment 8.9. How does the speaker engage with the audience? How does the speaker introduce the topic? What is the thesis? Two to three paragraphs.

Writing Tips Lesson Eight

Use of "One"

Some writers like to use the neutral "one" in their essays. Many teachers object to this, insisting that a writer is injecting an arbitrary character ("one") into their writing. Some professors are okay with the "one," because it avoids the problem of deciding whether to use "he" or "she" or "he/she" into the essay. If a student is worried about being politically correct for his professor, he could go ahead and use "one," but typically "he" is accepted as the universal reference to humankind. A diligent student will ask his professor or teacher which usage is preferred.

Note: the authors of this text are not offended by the use of the universal "he" referring to humankind.

Usage of he/she/they:

This common pronoun error causes more frustration with students than almost anything. To be sure your pronouns agree, make sure the tenses remain the same. If the subject is singular, the pronoun will be singular. For example, incorrect: "Each student must make sure their paper is stapled." The subject (student) is singular; therefore the pronoun must agree. "Each student must make sure his paper is stapled."

Note on political correctness: University professors and employers might insist that the generic pronoun "he" or "his" is sexist. They may require you to use "he/she" or "he or she." Historically the use of "he" referred to the generic, universal "human being."

The Second Canon:
Arrangement–Statement of Facts

In this part of discourse, the speaker must be very careful to shun every appearance of art and cunning. For there is no time at which the judge is more upon his guard, than when the pleader is relating facts. Let nothing then seem feigned: nothing anxiously concealed. Let all that is said, appear to arise from the cause itself, and not to be the work of the orator. (Blair, *Lectures on Belles Lettres*, Lecture 31)

Statement of Facts (*narratio*), the second division of a discourse, is also called **narration** or **explication** by more ancient scholars. The Statement of Facts must connect to the Introduction with a smooth transition. The final sentence or sentences of the Introduction must serve as a bridge from one to the next. In a court case, the prosecuting lawyer in Statement of Facts would set forth the essential facts of the case under consideration. The defending attorney might use this time to correct misstatements or add detail to the prosecutor's statements. Often in a ceremonial discourse which deals mostly in future events, a long statement of facts will not be necessary.

Statement of Facts is an *expository* section. It describes the facts that have to do with the topic, or simply reminds an audience before going on. Here the writer must state all the facts that need to be known, in a clear, lucid manner. Keep in mind that the writer or speaker has a goal of <u>transitioning</u> from the introduction to the main points of the case. This is the transition, or bridge, in which he lays out the points he will use or elaborate on later in his discourse. This section of the discourse provides <u>background</u> and <u>context</u> for the upcoming argument. Included here are <u>major terms</u> and their <u>definitions</u>: the who, what, when, where, and why. The introduction hooked the reader and provided the argument in capsule, and now the Statement of Facts widens the scope around the situation. Without directly saying, "Here is what I'm going to talk about," the writer is essentially saying it. This section is also orderly: Sometimes chronological order helps (Cicero recommends this order above all others), or from general to particular, or from the more familiar to the less familiar.

It's difficult, at times, to decide what to put into your Statement of Facts. Most often, students put too much in their Statement of Facts–everything but the kitchen sink, it seems. Remember the goal of your discourse is your Proof of Case (SEE: Lesson 10), so your Statement of Facts should <u>not</u> exceed its length. You're making things clear, and sometimes the most remotely connected piece of information is neither the clearest, nor the most helpful. Cicero advises that we should "not shift to another subject...trace the affair back to its remotest beginning, nor carry it too far forward, and...not omit anything pertinent;" in short: "begin it at the place at which we need to begin" and take it "to the point to which we need to go."[48] We must begin to use our judgment and discretion when deciding what to use in our discourses. Every single fact that you can possibly cram into your essay is wholly unnecessary; you'll bore your reader with extraneous details before you begin to prove your case!.

---

[48]   Cicero, *Ad Herennium*, 1.15, 14

Cicero says that "[a] Statement of Facts should have three qualities: <u>brevity</u>, <u>clarity</u>, and <u>plausibility</u>."[49] **Brevity:** a writer must be brief, only using as much time as it takes in proportion to the discourse. A short speech requires only a small statement of facts. Aristotle thought this was laughable, and asked, why can't the length be just right, instead of short or long? He believed that the length should be fitting to the subject at hand.

Clarity: the writer must be clear. Remember: the point of your discourse is to convince someone of something. If you're not clear, you're not going to be able to persuade. "Here we must see that our language is not confused, involved, or unfamiliar."[50] Use understandable language that appeals to and guides your audience. If you're explaining why something happened, providing a list of reasons or causes leading up to the event is helpful. Start the recital of facts at a point where it begins to concern the readers. Exclude all irrelevancies: Take out anything which neither adds to nor detracts from your discourse.

Plausible: When Cicero says "plausible," he's talking about believability. A writer or speaker is more plausible if he is ethical. If his authority and character are trusted, the discourse is bound to be more believable. We'll deal more with this in the lesson on *ethos* (SEE: Lesson 15).

Read the following paragraph from Hugh Blair's essay on Taste. This was a common Statement of Facts back when he wrote it.

> There are few subjects on which men talk more loosely and indistinctly than on taste; few which it is more difficult to explain with precision; and none which in this course of Lectures will appear more dry or abstract. What I have to say on the subject, shall be in the following order. I shall first explain the nature of Taste as a power or faculty in the human mind. I shall next consider, how far it is an improveable faculty. I shall show the sources of its improvement, and the characters of taste in its most perfect state. I shall then examine the various fluctuations to which it is liable, and inquire whether there be any standard to which we can bring the different tastes of men, in order to distinguish the corrupted from the true.[51]

Would the passage above serve as an effective Statement of Facts today? Why or why not?

Read Winston Churchill's speech "The Few" (1940). How does he use his Statement of Facts to prepare his audience for the actions England will be taking? Would this serve as an effective Statement of Facts today? Why or why not?

---

[49]   Cicero, *Ad Herennium*, 1.14

[50]   Cicero, *Ad Herennium*, 1.15

[51]   Hugh Blair, *Lectures on Rhetoric and Belles Lettres*, p. 87

In Summary, Lesson 9:

Statement of Facts is a bridge between…

Three Qualities of Statement of Facts:
- Brevity
- Clarity
- Plausibility

Terms to Remember:
- Cunning
- Feign
- Expository
- Lucid
- Brevity
- Clarity
- Plausible

Lesson Nine Assignments

Assignment 9.1

Read "Chronicle of an Undeception" by Michael Bauman. In three to four paragraphs, answer the following: Explain how paragraphs four through nine, as the Statement of Facts, lay out the facts that will be covered in this discourse. Why is it called the Statement of Facts? What is the thesis? Why/where found? What kind of discourse is this? Why? Complete the worksheet for this assignment and turn it in.

Assignment 9.2

Read Joseph Stalin's "Speech on Red Square on the Anniversary Celebration of the October Revolution." What type of Introduction does he use? Where does his Statement of Facts begin and end? Why? Make sure you prove your point by including brief quotes. Two to three paragraphs.

Assignment 9.3

Sometimes discourses make references to events or common phrases that have slipped out of usage today. That can make a discourse more difficult to understand. Become a student of history while at the same time studying rhetoric. For example, take a second look at "Chronicle of an Undeception." Take time to note some references that are not quite as clear today as they were in 1996, when this essay was published. Take time to research some of those terms and phrases, and spend time discussing them in class. What can you conclude about writing from this exercise?

Assignment 9.4

Read George W. Bush's speech "Freedom in Iraq and the Middle East." What type of Introduction does he use? Where does his Statement of Facts begin and end? Why? Make sure you prove your point by including brief quotes. Two to three paragraphs.

Writing Tips Lesson Nine

Double Quotes or Single Quotes?

When should you use a double quotation mark (") and a single quotation mark, or apostrophe (')? First let's eliminate the obvious: use an apostrophe when appropriate. Now, as for the use of the single quote, the ONLY time to employ it is when you have a quote within a quote.

Incorrect usage:

The news reporter referred to his source as a 'senior staff member.'

Correct usage:

The news reporter referred to his source as a "senior staff member."

Incorrect usage:

Chamberlain said, "In the German broadcast last night, which recited the 16 points of the proposals which they have put forward, there occurred this sentence: "In these circumstances the Reich Government considers its proposals rejected"" (6).

Correct usage:

Chamberlain said, "In the German broadcast last night, which recited the 16 points of the proposals which they have put forward, there occurred this sentence: 'In these circumstances the Reich Government considers its proposals rejected'" (6).

Note the placement of the citation in relation to the quotation marks and the period at the end of the sentence. The citation *always* goes at the end of the sentence. Always.

Many writers also attempt to use single quotes in the same way they would use air quotes. However, this is extremely informal. Find another way to demonstrate your sarcasm or verbal irony.

Lesson Ten

The Second Canon: Arrangement–Proof of Case (Confirmation)

> The entire hope of victory and entire method of persuasion rest on proof and refutation, for when we have submitted our arguments and destroyed those of the opposition, we have, of course, completely fulfilled the speaker's function. (Cicero, *Ad Herennium* 1.18)
>
> With regard to the different degrees of strength in arguments, the general rule is, to advance in the way of climax. This especially is to be the course, when the speaker has a clear cause, and is confident that he can prove it fully. He may then adventure to begin with feebler arguments; rising gradually, and not putting forth his whole strength till the last, when he can trust to his making a successful impression on the minds of hearers, prepared by what has gone before. But this rule is not to be always followed: for, if he distrusts his cause, and has but one material argument on which to lay the stress, putting less confidence in the rest, in this case, it is often proper for him to place this material argument in the front; to preoccupy the hearers early, and make the strongest effort at first; that, having removed prejudices, and disposed them to be favourable, the rest of his reasoning may be listened to with more candour. (Murray, *Murray's English Grammar*, 329)

Proof of the Case or Confirmation, is the third division of the discourse (*confirmatio*). This is the "meat" of the discourse, where we do what we started out to do—to prove our point. This is the main body, where we explain or persuade. The introduction of a discourse established what you would argue, the Statement of Facts provided context and definitions, and now the Proof of Case gets to the goal: the argument.

Once we have gone through the discovery process, we can arrange our Proofs. In this section, the largest and most significant of the discourse, we use the main bulk of information that was gathered during the process of invention. As we read and discover, we are mentally arranging the evidence. What points do we use, and in what order?

Organization of the Proof of Case

A writer has many options of methods for presenting information. These methods come from Aristotle and Cicero, and the final two on this list come from Hugh Blair.

- **Chronological**, sometimes in an expository discourse: we move from what happened first, to what followed next, and then next, and so forth. This is very likely in a courtroom, where the prosecutor presents events, one after the other, to prove where the accused was and what he has done, step by step. We could also see this in some deliberative or epideictic speeches, such as when Churchill brings his audience up to date on the events of the war.

- **From general to particular**, for a more complicated expository discourse: starting with broader ideas which the audience can understand, then narrowing our focus more and more.

This can be found where a leader tells his audience that the war has begun (general), and then he describes what must be done in order to win–on this front and in this region (particular).

- **From familiar to unknown**, also for complicated expository: our audience will nod in agreement because we have begun with topics or facts with which they are conversant. Once the audience agrees with the ideas with which they are more familiar, the speaker can move off into some (related) points, bringing his audience with him. Remember, this is to prove a point, so he needs to make sure that he doesn't head into the unknown too quickly, before gaining an understanding from the audience.

- A writer might **begin with the weakest argument and build up to the strongest argument** (an *a fortiori* approach, meaning "from the stronger"). This has the effect of gaining momentum throughout the discourse. It could prove to be a useful employment of *Ethos*. The *a fortiori* option is best, according to Aristotle. It leaves the strongest arguments as final thoughts in the audience's mind. Some rhetoricians vacillate on that point, as seen above in the quote by Murray, who names different scenarios in which weakest-to-strongest or strongest-to-weakest might be best.

- **Refute opposing arguments first and then present your arguments**. More discussion of Refutation will come in Lesson 11. A writer must be careful not to spend her entire time refuting. Too much, and the audience will begin to suspect that your only argument is that your opponent's case is flawed but then not know what kind of alternative you are presenting. Beware of this type of argument in political debates; it might signal that your argument is weak if you only spend time attacking your opponent.

- **Establish the case and then refute the opposition**. This can be effectively used alongside other proposed methods here. While presenting a chronological approach, the writer can describe, step-by-step, what happened and also refute the opposing side's description of the events.

- **Sandwich method:** Alternate refutation with proof, one argument at a time.

- **Analytic method (brick by brick):** the speaker or writer obscures the main points he wants to prove while he moves through his argument. Bit by bit he brings his audience to the point he tries to prove. As he progresses he moves his audience from one point to the next, until his audience sees what he's been trying to prove all along. In other words, he has built his argument, like a building, brick by brick. Not until the last brick is in place does the audience finally see the construction. In a sense he finally pulls back the curtain for the audience to see it full and complete. (This is the method C.S. Lewis uses in *Mere Christianity*, in which he begins with a basic agreement of a moral law existing in every person, and then he finally draws the reader to the conclusion that God, the author of the moral law, exists. The audience may not at first agree that God exists, but when a person agrees with the first point, the existence of a universal moral law, then he can then move on to the next point, and the next, until the conclusion is reached.)

- **Synthetic method:** This method seems to be the reverse of the analytic. Here the writer or speaker will tell his audience the point he wants to prove (the thesis), and then he spends the rest of his argument proving it. In other words, he would come very close to saying, simply, "This is what I am going to prove, and how I will prove it, so follow along with me."

- Sometimes **the nature of the topic will suggest the appropriate procedure**. Recognize that what works in one situation will not always work in every other. The writer or speaker must be aware of factors such as 1) the audience's familiarity with the subject, 2) the audience's mood toward the subject: are they angry? Scared? Do they need reassurance? Are they ready to take out their pocketbook and give money toward a cause?

Grounding your Proof of Case in the Three Appeals

Your Confirmation relies on the three appeals to work. Later lessons will discuss each of the different appeals in much greater detail, but it is important here to note that the three appeals (*Logos, Pathos, Ethos*) must work together to create a rhetorically sound discourse. One appeal should not stand alone as the only method of persuasion.

If a discourse *only* employs *logos*–reason–it can tend to appear dry, maybe only an extension of the Statement of Facts. Besides, humans are not persuaded solely by logic, as we're not from the planet Vulcan. We rely on emotion and ethics to add to the reasonable propositions given to us. At the same time, we tend to be persuaded more by emotion than anything else. Think about commercials from the ASPCA: there is no logical case provided for *why* you must help the animals at the Humane Society; all they have to do is show videos from an animal shelter so you can look into the eyes of an abused animal. Those ads focus on gut feeling and pity. People have gone to war merely because of anger, rather than looking at a logical process guiding them toward a conclusion.

The appeal that gets the least attention is *ethos*–ethical appeal–because more often than not, our relativistic world denies the existence of one consistent, absolute Truth; they say "your ethics are different than my ethics." As Christians, we know that there is <u>one</u> source of ethics: Scripture, and appealing to right and wrong should be based solely on the Bible. It is our measuring stick, our guide, and our authority.

Absolute truth is the linchpin of the Gospel. It is an attribute of God's character (John 14.6-7). Imagine someone trying to argue with you that the number four does not equal four! No, it's absolutely four! Think of different areas or topics in which someone might argue against an absolute truth. Would it work to go through life thinking that way?

The three appeals need to go hand in hand in order to persuade. Emotion may spark a conversation or the writing of a discourse, aiding in invention. We should argue rationally, ensuring that people are making decisions based upon careful consideration of facts. Finally, we should make sure that our decisions are based upon God's word, for we know that our reasoning cannot go against what the Bible says.

In Summary, Lesson 10:

Another name for Proof of Case:
    Confirmation

Purpose of Proof of Case...

Organization options for Proof:
- Chronological
- General to Particular
- Familiar to Unknown
- Nature of Topic may suggest the order
- From Weakest to Strongest
- Refute first, then argue
- Argue first, then refute
- Analytic
- Synthetic

Term to Remember:
    A fortiori

Lesson Ten Assignments

Assignment 10.1

Read Winston Churchill's "Be Ye Men of Valour" speech. What is the thesis? Where is the Proof of Case and how does he argue it? Answer this in two to three paragraphs. Complete the worksheet for this assignment and turn it in.

Assignment 10.2

Read Benjamin Netanyahu's speech "Against Iran's Nuclear Program" (you can also watch a video of this speech online). How does he introduce his topic? How does he ingratiate himself to his audience? Where is his Statement of Facts and how does he use it? How does he argue his thesis (and where is his Proof of Case contained)? Respond in three to five paragraphs.

Assignment 10.3

Read "On the Horrors of the Slave Trade" by William Wilberforce. How does he introduce his topic? How does he ingratiate himself to his audience? Where is his Statement of Facts and how does he use it? How does he argue his thesis (and where is his Proof of Case contained)? Respond in three to five paragraphs.

Writing Tips Lesson Ten

Use of numbers

Numbers must receive consistent treatment throughout your writing. When spelling out numerals, it's pretty straightforward. If you can spell out the numeral in two words or less, do it. If you need more than two words, use numerals. However, if you've got a lot of numbers in one sentence or paragraph that fall on either side of this rule, choose one and be consistent.

- One hundred vs. 101 (which would need to be spelled out as one hundred and one—just use the numeral!)
- Twenty-two vs. 222
- One-half vs. 1½

Never begin a sentence with a numeral. Spell out the number instead, or reword the sentence.

Dates should be treated consistently: May 9, 1995. Do not write May the 9th, 1995 or May 9th, 1995. A variation that works would be the ninth of May, 1995, or the twenty-fifth of May.

Lesson Eleven

The Second Canon: Arrangement–Refutation

When the pleader comes to refute the arguments employed by his adversary, he should be on his guard not to do them injustice, by disguising, or placing them in a false light. The deceit is soon discovered; it will not fail of being exposed; and tends to impress the judge and the hearers with distrust of the speaker, as one who either wants discernment to perceive, or wants fairness to admit, the strength of the reasoning on the other side. Whereas, when they see that he states, with accuracy and candour, the arguments which have been used against him, before he proceeds to combat them, a strong prejudice is created in his favour. They are naturally led to think, that he has a clear and full conception of all that can be said on both sides of the argument; that he has entire confidence in the goodness of his own cause; and does not attempt to support it by any artifice or concealment. The judge is thereby inclined to receive much more readily, the impressions which are given him by a speaker, who appears both so fair and so penetrating. There is no part of the discourse, in which the orator has greater opportunity of showing a masterly address, than when he sets himself to represent the reasonings of his antagonists, in order to refute them. (Hugh Blair, *Lectures on Belles Lettres*)

Refutation (*refutatio*) is the fourth division of the discourse.

Refutation means "rebuttal," or argument against the opposition. In this division a speaker refutes opposing views in debate or in writing. In a debate where both views are presented, the debater must refute his opponent as his topics are being presented. In writing, the writer has the option of addressing all opposing views, or just some of them. However logical and reasonable our arguments may be, doubts will remain in the minds of our audience if we do not anticipate the objections to our thesis and answer them.

In refutation the speaker or writer will identify the actual point of contention with others and address it. He does not argue what they agree on, but those aspects with which he and his opponents disagree–he exposes the inadequacies of opposing arguments.

If the audience has received the opposing views favorably, refute first, then present your argument. If the opposing argument is weak, present your argument, then refute your opponent. The sequence is not set in stone! Use what works best.

Remember that classical refutation is a section or division of a discourse. Often in contemporary discourses refutation is scattered throughout the discourse.

There are **four methods** by which a speaker can refute:

Refutation by Appeal to Reason (*Logos*). Here it is most helpful for students to remember their logic. In this method of refutation the speaker will prove the contradictory (or the impossibility) of his opponent's argument. (Remember your Logic: a thing cannot *be* and *not be* at the same time.) Demolish the arguments by which the proposition is supported: One side argues the feasibility of one point, and the other side would argue that his opponent's point is not feasible: a classic argument.

The speaker can deny the truth of one of the premises on which the argument rests and prove that the premise is false, through evidence or testimony, perhaps. He can object to the inferences drawn from the premises, by saying:

- "I admit the principle, but I deny that it leads to such a consequence."
- "I admit the principle but I deny that it applies in this case."
- "Your assertion is true, but it has no force as an argument to support your conclusion" (Corbett, *Classical Rhetoric*, 279).

Think of a current or recent event where some of this happens. Presidential politics, or examples of politicians' excuses for immoral behavior, are pretty good (irresistible) examples.

While there are ways to refute with logic, some arguments only use probabilities, which cannot be refuted by logic. While probabilities are more difficult to refute, the speaker can use examples or look for the missing premise (enthymeme), if there is one, and refute that by exposing the unspoken, underlying premise.

Refutation by Appeal to Emotion (*Pathos*). Here the speaker could appeal to the emotions of the audience, through pity or vivid descriptions, to sway their opinion and convince them that his argument is more valid than another's. It is important to know the audience here; an emotional appeal could blow up in your face if the audience is not receptive to emotional appeal or if your refutation is disproportionate in relation to the argument.

The speaker must gear his emotional refutation to appeal to the type of audience. Again, it is important to gauge the attitudes of the audience. Are they sympathetic to your case? In a largely mixed (heterogeneous) audience, you must decide which emotion will appeal to the largest majority of the audience as you refute your opponent.

Refutation by Appeal to Ethics (*Ethos*). Ethics must be present in every part of the discourse, but most importantly it must be maintained in the refutation. Aristotle said: "It is more fitting for a good man to display himself as an honest fellow than as a subtle reasoner."[52] Sometimes when our argument is weak, we carry weight if we are more ethical than our opponent.

Refutation by Wit.[53] The use of wit–humor–can catch an audience by surprise, perhaps defusing a tense moment of argumentation. "It is commonly said, and more particularly by Lord Shaftesbury, that ridicule is the best test of truth."[54] If what is alleged to be the truth can survive the

---

[52]   Aristotle, *Rhetoric* 3.17

[53]   Keep in mind that Wit–the use of humor–is not a means of persuasion, as are *pathos*, *ethos*, and *logos*. Some students can become confused.

[54]   Attributed to Philip Stanhope, 4th Earl of Chesterfield (https://libquotes.com/philip-stanhope)

onslaught of ridicule, it must really be the truth. One warning about ridicule, or wit: even though it is truth, it can still be rendered absurd in the minds of the audience, because wit can insult.

> It is the design of wit to excite in the mind an agreeable surprise, and that arising, not from any thing marvelous in the subject, but solely from the imagery she employs, or the strange assemblage of related ideas presented to the mind. This end is effected in one or other of these three ways: first in debasing things pompous or seemingly grave: I say seemingly grave, because to vilify what is truly grave has something shocking in it, which rarely fails to counteract the end: secondly, in aggrandizing things little and frivolous: thirdly, in setting ordinary objects, by means not only remote, but apparently contrary, in a particular and uncommon point of view.[55]

Wit and *ethos*

Jokes can be effective but used with utmost discretion. When refuting an opponent's claims, your audience may not appreciate a joke well, unless you know your audience well. Sarcasm and crass or obscene jokes are not welcomed and may jeopardize your *ethos*. If your argument is weak, wit might not be helpful, and it may also hurt your *ethos*.

Irony, Satire, and Deprecatory Humor

If your opponent is monotone and sober, wit can be used effectively to lighten the moment–just be sure your wit is appropriate to the topic. Some topics need to be treated soberly from beginning to end.

Irony can work as refutation, but some audiences might take the speaker seriously. Think of how Job uses irony when his "friends" come to comfort him. Instead of comfort, they point out the many reasons they can think of, for why he is in such a sorry state. He points that out with irony in Job 12.2: "No doubt you are the [only wise] people [in the world], and wisdom will die with you!" (*Amplified*).

Satire is a most popular form of wit—most of the great English satirists were schooled in rhetoric. Today satire can be found in political cartoons, in which an artist might exaggerate a flaw for effect, such as physical features of public figures (President Trump's hair, President Barack Obama's ears, or President Gerald Ford's habit of falling down in public).

Self-deprecation can be effective; it harms no one and may make a point. In a 1984 presidential debate against Walter Mondale, Ronald Reagan, one of the oldest candidates in history, said, "I will not make age an issue of this campaign. I am not going to exploit, for political purposes, my opponent's youth and inexperience." Here Reagan acknowledged some concerns about his advanced age, but he used it to his advantage and lightened the mood with a little joke on himself.

---

[55] Campbell, "The Philosophy of Rhetoric," *The Rhetoric of Blair, Whately and Campbell*, 150

In Summary, Lesson 11:

Four methods of Refutation

- Logos
- Pathos
- Ethos
- Wit

Terms to Remember:

- Artifice
- Heterogeneous
- Debase
- Pompous
- Vilify
- Aggrandize
- Frivolous
- Deprecatory
- Sarcasm
- Irony

Lesson Eleven Assignments

Assignment 11.1

Read then-Senator Richard Nixon's "Checkers" speech. Highlight the refutations you find, using paragraph numbers as reference points. Define at least 20 refutations, using just phrases instead of full sentences. Briefly identify all 4 types (even though we've not gone into detail in all 4 yet). Then look more closely at refutation by ethical appeal. Hindsight is always best, because we know about the scandal with which Nixon was involved as president. But be ready to discuss his ethical refutations. What can we conclude, in general, about someone's need to defend his ethics so vigorously?

Assignment 11.2

Read Mike Adams' article "I Used to Love Her but I Had To Kill Her" in *AFE*. He specifically and directly addresses four rebuttals and makes his own counterarguments as well. Which type(s) of refutation does he employ here? How does he go about actually employing refutation? Do his rebuttals work? Two to three pages.

Assignment 11.3

Read Wilberforce's "On the Horrors of the Slave Trade" again. What type of discourse is this? Find the thesis, the type of discourse, and tell what type of refutation you find. Discuss and show examples of his ethical appeal. Three paragraphs.

Assignment 11.4

Read Plato's "Apology of Socrates" again. List the refutations he employs, using paragraph numbers as reference points. (You should be very familiar with Socrates by now!) Complete the worksheet for this assignment and turn it in.

Assignment 11.5

Find a great political cartoon that employs satire. You can locate those at news sources online, or use a search on political satire cartoons. Locate a cartoon that pokes fun at some current topic today. Explain how the cartoonist (satirist) turned a current news item into humor. (In other words, did he exaggerate some flaw in a person? Did he use stereotypes? Did he make a play on words? Did he take a serious subject and, by twisting it, did he allow his audience to see it in a new light? What else did he do?) Be ready to show this in class and discuss it with your teacher and classmates.

Writing Tips Lesson Eleven

Long quotes

Just as a short quote is set apart from the text using quotation marks, a long quote should be set apart even more.

Requirements

A long quote...

- Consists of four or more full lines in the text (not <u>on</u> the fourth line, but it is four complete lines)
- Is indented 1/2 inch from the left margin. Hit Enter before typing the quote, as if you've made a new paragraph. Type or paste the quote. Then hit Enter again and continue the paragraph. Do not add extra space between the quote and the paragraph. See example, below. Make sure to cite the source.
- Does not use quotation marks
- Is the ONLY time when a citation goes after the final punctuation mark.

This example demonstrates the double-spacing and single-spacing you need to do correctly:

This text must go before the long quote. Remember that every quote must be "bookended," which means that you must surround your quote with your own words. Also note that this text, above the quote, is double-spaced. The space between this and the quote below must be only a double-space, no more.

> For we may rest assured that whenever we express ourselves ill, there is, besides the mismanagement of language, for the most part, some mistake in our manner of conceiving the subject. Embarrassed, obscure, and feeble sentences are generally, if not always, the result of embarrassed, obscure, and feeble thought. Thought and language act and re-act upon each other mutually. (Blair, *Lectures on Belles Lettres*)

Following the long quote is a continuation of this paragraph, above. Do not indent this first line, since it's still part of the above paragraph. Always bookend a quote. Also always provide good citation for a long quote.

The Second Canon: Arrangement–Conclusion

In all discourses, it is a matter of importance to hit the precise time of concluding, so as to bring our discourse just to a point; neither ending abruptly and unexpectedly; nor disappointing the expectation of the hearers, when they look for the close, and continuing to hover round and round the conclusion, till they become heartily tired of us. We should endeavour to go off with a good grace; not to end with a languishing and drawling sentence; but to close with dignity and spirit, that we may leave the minds of the hearers warm, and dismiss them with a favourable impression of the subject, and of the speaker. (Blair, quoted in Corbett, *Blair, Campbell,* 128)

The Epilogue has four parts. You must 1) make the audience well-disposed towards yourself and ill-disposed towards your opponent, 2) magnify or minimize the leading facts, 3) excite the required state of emotion in your hearers, and 4) refresh their memories. (Aristotle, *Rhetoric* 3.19)

Conclusion, fifth division of a discourse. *Epilogos* (to say in addition). Conclusion is the last impression we make on the audience. Without a conclusion, the discourse strikes us as merely stopping rather than ending with style. Our initial attempt might be to end with a flourish, with emotional intensity. Sometimes this is overdone and can detract from the solid achievements of the earlier parts of the discourse. Discretion is also important here.

Students agonize over writing an introduction and a conclusion in their essays or papers. Sometimes these sections feel false or forced. In his Book 3, Chapter 19, Aristotle gives his idea of what should be done in the Conclusion:

There are four approaches to the Conclusion:

*   To inspire the audience by disposing the hearer favorably towards oneself and unfavorably towards the adversary;

*   To amplify your points and depreciate the points of your opponent;

*   To excite the emotions of the hearer, rousing them to action;

*   To recapitulate.

    For after you have proved that you are truthful and that the adversary is false, the natural order of things is to praise ourselves, blame him, and put the finishing touches. One of two things should be aimed at: to show that you are either relatively or absolutely good and the adversary either relatively or absolutely bad. The topics which serve to represent men as good or bad have already been stated.[56]

Keeping in mind his formula, you might feel a bit more comfortable and may find a way through your writer's block.

---

[56] http://www.perseus.tufts.edu/hopper/collection?collection=Perseus:collection:Greco-Roman, bullets added.

Recapitulation (recap) in the conclusion. Here we restate in capsule form the important points. It might be helpful to remind the audience what has been said. Sometimes facts which may have seemed buried in the middle of our discourse might sit nicely in capsule here.

Recapitulation is vital in a court trial. After much testimony the final argument, or recapitulation, is important to remind the jury of the major points of the trial, and his client's argument.

Pathos can be best used here, and it is popular also, if used correctly and by a person of great *ethos*. An emotional appeal can be overdone, though. "Bombastic" emotional appeals are used less now than they were in the past. We rely more now on style and less on direct *pathos*. People tend to be suspicious of a bombastic style.

An emotional conclusion can be a call to action: it can inspire patriotism, incite people to war, or encourage people to band together to solve problems. A well-written conclusion can dispose the audience favorably toward the writer or speaker.

The ethical appeal in a conclusion is appropriate only if it has already been established earlier. Certain kinds of ethical appeal seem more appropriate in the conclusion:

- frank confession of our shortcomings
- honest acknowledgment of the strength of the opposing case
- magnanimous gestures toward vindictive opponents.

In Summary, Lesson 12:

Four approaches in Conclusion:

1. Inspire...
2. Amplify...
3. Excite...
4. Recapitulate

Terms to Remember:

- Epilogue
- Amplify
- Recapitulate
- Bombastic
- Magnanimous
- Vindictive

Lesson Twelve Assignments

Assignment 12.1

Read Neville Chamberlain's speech from 1939. Tell how he concludes, according to Aristotle's definition of conclusions. Also identify and discuss the thesis, type of discourse, type of introduction, and type(s) of refutation. One to two paragraphs. Complete the worksheet and turn it in.

Assignment 12.2

Persuasive piece REWRITE. Take one of the opinion pieces you have written this year, review all comments on it, and rewrite it. Hand in the original piece (version 1) <u>and</u> the rewrite (version 2), using the version numbers at the top of each, together. Post version 2 for comment by your classmates.

Assignment 12.3

Read Winston Churchill's "This Was Their Finest Hour." How does he conclude? What does he seek to do in his conclusion. One to two paragraphs.

Assignment 12.4

Reread "This House is Not for Sale" by Andy Rooney and "She Did Good" by Paul Harvey and identify the different parts of Arrangement. Do they have each of the parts? Are they in the proper order? Does this help or hurt? What would happen if something was rearranged? Does anything need to be added?

Assignment 12.5

Read "With Malice Toward None," Abraham Lincoln's second inaugural address. How does he conclude? What method does he use? How does it help him to accomplish his thesis' goal?

Assignment 12.6

Read the excerpt of this article about a BMW ad that was aired in early 2014. Perhaps you can find a video of it online.

RAM did it with Paul Harvey. Apple did it with Walt Whitman (by way of Robin Williams). Visa did it with Amelia Earhart. Now, it's BMW's turn to use the poetic words of a long-ago visionary to sell a modern product.

The automaker uses a recording of Arthur C. Clarke to celebrate the promise of the future, as realized today by the new BMW i-series of electric cars.

"Trying to predict the future is a discouraging and hazardous occupation," Clark says in the audio recording from 1964 which serves as the voiceover for BMW i's 60-second launch spot, "Hello Future." ...

Clark goes on: "If by some miracle a prophet could describe the future exactly as it was going to take place, his predictions would sound so absurd that people everyone would laugh him to scorn. The only thing we can be sure of about the future is that it will be absolutely fantastic. So, if what I say now seems to you to be very reasonable, then I will have failed completely. Only if what I tell you appears absolutely unbelievable have we any chance of visualizing the future as it really will happen."

Try to explain, in 250 words or less, what this quote by Clark says. Does it effectively communicate a clear message? Why would a car manufacturer choose to use this? Be ready to discuss in class.

Writing Tips Lesson Twelve

Use of titles and names

Remember that the standard for this textbook is MLA. When in doubt, look up usage standards in that style manual.

Names:

The first time a person is mentioned in your writing, refer to him using his full name. Thereafter you may use his last name or title. For example, "Winston Churchill" would be his full name, and then after the first mention you may refer to him as "Churchill." He also has a title, so you might refer to him as "Prime Minister Winston Churchill." Thereafter he could be called "Churchill" or "the Prime Minister." Never refer to him by his first name.

If someone has a readily identifiable other name, such as "Franklin Delano Roosevelt," you can (after referring to him properly the first time) call him "Roosevelt," "President Roosevelt," or "FDR."

Titles:

Book titles are ALWAYS italicized. Speech titles are in quotes.

Italicize these titles:
- Books
- Movies
- Ships' names (including names of spaceships)
- Plays
- Epic-length poems
- Television series or radio show series
- CD titles

These types of titles go in "quotation marks":
- Poems
- Speeches
- Songs (note: the CD title is italicized; the song is in quotes)
- Short stories
- Essays
- Articles from newspapers or magazines
- Episodes from television series or radio shows

The First Type of Appeal: Logic/Reason (*Logos*)
Introduction to *Logos* and Definitions

Of the modes of persuasion furnished by the spoken word there are three kinds. The first kind depends on the personal character of the speaker; the second on putting the audience into a certain frame of mind; the third on the proof, or apparent proof, provided by the words of the speech itself. Persuasion is achieved by **the speaker's personal character** when the speech is so spoken as to make us think him credible. We believe good men more fully and more readily than others: this is true generally whatever the question is, and absolutely true where exact certainty is impossible and opinions are divided. This kind of persuasion, like the others, should be achieved by what the speaker says, not by what people think of his character before he begins to speak. It is not true, as some writers assume in their treatises on rhetoric, that the personal goodness revealed by the speaker contributes nothing to his power of persuasion; on the contrary, his character may almost be called the most effective means of persuasion he possesses. Secondly, persuasion may come through the hearers, when **the speech stirs their emotions**. Our judgements when we are pleased and friendly are not the same as when we are pained and hostile. It is towards producing these effects, as we maintain, that present-day writers on rhetoric direct the whole of their efforts...Thirdly, persuasion is effected through the speech itself when we have **proved a truth or an apparent truth** by means of the persuasive arguments suitable to the case in question. (Aristotle, *The Rhetoric & The Poetics of Aristotle* 1.2, emphasis added)

Just as the soul animates the body, so, in a way, meaning breathes life into a word. (John of Salisbury, The Metalogicon of John of Salisbury: A Twelfth-Century Defense of the Verbal and Logical Arts of the Trivium)

This lesson reviews the prerequisite course of Logic for the rhetoric student (see "How to Use this Text"). If the student has not yet done so, or if it has been several years since his Logic course, these concepts will not be as easy to grasp in the context of rhetoric. We recommend *Introductory Logic* and *Intermediate Logic* by James Nance, both published by Canon Press.

Logic argues and draws conclusions from the premises. In logic, a conclusion is necessarily valid or invalid, true or false. In almost mathematical precision, logic enables the student to arrive at a conclusion.

Rhetoric, on the other hand, rests on probability. The conclusion is not arrived at with the same kind of mathematical certainty; rhetoric deals with whether someone can be persuaded of the possibility of something being true or valid. We will see that over and over throughout our study.

According to Aristotle, we persuade others by three means:
1. by appealing to their reason (*logos*)
2. by appealing to their emotions (*pathos*)

3. by appealing with our personality or character (*ethos*).

We call these the Three Appeals. One, two, or all three of these methods must be used in one discourse. The following factors will determine which of these methods we use:

- Our topic,
- The events surrounding our topic, and
- The audience for the discourse.

Everyone develops some instincts for adapting methods of persuasion to fit the subject, occasion, and audience, but experience and education will enable some people to cultivate their ability to persuade. This is where persuasion becomes more of an art. When persuasion is an art, it becomes rhetoric.

By observing how writers and speakers use these appeals, we can learn how to use them in our own writing.

Appeal to Reason (*logos*). Several different forms of persuasion fall under Appeal to Reason. The use of *definition*, *syllogism*, and *enthymeme* are just a few.

Definition is the foundation for the discussion of the rhetorical appeals to reason. Before anything else, we need to define our terms. When we begin to discuss with and debate one another, we need to clarify terms so that everyone involved uses the same terms with the same meaning. When there is a difference in definition of terms, we end up with confusion for both parties in a discourse, and nothing can be accomplished.

A definition is a statement that gives the meaning of a term. The **purposes for definitions** are listed below.

3. **To show relationships:** A *Connective Definition* demonstrates how one thing relates to another. Here you might define one idea as it relates to another. For example, a person might define marriage in the context of relationships, comparing it to other relationships, or to other marriages in the past.

4. **To remove ambiguity**: A *Lexical Definition* makes things clear, more specific. When a term has more than one meaning, a lexical definition removes verbal disagreement, which we will see later when discussing fallacies. For example, someone might say, "That guy is mad!" Another might answer, "I don't know what you did to make him so angry." To which the other would reply, "No, I mean he is really mad. You know, insane." Here "mad" has two different meanings. The person who uses that word must make his meanings clear.

5. **To reduce vagueness:** A *Precising Definition* is focused as to its extent. This is used when a term is vague or unclear. A term may have one single meaning, but its use or application may be unclear. A person may say it is hot outside, and another will want to know how hot. A precising definition will make that more clear.

6. **To increase vocabulary:** A *Stipulative Definition* is the creation or coining of a new term in order to label a concept.

7. **To explain theoretically:** A *Theoretical Definition* is a scientific or philosophical definition that will make a concept more clear. This is not the definition of something concrete like "flower," but rather something abstract like "love" or "life."

8. **To influence attitudes**: A *Persuasive Definition* is meant to change someone's opinions more than to define a term. This becomes vital in rhetoric, in which we attempt to influence our audience's attitudes. Some examples are:
   - abortion: murder or choice?
   - marriage: union of man and woman or union of two people regardless of sex?

Each of these definitions places the audience at a juncture of choice, almost a trap. The definition itself sets them up for a difficult decision, rather than simply defining a word for what it is. It puts baggage on the definition, a connotation to sway opinion. [57]

Six rules should be our standard for defining terms:[58]

1. *Defining terms should be clearer and more familiar than the term to be defined; do not be too broad or too narrow.* For example, the writer should define the word school as "an institution of higher learning," rather than something that is too unclear, such as "the place where students get tortured all day."

2. *A definition should not repeat the term to be defined* or use synonymous or derivative terms (an incorrect definition would be: "Abortion is the act of aborting a baby"). This is one rule our students learn very early in Rhetoric: It is illegal in our class to repeat the term when defining the word!

3. *A definition, whenever possible, should be stated positively, not negatively.* (It would not be: "Right to Life is against abortion." Instead it should be: "Right to Life advocates the choice of pregnancy over abortion").

4. *State the essential attributes of the term.* Adding to the definition with unnecessary words will not enhance the definition, but will take away from it. (A definition which does not just state the essential attributes of the term, but adds too many words, would be "To pause is to take one's time, to cease moving or acting, to rest in one's action or momentarily hesitate before going on.")

5. *A definition should not be figurative or unclear.* If, for example, the word "sun" is defined as "That great fiery orb that daily circles the globe," that definition is figurative; it is flowery. It is also unclear in that it does not adequately define the term.

6. *Nouns should define nouns; verbs should define verbs.* In other words, the definition should be of the same part of speech as the word to be defined. "Marrying is the state of a wedded union."

Types of Definition

For this section we will be covering six types of definition: Exposition, Essential, Synonym, Etymology, Description, and Example.

---

[57] This information taken with permission from James Nance's *Introductory Logic*, Mars Hill publication of Canon Press.

[58] These rules were found in two sources: Corbett, p. 37, and Nance's *Introductory Logic*, p. 24-25.

A. An Exposition (expository work) is a form of definition, an explanatory work or speech. A dictionary is an explanatory work which defines words. A how-to book or manual explains or defines how something works or operates. And discourses that analyze or classify are also expository definitions.

B. An Essential definition is a term that designates *what something is* (a noun) and *distinguishes it from all other things*; it spells out a thing's fundamental nature. "Man is a rational animal" cannot be true of any other being. That would be an essential definition; it distinguishes "man" from all other things.

A **Genus** is the general class of the thing to be defined. A **Differentia** distinguishes a term from every other thing. The plural of differentia is *differentiae*. (Genus can be remembered as the general term; differentia is the term that makes a difference between it and other similar terms.) Genus in the above definition would be "animal;" "rational" would be the differentia. In the above definition, "a rational animal" is the differentia. If we were to define bird as "an animal with wings," the term "with wings" would be the differentia, as it separates birds from all other animals.

In the definition, "An airplane is a winged vehicle that flies in the sky," the genus is "vehicle" and the differentiae are "winged" and "flies in the sky." Does this differentiate "airplane" from "helicopter"? How would you define "helicopter" in a way that it differs from "airplane"?

Aristotle, in his treatise on *Physics*,[59] speaks to the need of understanding *why* something is, in order to truly understand its ultimate meaning and impact on the world.

> Knowledge is the object of our inquiry, and men do not think they know a thing till they have grasped the 'why' of (which is to grasp its primary cause). So clearly we too must do this as regards both coming to be and passing away and every kind of physical change, in order that, knowing their principles, we may try to refer to these principles each of our problems. (Aristotle, *Physics*, Book II Part 3)

What separates something from everything else? This is the work of the differentia.

Differentiae in a definition often specify one or more of the four causes of a thing: the **material**, the **formal**, the **efficient**, and the **final**.

- The **material** cause is what makes up the thing. Aristotle describes the material cause as "that out of which a thing comes to be and which persists, is called 'cause', e.g. the bronze of the statue, the silver of the bowl, and the genera of which the bronze and the silver are species."[60] The genus in this case is the statue or the bowl, while the differentiae are the bronze or the silver.

- The **formal** cause is the physical description of the thing or "the statement of the essence,"[61] the expression of the material cause.

- The **efficient** cause is the producer or maker of the thing; what caused it to become that thing. This is "the primary source of the change or coming to rest; e.g. the man who gave advice is a cause, the father is cause of the child, and generally what makes of what is made

---

[59] http://classics.mit.edu/Aristotle/physics.2.ii.html

[60] Ibid

[61] Ibid

and what causes change of what is changed."[62] For the bronze statue or the silver bowl, an artist is the efficient cause.

- And the **final** cause is the end use or purpose of the thing: "'that for the sake of which' a thing is done, e.g. health is the cause of walking about. ('Why is he walking about?' we say. 'To be healthy', and, having said that, we think we have assigned the cause.) The same is true also of all the intermediate steps which are brought about through the action of something else as means towards the end, e.g. reduction of flesh, purging, drugs, or surgical instruments are means towards health. All these things are 'for the sake of' the end, though they differ from one another in that some are activities, others instruments."[63] This is the why, the function, the aim.

Here in the (somewhat simplified) definition of "flute" we can see the use of the four causes and the genus:

A Flute is a musical instrument (genus) usually made of silver or nickel (material cause). It is long and hollow with keypads covering the holes (formal cause). A flute is made by an instrument maker or craftsman (efficient cause), and it is played by blowing across one end, which produces a high musical sound (final cause).

Keep in mind that the differentiae would change if we would attempt to define various kinds of musical instruments. The causes will not always appear in that order, and in some definitions a person will not always see every cause. For example, we may not always know the specific person who designed the flute, though we can likely know the manufacturer (and at times a little bit of research is needed to arrive at that information). Further, we know that it has been made by a person; it didn't just arise on its own.

Look in a dictionary at a noun. You will find that most definitions use Aristotle's method of definition: the substantive is assigned to a general class and then differentiated in one or more ways. This is simple with basic nouns but becomes more complex with more abstract things.

C. Synonyms are words that mean the same. A writer will define using words that can be understood. Some words do not have synonyms, some synonyms may be hard to understand, and some synonyms do not have exact meanings.

Aristotle disliked this method of definition (synonyms), saying that a real definition could only be given within a phrase. This is correct; to understand the real meaning of a word, we must understand it within the context of its presentation.

However, by comparison and contrast, synonyms can help us understand a more precise meaning of a word. Instead of using the word "go," which is imprecise, we should use synonyms to clarify: run, walk, amble, drive, fly. Each of this is more specific and makes the word "go" better understood. English teachers want to see their students use better synonyms in their writing. Why use the word "said" over and over again when there are so many better, more evocative words like announced, mumbled, shouted, commented, or dozens of other words?

D. Etymology is another way to define. Here a person will describe the roots and history of a word. An etymological dictionary details the history of words. Students of rhetoric who have taken

---

[62]   Ibid

[63]   Ibid

Latin will recognize the Latin roots of many words we cover in this class. Here are some examples of etymology:

Essential: from Fr. Esse, to be. Latin ens, a thing.

Some meanings drift far from the etymology of the word. For example, the word *Read* is related to the Anglo-Saxon *raedan*, which means to counsel, consult, interpret. It is also related to the Latin, *reri*, to think. It is not always a close relationship to the origin. However, this helps to understand the fuller meaning of a word, how it came to be.

E. Description is another method of definition. Types of Description include the following:

- Comparisons. A person defines by comparison when relating one thing to another similar item. In comparing a writer could also contrast items.

- Analogy. The writer may also define by analogy much like Jesus did when speaking in parables. When he tells the parable of the Good Samaritan, he is drawing an analogy in order to define "neighbor."

- Metaphors. A metaphor defines in a more poetic way. A thing is described as being something else. For example, "Her teeth were pearls lined up in a row."

- Similes. Similar to a metaphor, this term compares one thing to another using the words *like* or *as*. For example, "The kingdom of heaven is like a pearl of great price."

F. Defining by Example (*exemplum*) will define by providing a similar, meaningful illustration. ("Faith" is leaning on someone because you trust him.)

In Summary, Lesson 13:

Definition purposes:
1. Show relationships
2. Remove ambiguity
3. Reduce vagueness
4. Increase vocabulary
5. Explain theoretically
6. Influence attitudes

Types of definitions
A. Exposition
B. Essential
C. Synonyms
D. Etymology
E. Description
F. Example

Four causes:
- Material
- Formal
- Efficient
- Final

Six rules for defining
1. Should be clearer
2. Should not repeat
3. State positively
4. State essential attributes
5. Do not be figurative
6. Define using the same part of speech

Terms to Remember:
- Ambiguity
- Lexical
- Genus
- Differentia
- Evocative
- Etymology

Lesson Thirteen Assignments

Assignment 13.1

Find a newspaper or magazine article (not an advertisement!) in which there is a definition. Answer the following questions in short answer form. Include a copy of the article with the paragraph in which you found the definition.

- What is defined?

- What kind of definition is it (from "types of definition," above; i.e., synonym, essential, exposition, etc.)?

- How could the author of the article be trying to influence attitudes with his definition? (For example, an article about the galaxies and stars might include a definition about the beginning of the universe and therefore he is reinforcing evolutionary theory.)

Assignment 13.2

Look online to find the opinion piece titled "The AP Stylebook is Getting Crazy" by Brent Bozell (2017) and answer the following questions in two to three paragraphs. How is the AP Stylebook using definitions to shape public opinion? Be specific about what words and phrases are changing in definition. How would these changes influence people's viewpoints?

Assignment 13.3

Take a look at the essay "Pretty Stones and Dead Babies: Abortion's New Language" by Charles Colson in *AFE*. Take time to read it together in class. Colson exposes the worldview of the abortion industry. Obviously the people in his column see that their former "clients" experience deep remorse for what they have done, and they try to reduce that remorse. Here is a clear exposure of a faulty worldview. Take time to discuss it. Apply your critical thinking.

Anyone espousing a worldview (and that means every single person in the world) must be able to defend his worldview. When students of Rhetoric refute a worldview, they should help their audience break down the logical application of the worldview. In other words, follow that worldview all the way to its logical conclusion. A worldview must be logically consistent all the way to its conclusion.

Keep this in mind when examining the worldview these abortionists display. Where is it inconsistent? Where/how does it fall apart? What does he define? What is his purpose? What is his thesis? Complete the worksheet for this assignment and turn it in.

Assignment 13.4

This is a three-part assignment. Complete the worksheet for this assignment and turn it in.
1. Look up the following ten nouns in the dictionary. Write out the most complete definition you can find. (Use ONE definition, even if the dictionary gives you more than one.) Then identify and label the differentiae (efficient cause, formal cause, etc.). You might not find every cause! Nouns to define: **church, restaurant, carpet, desk, cross, hymnal, dictionary, piano, Bible, plate**.
2. Take two of the above nouns and write your own complete definitions, using the genus and every cause. Label/color the causes. Do this on a separate page.

3. Make up your own noun and define it **using genus and all four differentiae.**

Assignment 13.5
Below are words and verses that correspond. Each verse defines that word. For each verse, write the phrase in which the word is used, and define the word as it is used. You may use a dictionary, your Bible's notes, commentaries, etc.

For example:
Word: Seal

1st Verse: Eph 1.13-14.

<u>Phrase that includes the word:</u> "sealed with the Holy Spirit of promise."

<u>Means in this context:</u> A sign or pledge of promise.

2nd Verse: 2 Cor 1.22

<u>Phrase that includes the word:</u> "who also sealed us and gave us the Spirit in our hearts as a pledge."

<u>Means in this context:</u> Joined us to Him. (Like sealing an envelope.)

3rd Verse: John 6.27

<u>Phrase that includes the word:</u> "on Him the Father, even God, has set His seal"

<u>Means in this context:</u> Mark of ownership.

Your words to define:
Glory
Ephesians 1.6, 12, 14 (one definition), Luke 2.32, 2 Corinthians 3.7

Wisdom
James 3.15, James 3.17

Holy
Exodus 3.5, Joel 3.17, 1 Peter 1.13-16

Grace
Acts 14.3, Romans 11.6, 2 Corinthians 8.7, Galatians 1.3

Assignment 13.6
Write an essay in which you define "life." You must give a full essay, including examples and discussing where, why, how, etc. Your essay must have a worldview reflecting your definition, or reflected in your definition. For example, if you take the pro-abortion point of view, your definition of life would be very different from the pro-life definition of life. 500 words.

Assignment 13.7

Comment on three of your classmates' opinion piece rewrites. Pay attention to the changes that were made. Be constructive, and watch for excellent writing!

Assignment 13.8

Discuss the logical presentation in this passage:

"After the Diet of Worms the conflict between Protestants and Rome escalated. The issues at once proliferated far beyond the matter of indulgences, yet they focused chiefly on the substantive issue of justification by faith alone. It has often been noted by the use of an ancient Aristotelian distinction between form and matter that the formal cause of the Reformation was the issue of authority (*sola Scriptura*) and that the material cause was the issue of justification (*sola fide*)" (R.C. Sproul, *Faith Alone*. Grand Rapids: Baker Books, 2004).

Assignment 13.9

Read "I Used to Love Her But I Had to Kill Her" by Mike Adams alongside Colson's "Pretty Stones and Dead Babies." What do these two different approaches say about the practice and definition of abortion?

Assignment 13.10

Read Mother Teresa's speech: "Whatever You Did Unto the Least of These, You Did Unto Me" and examine her appeals: how does she differ from Adams and Colson? How is she similar? What is the basis for her argument? Do you agree or disagree? Three paragraphs.

Assignment 13.11, Group Discussion

Read Proverbs 26.4-5. These two verses appear to contradict one another. Within a small group discuss the two verses. Do they contradict? Look carefully and examine what the verses really communicate. What is the definition of "fool" in this context?

Assignment 13.12

Read paragraph 22 of Edmund Burke's "Letter to a Noble Lord." What does he define? How does he define his terms, according to what we have just learned? Break down his method and be ready to discuss in class.

Writing Tips Lesson Thirteen

Usage errors

The list below contains the most common problems with student writing.

Error	Correction
Prophecy/prophesy	Prophesy/prophesies is the <u>verb</u>.
Prophecies/prophesies	Prophecy/prophecies is the <u>noun</u>
Less/fewer	Fewer deals with the number of things: "Fewer mistakes." Less concerns the degree of things: "I am less concerned about your errors now."
Further/farther	"Farther" relates to distance. "Further" relates to ideas.
Towards/toward	"Towards" is not a proper word for writing
Lead/led	The past tense of "lead" is "led." "He <u>led</u> them in a discussion."
Based off of/based on	Somehow students tend to say things like "His ideas are based off of…" when instead they should say "His ideas are based on…"
Anyways	Not a word!
Irregardless	Not a word!
Orientated	Not a word!
Affect/Effect	<u>"Affect" is the verb; "Effect" is the noun</u>. The only exception is when Effect is used as a transitive verb: "The government was able to effect a change in taxation." The meaning here generally would be to bring about.
Accept/Except	Students know the difference; they just don't always proofread carefully. "Accept" means to receive or admit. "Except" means to exclude or leave out, or is a conditional term.
Its/it's	This is a common error we want you to overcome! "Its" means "belonging to it," as in "The Garden Club announced the winner of its first writing contest." "It's" is the contraction of "it is," as in "It's the most popular writing contest in the county."
Myriad	"Myriad" means "many." Remember that alliterative sentence when you use the word. Incorrect: "I have myriad of examples of poor grammar." Correct: "I have myriad examples of poor grammar." Or less passive: "Myriad examples of poor grammar abound."

Myriad other usage errors exist. You may want to add more of your own.

Hyphenated words used as adjectives:

When describing a noun, sometimes words are grouped together and would be better treated with a hyphen. Example:

The often used term…

Might be better as: The often-used term…

Oil rich countries sell their product at a huge profit.

Might be better as: Oil-rich countries sell their product at a huge profit.

The First Type of Appeal: Logic/Reason (*Logos*)
Enthymeme, Example, Fallacies

"Logic!" said the Professor half to himself. "Why don't they teach logic at these schools? There are only three possibilities. Either your sister is telling lies, or she is mad, or she is telling the truth. You know she doesn't tell lies and it is obvious that she is not mad. For the moment then and unless any further evidence turns up, we must assume that she is telling the truth." (CS Lewis, *The Lion, the Witch, and the Wardrobe*)

Actually I'm highly logical which allows me to look past extraneous detail and perceive clearly that which others overlook. (J.K. Rowling, *Harry Potter and the Deathly Hallows*)

Another logical form of persuasion: syllogism and enthymeme

Aristotle invented syllogisms and enthymemes to analyze and test deductive reasoning. Here we can see some of the difference between the focus of Logic and that of rhetoric. Logic works with proofs, reaching conclusions by using statements. <u>Rhetoric, on the other hand, works with probability rather than proof.</u> Rhetoric may not always rely on provable statements, but rather on <u>probable</u> ones which may not always be true. (Thus, we see the negative side of rhetoric: it might not always use truth, but it will always try to persuade. Hence its shaky reputation today.)

Ancient orators preferred to argue probabilities rather than cold hard evidence because, they argued, evidence can be manufactured and witnesses could be bribed. Later speakers, including those of today, tended to rely on probabilities, coupled with charming oratory and popular personality, to convince their audience.[64]

Keep all this in mind as you read and study discourses. Note places in which the orator uses sound logic in order to persuade, or when he builds a shaky argument on an unsteady foundation.

Syllogisms: A Quick Review

Remember that a syllogism is an argument with a logical flow containing two premises and a conclusion. The syllogism can be "valid," meaning its construction is sound and its conclusion can be drawn from the premises. For example (and probably the most famous one):

All men are mortal.
Socrates is a man.
Therefore Socrates is mortal.

This argument uses a major premise (all men are mortal), minor premise (Socrates is a man), and conclusion (Socrates is mortal). We say this is both valid and true.

---

[64]   Kennedy, *Classical Rhetoric*, 21

Some syllogisms can be valid but untrue, meaning they can have the right structure, but the *truth value* of the conclusion is false. For example:

All dogs are four-legged animals.
All dogs are furry animals.
Therefore, all furry animals are four-legged animals.

 While this fits the <u>form</u> of a valid syllogism, the conclusion is <u>false</u>; it cannot be drawn from the premises.

A great number of arguments contain logic but might not fit the pattern of formal logic. Look at the logical progression in John 14.23-24:

> Jesus answered him, "If anyone loves me, he will keep my word, and my Father will love him, and we will come to him and make our home with him. Whoever does not love me does not keep my words. And the word that you hear is not mine but the Father's who sent me." (*ESV*)

This progression follows the *a fortiori* form, building in strength as it moves along.

Enthymemes: Most persuasive arguments are not going to come in the form of a syllogism. Many will (and should) use logic to move their audiences to a conclusion; they just won't have that formal pattern. So many will contain the form of an *enthymeme* ("INTH-uh-meem").

An enthymeme is a <u>syllogism with a missing premise</u>. Aristotle notes:

> The enthymeme must consist of few propositions, fewer often than those which make up the normal syllogism. For if any of these propositions is a familiar fact, there is no need even to mention it; *the hearer adds it himself.* Thus, to show that Dorieus has been victor in a contest for which the prize is a crown, it is enough to say "For he has been victor in the Olympic games," without adding "And in the Olympic games the prize is a crown," a fact which everybody knows.[65]

Take note of the phrase above: "the hearer adds it himself." The speaker must know that his audience is astute enough to fill in the missing premise in their own minds in order to come to the conclusion he wants them to.

An enthymeme is persuasive but not conclusive. If he cannot *convince* his audience, the writer or speaker must *persuade* them. Rhetoric can persuade according to what is probable, what people believe *might* happen. He should not expect them to make huge leaps from one point to another unless he knows they all understand his meaning.

Deductive reasoning in the case of enthymemes is peculiar to rhetoric; here we must look at the implied premise. For example: "Tomorrow is testing day since we finished Chapter 7." The missing, implied premise here (understood by everyone in the class if they've paid attention) is: when we finish a chapter, we always take a test.

Another example is "He must be a right-wing bigot because he says he is a Christian." The implied premise may be faulty: "All Christians are right-wing bigots." The argument may be logically true (meaning the form or structure of the argument makes sense), but the implied premise is false. In rhetoric, then, our job is to refute this implied premise. That implied premise may be the vulnerable spot in the other person's argument. Aim your argumentative weapons there first.

---

[65]   Aristotle, *Rhetoric* 1.2, emphasis added.

Reasoning by Example

The **example** is another form of persuasion by reason. It uses inductive reasoning, going from the particular to the general. The example also uses verifiable phenomena.

> [Its] relation to the proposition it supports is not that of part to whole, nor whole to part, nor whole to whole, but of part to part, or like to like. When two statements are of the same order, but one is more familiar than the other, the former is an "example." The argument may, for instance, be that Dionysius, in asking as he does for a bodyguard, is scheming to make himself a despot. For in the past Peisistratus kept asking for a bodyguard in order to carry out such a scheme, and did make himself a despot as soon as he got it; and so did Theagenes at Megara; and in the same way all other instances known to the speaker are made into examples, in order to show what is not yet known, that Dionysius has the same purpose in making the same request: all these being instances of the one general principle, that a man who asks for a bodyguard is scheming to make himself a despot.[66]

A person can counteract an example by citing a valid example where the outcome is the opposite of the one given. An argument cannot solely rely on the example because it does not constitute real proof; it is mostly a probability. It is, of itself, persuasive. But it is vital to remind an audience that if someone has used example, one example does not prove the point–there's quite often an exception to a rule demonstrated by example.

The Fallacies

A fallacy is an error in reasoning; it is a false statement, an untruth which has to do with the *matter* or *form* of the argument. A fallacy can be a deliberate manipulation of argumentation, or it can arise from poor logic.

Here again it is important for the student of rhetoric to have an understanding of logic. If it has been a couple of years since logic has been studied, take time to become familiar with that subject again.

Because they are errors in reasoning, we can easily conclude that fallacies can be proven false. Every statement can be analyzed and its veracity or fallacy detected only by a person's knowledge of the facts and the structure of the argument itself. Here, for the student of rhetoric, lies the reason for the need to know great amounts of information. How can you prove anything true or false if you know nothing about it, or you even lack the ability of finding reliable sources of information so you can learn about it?

Note that we have grouped the following fallacies by their forms. Not every expert categorizes fallacies the same.

---

[66]   Aristotle, *Rhetoric* Book 1 Chapter 2

Deductive Fallacies

Fallacies of reasoning in deduction occur due to the logical structure of an argument (or better put: lack of logical structure)

1. **Undistributed Middle Term** does not supply a logical flow of the arguments. For example: "All Baptists are people. All Americans are people. Therefore all Americans are Baptists." In other words, a person cannot draw a conclusion from the supplied premises. There's no connection between the terms in the conclusion, which means the conclusion cannot follow from the premises. (If you have had Logic, you will remember this as one of the tests of the validity of a syllogism. This will be difficult to understand if Logic is not fresh in your mind.)

2. **Conclusion from Two Negative Premises**. The logician cannot arrive at a negative conclusion with two negative premises. This does not establish a relationship among all three terms in a syllogistic chain of reasoning. For example: "No Protestants are Catholics, and no Catholics are Baptists, therefore no Protestants are Baptists." The premises do not lead to this conclusion and are faulty because they are negative.

3. **Affirmative Conclusion from a Negative Premise**. No affirmative conclusion can be drawn from negative premises. For example, "No believers are slaves, and no slaves are free men. Therefore, some believers are free men." Even though the conclusion may be true, you cannot logically draw that conclusion from the supplied premises.

4. **Fallacy of Asserting the Consequent** uses a hypothetical proposition. This is also called a *non sequitur*. Here the premises don't support the conclusion. For example: "If I take driver's education I can drive the car. I drove the car, therefore I took driver's education." What if she took the car out for a ride without permission? It does not necessarily follow that she took driver's education.

5. **Fallacy of Denying the Antecedent** also reasons from hypothetical propositions. For example: "If I take driver's education I can drive the car. I didn't take driver's education, so I didn't drive the car." Again, it's not legal to get a license without taking driver's education, but a determined individual will not let that detail get in his way!

6. **Either/or** fallacy oversimplifies the choices. "Where is she? She's late! Either she got lost or she's been eaten by a bear!" But what if she forgot or had mechanical failure? (This can also be called "False Dilemma.")

Inductive Fallacies

In these cases, the conclusion cannot be legitimately gotten from the weak premises of the argument.

1. **Appeals to Authority**
    a. *Ipse Dixit* **(he said it himself):** Faulty generalization based on evidence derived from authority when <u>the authority quoted is biased or prejudiced, incompetent, or outmoded</u>. For example: "I tend to believe that the United States is a hateful country, because for several generations the rulers of North Korea have called it 'the Great Satan.'" Furthermore, the authors of this textbook are not authorities on quantum physics (though maybe as far as science fiction can go), but they are authorities in terms of rhetoric, logic, literature, and writing. It's important to understand when people both have earned and demonstrate authority before using them to support arguments. Furthermore, when in a debate or discussion with someone, it's even more important to recognize when the sources your opponent uses are questionable.

b. **Misuse of Authority:** A competent authority is inaccurately quoted, misinterpreted, or quoted out of context. Through no fault of the authority, then, someone can intentionally or mistakenly refer to or quote an authority to suit his own agenda. This can also be called over-generalization or unrepresentative example. For example, "I eat a lot of candy, and my dentist says my teeth are in great shape. So the argument that sugary foods are bad for the teeth is just a lot of rubbish."

2. **Apriorism—a sweeping or hasty generalization.**[67] <u>Jumps to a conclusion too quickly and easily.</u> Some possibilities of faulty generalization arise when the particulars may be irrelevant, unrepresentative, or not enough to warrant the conclusion. For example, two young brothers scooped some soil from a California creek bed and panned for gold. After a few shovelfuls came up empty, they declared that there was no gold in all of California. This causes us to speculate that all adolescent boys commit this fallacy. Yes, we just committed a fallacy! See how easy it is? This can also be called a **"faulty causal generalization"** when we make an assumption that observes an effect and assigns the wrong cause to it. For instance, in his book *The Cave Painting: A Parable of Science*, author Roddy Bullock imagines a place where animal paintings were found on the walls of a cave which periodically has seen the rise and fall of floods. In his story, experts declare that the pictures arose naturally; when they receded, the waters left these pictures on the walls. His allegory points out the faulty assumptions of our own world, in which naturalists refuse to believe that the universe was created by a sovereign God.

3. *Post hoc ergo propter hoc* (after this, therefore because of this). Fails to take into account that the same cause can produce diverse effects. For example, "Things started to go badly as soon as you came into the room. Go away!"

4. **Faulty Analogy.** Assumes that if two things are alike in one certain aspect, they must be alike in many more ways. This is a much more subtle fallacy, and some audience members might not recognize it as such. "The God of the Jewish people is the same God of Christianity, and both of them read the Law and the Prophets. So the two religions are basically the same."

5. **Slippery Slope** occurs when someone lists events that occur from point A to point D, but one does not exactly lead to the other. In other words, you cannot get to D from A. Example: "Drinking can lead to the use of marijuana. Marijuana use can lead to harder drugs. Harder drugs can lead to heroin. Therefore, people should not drink because they will end up on heroin." Also called "*Reductio ad absurdum.*"

---

[67] This fallacy can also be categorized as hyperbole, a Figure of Speech we will study later on in rhetoric.

Fallacies of Ambiguity

Ambiguity muddies the water a bit, so that the premises or the conclusion (or both) aren't very clear. When you muddy the water, you are purposefully drawing attention away from your weak argument.

1. **Equivocation** attempts to cloud the argument by using a term that contains two or more meanings. The argument may hinge on someone defining a word two different ways. For example, one person will say that Jane is mad (meaning angry), but the other may understand Jane to be mad (meaning insane). Either way, poor Jane is not good company.

2. **Accent** is a form of equivocation. Change the meaning of a sentence not through definition, but by emphasizing different words. For example, "We should never shout fire in a crowded auditorium" can be accented different ways. With the emphasis on the *we*, one might think that other disinterested parties can do the shouting. Emphasizing *should* might imply that even if we shouldn't, we might go ahead and do it ourselves. If we emphasize *never*, it would actually imply what the speaker intends: this is something we should never do. Emphasis helps immensely.

3. *Petitio principii* is also called Begging the Question or circular reasoning. Here a person assumes what must be proven. "Why do you insist that this conference speaker is going to be a reliable expert?" "Because I met him last year, and he told me he was a reliable expert."

4. **Amphiboly:** The fallacy here lies in the structure of the sentence. The sentence is structured in such a way as to confuse or mislead the listener. Often found in headlines. A famous amphiboly would be "Mary had a little lamb. I'll bet the doctor was surprised." Or "Iraqi head searches for arms." A recent surprising headline read "Thousands of CA national guard soldiers paid $150 million in bonuses to keep money." What exactly does it mean?

5. **Composition:** This fallacy comes in when a person believes that since the parts that make up the whole have one certain quality, the whole will also have that quality. For example, "Women are the ones who have abortions, therefore all women should be pro-abortion." Or, "My sister is stupid and she voted for President George W. Bush. That means all Bush supporters are stupid."

6. **Division:** This is the opposite of Composition. In this fallacy, one makes the mistake of supposing that since the whole thing has a certain attribute, the parts that make up the whole also have the same attribute. For example, "Super-genius Unlimited Corp. collapsed because it is an unstable, dishonest company. That means all those employees were dishonest and unstable as well."

Fallacies of Relevance

Relevance claims to have the right answers, but the answers–or the path you take to get to the answers–are irrelevant to the argument. Remember *Ad hominem* from logic? It's the very childish pattern: "I'm right and you know it!" "Oh yeah, well your shirt doesn't match your pants." What does one have to do with the other? Not a thing, but if I can draw you off the topic by slipping in an unrelated argument, then I've won.

1. *Ad hominem* (to the man) distracts from the main point of the argument or discussion and becomes an attack on the opponent. It may be reduced to name-calling or other insults. "Don't listen to Senator MacSnide; he is an idiot." Related:

a. **Bulverism** discounts a person's reliability by assigning him with a negative quality. "It figures you would get in trouble in her class. Female teachers can be so mean!" This fallacy was suggested by C.S. Lewis.

b. **Genetic Fallacy:** Similar to *ad hominem* or Bulverism, this fallacy discounts or validates the reliability of a statement because of its source. "My mom said it, so it must be true." "I don't trust anything that comes out of the White House." Or "You really can't rely on anything a scientist says."

2. **Straw man** oversimplifies an opponent's argument before refuting it. "Senator Pennywhistle says he is a Christian. I can't vote for anyone who is an anti-science bigot." The speaker deduced a lot from that one simple statement. Perhaps the Senator was a scientist before he entered politics. We just don't know, either, that he is a bigot, because the speaker has not presented that information.

3. *Ad populum* (to the people) is another fallacy of distraction and takes several forms:

a. *Ad populum*: the speaker draws the argument away from the issue by appealing to emotions. It capitalizes on people's fears and prejudices and allows that, instead of the issue, to become the topic. For example, Hitler's rise to power exploited post-World War I depression and fear among the German people by giving them someone on whom they could place all their aggression: the Jewish people. This is also called the **Bandwagon Fallacy,** which persuades an audience to do something because everyone else does it: "Come on, the whole class is doing it!"

b. The fallacy of *ad invidiam* is also similar to *ad populum*. Called Appeal to Envy, it capitalizes on strong negative emotions like hatred, dislike, or prejudice. As with *ad populum*, all Hitler and his minions had to do was point out the facts that many Jews were wealthy and successful in business, and tell his people that Jews were stealing from the Germans. He successfully directed all their post-World War I anger and frustration to the Jews. The truth did not matter.

c. *Ad verecundiam*, appeal to authority, is similar to *ad populum* in that it appeals to an improper authority, generally based in positive emotions or prejudices. This could legitimately appear similar to **Faulty Generalization** in which one tries to make a case based on an illegitimate authority. "I just bought a vitamin called 'Super-Dee-Dooper Men's Health.' Gerald Smith, a doctor on the TV show *Super-Doc*, recommends it, so it must be good." *Ad verecundiam* could also include appealing to the reverence for certain institutions (allegiance to the flag, country, school, political party, church) rather than an argument about the issue itself.

d. **Appeal to vanity** causes envy, making a person feel as if he is truly missing out on something someone else has. An ad making someone want to be thin, athletic, sexy, etc. is an appeal to vanity.

e. **"Red Herring"** is a fallacy of distraction where an opponent dodges the issue by changing the subject. Students like to call this one the "rabbit trail" fallacy, in which the speaker may divert attention from the main point by letting himself get sidetracked. The politician might say, "You say I have lied while in office. But look at how strong the economy is."

4. **Appeal to Pity**, also called *ad misericordiam,* is a tear-jerking story intended to provoke sympathy and a response. "You have to give me an A in this class! My poor dying grandmother needs to see me graduate with honors!" Refer to Lesson 16 and Assignment 16.2 for a discussion of Appeal to Pity.

5. *Tu quoque* (also called *ad hominem tu quoque*): This is a "you do it too" fallacy. A teenager might point out that his parent smoked when he was a teenager, so the son can smoke as well. The teen might accuse his parent of hypocrisy. However, this parent is operating on a lifetime of facts and experience when telling his son not to smoke, so the parent is not a hypocrite. The teen, however, is using this fallacy to win an argument with his dad. Who will win this debate?

6. **Chronological snobbery:** The faulty logician commits this fallacy by assuming that because of the age of an individual or a thing, it is either good or bad. For example, "No one can rely on the Bible. It is outdated." Or, "My encyclopedia from 1942 is the best and most reliable because it was written so long ago." Or, "That kid must be doing something bad. He's a teenager, isn't he?"

7. **Appeal to Tradition:** Many students like to point this one out to their parents or grandparents. The older generation might say, "It's always been done this way," to which a young man or women might answer, "That doesn't make it the right way!" You might want to classify this as another form of **Chronological Snobbery.** If you do, remember that it goes both ways: Just because it has always been done this way, doesn't make it wrong. Conversely, deciding to do something else because you're tired of always doing it the way your parents want, doesn't mean that your method is better than the old way!

8. **Relative Privation:** This is the "it could be better/worse" fallacy. Trying to argue that this is the best or the worst case. Arguing from the negative produces a weak result that can easily be defeated. "I know you don't like the new team member we hired. But at least she's not as incompetent as the last guy we fired." Or: "Sure, you got 9 out of 10 answers correct. But you've gotten one wrong. That's not good enough."

Fallacies of Omission

An argument needs to have complete information in order to be effective–or for its errors to be clearly seen. Statements or arguments that leave out something important are quite often fallacies of omission.

1. **The Complex Question** is a question framed in such a way as to exclude the only legitimate response. It sets someone up with a question: "When did you stop beating your wife?" There is no good way to answer that, so the accused must step back and point out the illogic of that question. It would be necessary to break it apart and answer each point. Today this is also called the "gotcha" question. It is very similar to the Either/Or fallacy.

2. *Ad ignorantiam* concludes something in the absence of proof. It might also assume something because the opposite cannot be proven. "Because I can't see God, he does not exist." Essentially, this uses the absence of proof as proof. This cannot work because, as Hermione Granger points out: "I mean, you could claim that anything's real if the only basis for believing in it is that nobody's proved it doesn't exist!"[68]

3. *Ad baculum* (appeal to the stick) is committed when the speaker or writer uses a veiled threat to convince his audience to do something or believe something. The audience members believe what they are told because they fear for their physical well-being. This appeals to people's personal anxiety. "A vote for Republicans is a vote to pollute the air and the environment."

---

[68]   Rowling, J. K. *Harry Potter and the Deathly Hallows.* New York, Scholastic Inc., 2007.

4. **No True Scotsman:** Perhaps close to Bulverism, this fallacy occurs when the speaker seeks to discount a person (or his argument) by eliminating the possibility of a legitimate counterexample. The philosopher Antony Flew proposed this fallacy with the following example: "Imagine Hamish McDonald, a Scotsman, sitting down with his *Glasgow Morning Herald* and seeing an article about how the 'Brighton Sex Maniac Strikes Again.' Hamish is shocked and declares that 'No Scotsman would do such a thing.' The next day he sits down to read his *Glasgow Morning Herald* again; and, this time, finds an article about an Aberdeen man whose brutal actions make the Brighton sex maniac seem almost gentlemanly. This fact shows that Hamish was wrong in his opinion, but is he going to admit this? Not likely. This time he says: 'No *true* Scotsman would do such a thing.'"[69]

5. **Stacking the Deck:** Propaganda employs this fallacy, in which any opposing arguments or examples are ignored or omitted. If your argument is weak, you certainly don't want to hear much from the opposition, so you will "stack the deck" in your favor. Perhaps your method of stacking the deck is to shout loudly so no one can hear your opponent.

6. *Ad captandum* occurs when a speaker has a captivating manner, and because of it, the audience believes him whether it's true or not. It could be argued that this is not a legitimate fallacy, so rhetoricians need to consider not just the speaker's charismatic presence. Rule of thumb: consider whether the audience believes (or disbelieves) the speaker/author just because of who he is, rather than the logic of his argument.

From this point, you should be able to recognize persuasion by logic, as well as begin to identify fallacies in whatever you read for this class.

---

[69]   Flew, Antony (1975), *Thinking About Thinking: Do I Sincerely Want to Be Right?*, London: Collins Fontana, p. 47

119

In Summary, Lesson 14:

The difference between Logic and Rhetoric:

The difference between enthymemes and syllogisms:

The _____ **may be the vulnerable spot in the other person's argument.**

Reasoning by Example:
    A person can counteract an example by citing _____.

Terms to Remember
* Fallacy
* Deductive (or deduction, as in reasoning)
* Inductive (or induction, as in reasoning)
* Each of the fallacies and the categories into which they fit

Lesson Fourteen Assignments

Assignment 14.1

Work through the Enthymeme worksheet, found in Teacher version. Find the implied premise. Some of these are much harder than others! Method: either rewrite as standard syllogisms to supply the missing premise, or just work through it by finding the conclusion. Only provide the missing premise.

Assignment 14.2

Find the implied premise(s) in the following verses. Explain your reasons. Use the same method as above. Give simple answers, supplying only the missing premise and one or two sentences as reasoning.

- Matthew 13.20-21–"As for what was sown on rocky ground, this is the one who hears the word and immediately receives it with joy, yet he has no root in himself, but endures for a while, and when tribulation or persecution arises on account of the word, immediately he falls away."
- Matthew 27.6–"But the chief priests, taking the pieces of silver, said, 'It is not lawful to put them into the treasury, since it is blood money.'"
- Matthew 6.12–"And forgive us our debts, as we also have forgiven our debtors." (*ESV*)

Assignment 14.3

Read Huss: "The Church—Not Man but Christ" (1415) in *AFE*. Analyze his logical appeal. Discuss the logical techniques he uses to communicate his thesis (What does he define? How does this support his thesis?). What is his thesis? Discuss in two to three paragraphs.

Assignment 14.4

Complete the fallacies worksheet (found in the Teacher Version), either together in class or on your own.

Assignment 14.5

Read Chuck Colson's *Breakpoint* Article, "A History of God—Who's Got it Right?" Without naming the fallacy, Colson has pointed it out and corrected it. What is the fallacy (or are there more than one?)? How else would you counter this fallacy/fallacies? Discuss in 2-3 paragraphs.

Assignment 14.6

Read the passage on rhetoric and Logic by Martin Luther ("On the Dialectic"). Discuss its meaning and application directly regarding what we do here in rhetoric, and how Luther applies a biblical worldview to the study of rhetoric and logic.

Assignment 14.7

Compare Winston Churchill's five speeches contained in *AFE*. Examine how he uses *logos* in his discourses. In each case, identify his goal for his logical appeal and evaluate how successful he is in accomplishing that goal. Two to three pages.

Writing Tips Lesson Fourteen

Be aware of your audience

It's not difficult for the Rhetoric student to understand our main points throughout this text. One topic we address consistently is **"Be aware of your audience!"** Read this article about careful writing and work on building awareness of how your audience receives what you write.

Careful Writing Cares for Your Audience[70]

By Shaunna Howat, 2017

The audience of a high school student is usually only one person: the teacher. A conscientious student will make sure to stay within the guidelines of that assignment, including careful editing. But as they go on into university and/or the "real world," young people would do well to continue caring for their varied audiences. Grammar, spelling, punctuation–and the message–remain important, regardless of the audience or the writer.

I try very hard not to be obnoxious about it (really, I do!), but I begin twitching when I see poor writing. Bad grammar, spelling, and punctuation–at least to me–communicates that you do not care enough to try to get it right. Please don't get me wrong: I don't judge your character or level of education, and I admire that you are in business. Just spend a few extra dollars to have someone make sure you communicate well to your audience–and in this case, your customers.

Here are a few examples.

1. Waiting for a local stage production to begin, we glanced at the ads flashing on the screen. A local fundraiser advertised a **"Pankake Breakfast."** Wondering whether they meant to write it that way (*twitch*), I went to their website. No, it's spelled correctly there, but some of their pages give evidence to their lack of care. One link was titled **"Comming events."** Okay, local group, done quickly perhaps.

2. But then there's Trader Joe's, a great chain, one of my favorites. On the box for a Chocolate Pecan Pie Bar, the description below the name says **"Rich chocolate and pecans in a buttery, tart shell."** Set aside for a moment the distraction from how amazing the dessert sounds. My questions, upon reading this, are twofold: Is the shell buttery and tart (meaning acidic), or is it in a buttery pastry-tart shell? If the latter, that comma shouldn't be there. If the former, why would you buy it? Think of the comma as meaning "and" in a list.

3. And finally, this is most disturbing if you like cats. (I don't, so I found it more amusing than troubling). In the calendar section of our local paper sits a photo of a not-very-happy-looking cat in a cage. Directly below the photo is the following event: **"Another Chance Animal Welfare League hosts its Korean Barbecue and Breakfast fundraiser from 10 a.m. on Sept. 9 at Another Chance Animal Welfare League. Attendees can**

---

[70] Adapted from https://writingrhetorically.com/2017/12/11/careful-writing-cares-for-your-audience/

choose from a Korean barbecue meal or a burrito breakfast with sides and drinks. Both are $5 each at the door. Another Chance Animal Welfare League will also host a parking lot sale and animal adoptions in conjunction with this event." Remember that you are reading about a barbecue while looking at a photo of a cat. Two questions immediately arise: Really, would this poor feline be a main course in the fundraiser? (That's what it looks like to the audience!) And who is going to buy a parking lot, even for a charity? This newspaper's editors may need to take a moment to find a good proofreader–or perhaps a course in sensitivity toward animals.

So take my advice, whether you are a student or a business person: Spend a few extra moments checking your work–essay, ad, news article, etc.–or find someone who can do it for you. It will save you some embarrassing moments, poor grades, or lost revenue. If you don't care, that's fine too. But I'm sure you'll hear me *twitching*.

The Second Type of Appeal: Ethics (*Ethos*)

In the first place, what stands highest in the order of means, is personal character and disposition. In order to be a truly eloquent or persuasive speaker, nothing is more necessary than to be a virtuous man.

Bad as the world is, nothing has so great and universal a command over the minds of men as virtue. …Nothing, therefore, is more necessary for those who would excel in any of the higher kinds of oratory, than to cultivate habits of the several virtues, and to refine and improve all their moral feelings. Whenever these become dead, or callous, they may be assured, that, on every occasion, they will speak with less power, and less success. The sentiments and dispositions particularly requisite for them to cultivate, are the following: The love of justice and order and indignation at insolence and oppression; the love of honesty and truth, and detestation of fraud, meanness, and corruption; magnanimity of spirit; the love of liberty, of their country, and the public; zeal for all great and noble designs, and reverence for all worthy and heroic characters. (Blair, qtd. in *Blair, Campbell* 129-130)

Rhetoric in its truest sense seeks to perfect men by showing them better versions of themselves, links in that chain extending up toward the ideal.
(Richard Weaver, *The Ethics of Rhetoric*)

The great enemy of clear language is insincerity. When there is a gap between one's real and one's declared aims, one turns, as it were, instinctively to long words and exhausted idioms, like a cuttlefish squirting out ink. (George Orwell)[71]

Many consider ethical appeal to be the "hidden persuader." A writer or speaker is not going to step up and tell his audience, "I have great ethics! Let me tell you how and why!" His tone and content must display his ethics, but before he opens his mouth (or puts words on paper), his life must display his ethics. "The good person out of the good treasure of his heart produces good, and the evil person out of his evil treasure produces evil, for out of the abundance of the heart his mouth speaks" (*ESV*, Luke 6.45). It's a truth that what's inside you will naturally spill out and give evidence of the condition of your heart to anyone around you!

Even the most ingenious and logical appeal or the most impassioned plea could fall on deaf ears if the audience reacted unfavorably to the speaker's character. Quintilian said: "For he, who would have all men trust his judgment as to what is expedient and honourable, should both possess and be regarded as possessing genuine wisdom and excellence of character."[72] Character does become

---

[71] https://www.goodreads.com/quotes/342655-the-great-enemy-of-clear-language-is-insincerity-when-there
[72] Quintilian, *Institutio Oratoria, Book 3*

extremely important when a writer or speaker wants his audience to believe him as a credible source, or when he attempts to attack the credibility of his opponent.

In a discourse in which the speaker or writer is attempting to impress the audience of his ethics, his words should demonstrate his wisdom, his virtue, and his good will. The discourse must exhibit the speaker's ethics and good sense. He must show that he knows how to reason, that he can be fairly objective in his argument, and that he knows a lot about this and other subjects.

So when you analyze a discourse for its *ethos*, consider what's underneath, or behind, the speaker's words. Consider what has spurred him to speak. And consider what he wants his audience to take away from it.

We can find ethical appeal throughout Scripture (and well we should!). Take a look at Psalm 37. Make a list of all verbs and adjectives that speak of ethics. The reader may be dismayed by the list, until he discovers what the psalmists did: I cannot do all this on my own! Indeed we cannot; it is God who wills and works in us (*ESV*, Philippians 2.12-13). It is only by His power that we are able to both <u>want</u> to obey and <u>actually obey</u>.

Emperor Marcus Aurelius declared, "No longer talk at all about the kind of man that a good man ought to be, but be such."[73] Someone cannot simply declare his integrity by saying, "I am a righteous man!" He must demonstrate it, yes, through words he says, and by exhibiting that his words are truly lived out, he gains the audience's trust. Just as James 2 says that faith without works is dead; words without actions are hollow.

The discourse needs to genuinely reflect the writer's virtues or morals. Does his discourse show that he:

- abhors dishonest methods of proof,
- respects and honors virtues that are common to all humanity,
- displays an unwavering integrity,
- truly cares about the welfare of the audience, and
- is ready to sacrifice any opportunity to make more of himself if his argument conflicts with the best interest of others?[74]

It must also exhibit his understanding of human psychology, being aware of the needs and emotions of people of different ages and in different stages of life (young/middle aged/old, wealthy/poor, educated/illiterate, well/sick, men/women). The writer should adapt his tone and sentiments to fit the audience, without compromising his ethical tone.

A writer or speaker's ethical appeal is jeopardized by a slip of behavior or words that might belie a false front. If one's integrity has come into question during the discourse, or he becomes irate or ill-tempered; if he has used false information or poor logic, his ethical appeal has been jeopardized.

In today's social media-driven society, almost everything is exposed for public scrutiny, and *ethos* is difficult to maintain. From Presidential candidates to businessmen to pastors to teachers and even to students, *ethos* is essential to all aspects of our lives–damaging your *ethos* can harm reputation, job prospects, and even university admission.

---

[73] http://classics.mit.edu/Antoninus/meditations.10.ten.html

[74] Adapted from Corbett, *Classical Rhetoric*.

Keep an eye on the news, in whatever form you can. Politics provides ample material to view the different types of persuasion. For example, in September of 2017, US Senator Diane Feinstein served on a Senate committee tasked with approving presidential nominations for Federal Judge appointments. The senator scornfully told the nominee, Amy Barrett, a Catholic, "the dogma lives loudly within you." The senator did not expect Christians to adopt what she had thought was a badge of shame, and proudly declare that the dogma lives loudly within them, too. This causes us to remember Genesis 50.19-21, when Joseph told his brothers, "As for you, you meant evil against me, but God meant it for good." It may confound unbelievers to see that what the Senator meant to be a disdainful rebuke actually became a rallying cry among Christians, an excellent example of *ethos*.

Rhetoricians can use all kinds of language in order to persuade. Do not expect someone to use only one mode of persuasion (*logos*, *ethos*, *pathos*). The point–the goal–is to persuade. Can rhetoric offend? Recall the Old Testament prophets–could they have offered some nice, flowery prose? Certainly not when they were warning Israel to repent! Think of Jesus' Sermon on the Mount, and contrast that with his "brood of vipers" invective against the Pharisees.

A Lesson in Identifying Ethos

Let's take a look at Churchill's "Blood, Toil, Tears, and Sweat" speech, the last few paragraphs, with regard to his use of *ethos*.

> To form an Administration of this scale and complexity is a serious undertaking in itself, but it must be remembered that we are in the preliminary stage of one of the greatest battles in history, that we are in action at many other points in Norway and in Holland, that we have to be prepared in the Mediterranean, that the air battle is continuous and that many preparations, such as have been indicated by my honorable friends below the Gangway, have to be made here at home. In this crisis I hope I may be pardoned if I do not address the House at any length today. I hope that any of my friends and colleagues, or former colleagues, who are affected by the political reconstruction, will make allowance, all allowance, for any lack of ceremony with which it has been necessary to act. I would say to the House, as I said to those who have joined this government: "I have nothing to offer but blood, toil, tears and sweat."

> We have before us an ordeal of the most grievous kind. We have before us many, many long months of struggle and of suffering. You ask, what is our policy? I can say: It is to wage war, by sea, land and air, with all our might and with all the strength that God can give us; to wage war against a monstrous tyranny, never surpassed in the dark, lamentable catalogue of human crime. That is our policy. You ask, what is our aim? I can answer in one word: It is victory, victory at all costs, victory in spite of all terror, victory, however long and hard the road may be; for without victory, there is no survival. Let that be realised; no survival for the British Empire, no survival for all that the British Empire has stood for, no survival for the urge and impulse of the ages, that mankind will move forward toward its goal. But I take up my task with buoyancy and hope. I feel sure that our cause will not be suffered to fail among men. At this time I feel entitled to claim the aid of all, and I say, "come then, let us go forward together with our united strength."

Take note of words and phrases that seem to be communicating *ethos*, or strong character. Churchill may want to show his audience that he is a man of high ethics; he may also want to point out the high (or low) ethics of others. Remember the times in which he speaks. Who/what is the enemy? We will identify emotional appeal (*pathos*) in the next lesson, so pay attention to words and phrases that sound like *ethos* here.

- serious undertaking
- honorable
- I have nothing to offer but blood, toil, tears and sweat
- with all our might
- with all the strength that God can give us
- wage war against a monstrous tyranny
- victory, however long and hard the road may be
- the urge and impulse of the ages
- mankind will move forward toward its goal
- I take up my task
- our cause will not be suffered to fail among men
- I feel entitled to claim the aid of all
- come then, let us go forward together with our united strength

You might not have thought that there are so many ethical appeals in just two paragraphs! But take a look at this list. Think of what he is communicating. What's his goal? To unite the country against an evil power that wants to dominate the world.

Some of these may not seem ethical. But put them in other words. For example, how is "I take up my task" ethical? Consider what he is communicating here. "I am rolling up my sleeves to do this job. I am brave and tireless." The same can be said for "I have nothing to offer but blood, toil, tears, and sweat." You might agree that he says he will do this job with every fiber of his being, that this is a cause worth fighting for, even dying for. And notice how strong that sentence is. He didn't say "I will work hard." No, he used strong metaphors to communicate his dedication to the task at hand.

In Summary, Lesson 15:

Analyze the speaker's ethics: He...

1. Abhors...
2. Respects and honors...
3. Displays...
4. Truly...
5. Is ready...

Terms to Remember:

- Insolence
- Indignation
- Idiom
- Integrity
- Dogma

Lesson Fifteen Assignments

Assignment 15.1

Read Joel Belz's "The Lie is Marching On" and analyze its use of ethical appeal. What kind of ethical appeal does he use, and where? Remember to consider what the thesis is and how he supports it, as well as what kind of introduction it is. Can you find any areas where he might actually jeopardize his own ethical appeal? Two to three paragraphs.

Assignment 15.2

Read Vaclav Havel's "A Contaminated Moral Environment" and analyze his employment of the appeal to *ethos*. It's the underpinning of everything he says: how does he do it? How does he also use the other appeals to support *ethos*?

Assignment 15.3

Look up "ethics in politics" OR "ethics in medicine" online. Find some articles that discuss this subject and write an essay discussing the world's definition of ethics today. You might compare what you find to what scripture says about moral and ethical behavior. Compare the original AND a modern version of the Hippocratic Oath and compare. You could also compare it to what Blair says in the passage above.

Assignment 15.4

Read and watch a video of President George W. Bush's "Axis of Evil" speech, which was his first State of the Union address after the September 11, 2001 terrorist attacks. How does Bush use *ethos* here? How does he combine *ethos* with rebuke and refutation? In this speech, he both defends an ideology and condemns another. How does he do this, and is he successful?

Assignment 15.5

Look up videos of past presidential speeches (choose at least two different presidents—look in *AFE* for ideas, or a website like AmericanRhetoric.com). Take note of ethical appeal in these speeches. Transcribe the passages to which you are referring, and discuss, in 300-500 words, the speakers' use of ethics. Take into account the times in which the president speaks, the audience, and what the audience needed to hear. Do you find the use of ethical appeal to be genuine, or is it lacking in something? Does your historical perspective color how you view the speaker's ethical appeal? Be ready to discuss.

Assignment 15.6

Read King George VI "In This Grave Hour." Keep in mind what is going on in history at the time of his address, and discuss his use of ethos. 300-500 words.

Writing Tips Lesson Fifteen

Using and quoting Bible passages

You will find many opportunities to use passages from the Bible in what you write for this course. Be sure to follow some quick guidelines before you do.

- **Be aware of the full context of what you're quoting**. This means you must not pull a few words out of a verse in order to make your point, while ignoring the larger context of the passage from which you have drawn your quote. For example, do not use the passage from Ephesians 5, instructing wives to submit to their husbands, if you plan to teach about the proper place for wives (5.22-24), you must also make note of what follows that passage. In the next three verses, men are told to love their wives as Christ loved the Church.

- **Notice what the "therefore" is there for!** Take what a passage is teaching and use it; don't twist the passage so completely out of shape that your reader begins to wonder where you're going. If a passage says "therefore," look at what is written before the "therefore"! It's there for a reason!

- **Refer to the MLA for requirements** regarding Bible passage citation. Notice the way we have cited scripture in this textbook, which complies with MLA 8th edition.

The Third Type of Appeal: Emotions (*Pathos*)

You can sway a thousand men by appealing to their prejudices quicker than you can convince one man by logic. (Robert A. Heinlein, *Revolt in 2100*)

It is not right to pervert the judge by moving him to anger or envy or pity—one might as well warp a carpenter's rule before using it. ...[A] litigant has clearly nothing to do but to show that the alleged fact is so or is not so, that it has or has not happened. (Aristotle, *The Rhetoric & The Poetics of Aristotle* 1.1)

Many Christians today can point to a pivotal moment at which their emotions were stirred and they were saved. Yet it's not that alone. We can recognize that God stirs the emotions (because we are emotional creatures) and convicts us of our sins, and that his written Word informs, instructs, and feeds our faith. Our faith is not solely emotional. If it is, it will soon wane and wither.

Thus we understand why emotional appeal–*pathos*–is only one of three methods of persuasion; communicators will stir emotions, but they will need to use a combination of the three methods in order to persuade effectively.

Many of our actions are prompted by the stimulus of our emotions or combination of reason and emotion. In other words, we will respond to emotions alone, or reason and emotion combined. Aristotle cautions speakers and audiences against *pathos* alone: "Besides, an emotional speaker always makes his audience feel with him, even when there is nothing in his arguments; which is why many speakers try to overwhelm their audience by mere noise."[75] This is important to consider as communicators; our argument should appeal to more than just reason (or emotion) alone, or else we might be swindled by "mere noise," rather than true substance.

Aristotle said we can analyze emotions from three angles: their <u>nature</u>, their <u>object</u> (the people or things toward whom we experience the emotion), and their <u>exciting causes</u> (what brings about the emotion?). We need to know <u>all three things</u> about an emotion if we hope to arouse it in others. Aristotle spent a great deal of his *Rhetoric* examining emotions and their opposites. No wonder, then, that he is considered a philosopher as well as a psychologist of sorts.

Our will does not have direct control of our emotions. It is dangerous to announce to an audience that we are going to play on their emotions. We must get at the emotions in a roundabout manner, rather than outright stating that we will be twisting their emotions. We might reflect upon the thing that would arouse emotions. For example, think of advertisement by an animal shelter urging people to donate money or adopt a homeless dog or cat. Sad photos and an equally sad commentator will pull at your heart strings in order to evoke pity. (Take a moment to recall what fallacy this would be!)

Hugh Blair emphasizes that though emotional appeals are important, the communicator must use an even tone in his emotions. He does not want the speaker to heat up his emotions too soon

---

[75]   Aristotle *Rhetoric* 3.7

and wear out the audience. Highly intense emotions throughout the speech will also exhaust the topic. So the speaker must intensify his emotional appeal gradually and organize his speech in order to build up to that intensity.

Aristotle agrees with Blair that emotional persuasion must fall in line with the situation that warrants them: "To express emotion, you will employ the language of anger in speaking of outrage; the language of disgust and discreet reluctance to utter a word when speaking of impiety or foulness; the language of exultation for a tale of glory, and that of humiliation for a tale of pity and so in all other cases."[76] This calls for accuracy–this calls for a sense of logic and order in the presentation of emotional arguments. We cannot simply fly off the handle when seized with emotion; rather, we must *use* our God-given emotions to fuel good, well structured arguments that will compel the mind and emotion.

Passionate emotions can be aroused even by unemotional descriptions. Someone who wants his audience to be outraged at high taxes might describe how the average citizen, who scrapes to make ends meet, ends up in poverty because he can't pay his property taxes. The speaker must appeal to the imagination, creating a word-painting by use of sensory, specific detail. His evenly-toned description can itself arouse emotions; he may not need to act emotionally himself. Think of how vivid descriptions can move someone to think a certain way, react in a certain manner, or arouse certain emotions.

A *logical argument*, which appeals to reason, produces conviction about the practicality of the means to the desired end: use logic to persuade that voting for this candidate is reasonable based upon his views regarding the issues at stake. An *emotional argument* makes the end seem desirable: use emotions to persuade that this candidate is more appealing than–or not as bad as–his opponent. Notice that the argument or stance of the candidates can tend to be bypassed in this type of appeal, leading to fallacious reasoning like the Straw Man, *ad hominem*, or Bulverism (to name a few). Emotions can quite easily distract from the issue at hand, rather than being utilized as a tool for the rhetorician to use *alongside* a *logos* argument.

---

[76]   Ibid.

A lesson in identifying *Pathos*

Let's take a look at Churchill's "Blood, Toil, Tears, and Sweat" speech, the last few paragraphs, with regard to his use of *pathos*:

> To form an Administration of this scale and complexity is a serious undertaking in itself, but it must be remembered that we are in the preliminary stage of one of the greatest battles in history, that we are in action at many other points in Norway and in Holland, that we have to be prepared in the Mediterranean, that the air battle is continuous and that many preparations, such as have been indicated by my honorable friends below the Gangway, have to be made here at home. In this crisis I hope I may be pardoned if I do not address the House at any length today. I hope that any of my friends and colleagues, or former colleagues, who are affected by the political reconstruction, will make allowance, all allowance, for any lack of ceremony with which it has been necessary to act. I would say to the House, as I said to those who have joined this government: "I have nothing to offer but blood, toil, tears and sweat."
>
> We have before us an ordeal of the most grievous kind. We have before us many, many long months of struggle and of suffering. You ask, what is our policy? I can say: It is to wage war, by sea, land and air, with all our might and with all the strength that God can give us; to wage war against a monstrous tyranny, never surpassed in the dark, lamentable catalogue of human crime. That is our policy. You ask, what is our aim? I can answer in one word: It is victory, victory at all costs, victory in spite of all terror, victory, however long and hard the road may be; for without victory, there is no survival. Let that be realised; no survival for the British Empire, no survival for all that the British Empire has stood for, no survival for the urge and impulse of the ages, that mankind will move forward toward its goal. But I take up my task with buoyancy and hope. I feel sure that our cause will not be suffered to fail among men. At this time I feel entitled to claim the aid of all, and I say, "come then, let us go forward together with our united strength."

First we need to find the words and phrases that convey emotion; they tug on the emotions of his audience. Be aware that some words and phrases can also contain some ethical or logical appeal.

- one of the greatest battles in history
- blood, toil, tears and sweat
- ordeal of the most grievous kind
- many, many long months of struggle and of suffering
- monstrous tyranny
- dark, lamentable catalogue of human crime
- victory (note how many times it is used here)
- terror
- no survival (note how many times that phrase is used)
- buoyancy
- hope

When analyzing the use of *pathos*, we cannot analyze any discourse without taking into account the moment in history in which the speech is given. What's going on in the world at the time? If you

133

are unable to place a discourse in a specific time in history, you will most likely miss the impact of its words.

Take note of which emotions are elicited. Look for positive and negative ones. Consider how Churchill might want his audience to respond. Will he want them to be angry at that which makes him angry? Will he urge them to action? More simply put, does he want them to be depressed, angry, hopeful, patriotic? Which words and phrases are particularly effective and emotion-laden? With regard to the repetitions noted above, what impact is that going to have on his audience? Why repeat them?

Notice that Churchill does not begin with *pathos*. The two paragraphs we have quoted are the final paragraphs of his speech. He chose to lay the groundwork for his emotional appeal first.

A caution regarding emotional appeal: Some people exploit emotions for unscrupulous purposes, and we will come across several examples in this rhetoric course. Some will ignore a logical or ethical appeal in exchange for an outright play on people's emotions. This comes up in politics with predictable regularity. A politician will tell his audience "I feel your pain" so that they feel like he knows what they're going through. Another will advertise with emotionally-laden photos, artwork, sound bites, or catchy phrases in order to sway voters.

Those who study human personality know that people do things, or avoid doing things, based on their emotional condition. Advertisers have always taken advantage of this. Sometimes, though, we can recognize when someone is tugging just a little too much on our emotions, and we dig in our heels. So what's the best way to persuade an audience?

Consider advertisements, which typically utilize *pathos* (often in lieu of *logos*) to persuade their audience to purchase something.

Pathos in an advertisement

Read the text for the following ad, taken from the radio. (If possible, see if you can locate an audio file of this ad on the internet.) Consider how well or how poorly emotion is used here. Be ready to discuss in class. See Assignment 16.10.

> Somebody just died…while you're listening to me. And that somebody is somebody's sister, brother, mom, dad, daughter, son or friend. 450 people die a day. 19 an hour. From Lung Cancer. Six-hundred and fifty thousand people will die of the world's DEADLIEST cancer by the year 2010 if we don't do something now. Where's the outrage? Lung Cancer Matters Too. It's not what you think. It's not what you've heard. Don't believe that if you don't smoke you can NEVER get lung cancer. I'm Deborah Morosini and I lost my sister, Dana Reeve, to lung cancer. Please help us save lives at the Bonnie J. Addario Lung Cancer Foundation. Because we can.
>
> Donate today at www lung cancer foundation dot org or call 866.926.LUNG. Lung Cancer Matters Too. And so does EVERYONE we love.
>
> (Radio PSA from the Lung Cancer Foundation, 2007-08)

The United States in the 1970s sat up and noticed the smog and pollution that fouled the land. TV viewers watched advertisements aimed at encouraging citizens to clean up their land. One series of ads featured a Native American named Iron Eyes Cody, who shed a large tear as he roamed through the land. Search his name and his "Make America Beautiful" commercials. Take note of the visual message and the emotions aroused.

Sensing emotions and how to address them is instinctual for some. Others may have to work on understanding and employing this concept. Intellectual appeal is often not enough to move people's will to act, so the rhetorician who decides to forego all emotional appeal might just lose the argument because he didn't pay close enough attention to the needs of his audience.

As an audience member, be alert for emotional appeals from others. What is that commercial trying to get you to feel? (Christians must always be aware of the underlying presuppositions which drive certain ideas and actions, and prompt certain emotions.)

Be natural; let the nature of the subject matter, the occasion, or the audience elicit the appropriate kind and the right amount of emotional appeal.

"The Emphatic" as a type of *pathos*

We have said that *pathos* has a unique impact on an audience. One type of *pathos*, not mentioned by Aristotle or Cicero, we will call "The Emphatic." This kind of *pathos* depends on the speaker sounding believable. The Emphatic comes across as a promise to the audience. Politicians imply a promise, saying, in so many words, "you can trust what I've said here." In the following article are several examples of the Emphatic. We add another, more recent example: U.S. President Donald Trump made countless promises during his campaign–as do all politicians–and his usually came with the phrase *believe me*: "We are now, under the Trump Administration, reclaiming our heritage as a manufacturing nation. We are fighting to provide a level playing field for American Workers and Industries. Other countries will cease taking advantage of us, believe me." [77] For more examples of the Emphatic, read the following discourse and discuss it with your class.

---

[77] https://www.whitehouse.gov/the-press-office/2017/07/21/president-donald-j-trumps-weekly-address

Read My Lips...Period: The Use of the Emphatic in Rhetoric[78]

By Shaunna Howat, 2013

Sometimes speakers (in politics, religion, and other public venues) forget the power of their words to move an audience. Sometimes they capitalize on it. Words strung together to project a thought or an idea–they have meaning. Words have permanence. And words, misused or abused, will sometimes swing right back around and smack the speaker in the mouth. Words have meaning.

A few years ago President George H.W. Bush made a promise: "Read my lips: No new taxes." When shortly thereafter he raised taxes, his recorded words proved that he had not carried out his pledge. That broken promise effectively lost his chance for reelection. How do we know it was a promise? He used the emphatic: Read my lips. He didn't need to say "I promise you." His emphatic rhetoric, "Read my lips," was his vow. And the country knew he had broken his promise.

Emphatic rhetoric can take place not just with words but also with physical gestures. President Bill Clinton pointed at and looked directly into the cameras, and jabbed his finger with every sentence: "I did not. Have sexual relations. With that woman [Monica Lewinsky]." His physical gestures, along with the emphasis he made as he spoke (including the fact that he effectively looked us in the eye), implied a promise or a vow, almost daring the reporters to prove him wrong. As the world knows, he had lied to the American people, and he was impeached for lying under oath not long afterward. He lost credibility, and he is now a joke among late night TV hosts. His reputation is forever tarnished.

President Richard Nixon, like Clinton, looked into the cameras and made his famous avowal: "Let me be perfectly clear." He averred that he was not a crook. As the world found out, Nixon was up to his eyeballs in the Watergate scandal. He left the office of the president shortly thereafter. He too is a byword; his name will forever be associated with the scandal he launched.

Promises are made with the use of the emphatic, and they can be words alone, or words and gestures together. We as the audience understand the emphatic. We remember it. We hold the speakers accountable for it.

This is why President Barack Obama has found himself in such hot water. He used the emphatic, time and time again (one news outlet counted 26 different speeches), to promise that [with his signature health care bill, now called ObamaCare] if Americans like their current health insurance plan and liked their doctor, "you can keep them. Period."

The use of the emphatic "period" is what has ensnared him. He cannot get away from it. The "period" was his promise. His audiences saw it as his pledge to them, and they held him to it. Upon finding out that they indeed could not keep their plans or their doctors [under ObamaCare], Americans registered their outrage. The president's reputation, and his opinion polls, have been on a downward spiral since. Not only did he break his promise, but documents are beginning to show that he knew this was a broken promise a couple of years before his health care law was launched in October of 2013. Yet he continued to repeat the pledge time and again.

Don't make the mistake of thinking that this emphatic promise was a mistake, that he misspoke. Presidents do not often make impromptu claims or commitments, and certainly not 26

---

[78] https://writingrhetorically.com/2013/11/14/read-my-lips-period-the-use-of-the-emphatic-in-rhetoric/

times in a space of three or four years. Whether his supporters want to agree or not, he made a pledge–a promise–using the language of the emphatic, and he cannot excuse it away. He also cannot, as he tried in the weeks afterward, "unspeak" his promise, or re-interpret it. In an age of video recordings available to anyone, anytime, people can see the speaker and hear his words for themselves; the promise cannot be erased.

The use of the emphatic is intentional. The speaker does not have to say "I promise" for it to be understood as a guarantee. The speaker pledges his reputation on such an emphasis, and the audience reads it as a serious promise.

Jesus used the emphatic with his "verily, verily I say unto you," also translated as "truly I say to you." He effectively said to his hearers, "listen up: what I am about to say is true." He did not prevaricate; he did not equivocate. What he said could be taken as true because he led up to it with such a pledge.

The fact remains that people will believe you if you use emphatic rhetoric, both in word and in gesture. God's word reminds people to take words seriously. "But above all, my brothers, do not swear, either by heaven or by earth or by any other oath, but let your 'yes' be yes and your 'no' be no, so that you may not fall under condemnation" (*ESV*, James 5.12). In other words, understand that the implied promise of the emphatic word or gesture will be taken as truth, and you have staked your reputation on it.

Discussion on Pathos and Ad Misericordiam

The following exchange by two former students took place in a classroom discussion board. See what you can add or contribute to the discussion.

"When the mind is freely exerted, its reasoning is sound; but passion, if it gain possession of it, becomes its tyrant, and reason is powerless…

"But to what end, in the name of the eternal gods! was such eloquence directed? Was it intended to render you indignant at the conspiracy? A speech, no doubt, will inflame him whom so frightful and monstrous a reality has not provoked!"

I have been thinking recently about the proper use of emotional appeal. In particular, I am wondering where real, useful, proper *pathos* (a legitimate appeal) ends and where puny *ad misericordiam* (a fallacy) begins. Julius Caesar was evidently not an advocate of firing up one's audience, as if the bare facts won't do enough. He brings up a good point: that truth should be sufficient to convince. However, there may be a loophole in his argument about reason being sound, since human reason is corrupted. So I suppose that one use of *pathos* would be to restore reason, through emotion, to its proper state.

There is a tendency to dismiss emotion as limiting and unnecessary, something we should strive to liberate ourselves from. While emotion has definite dangers, and while I (at least theoretically) dislike emotional appeal in general, it does seem that since God gave us emotions, they are valid, just as reason is valid. Perhaps emotion was created specifically for the purpose of restoring our warped rationality. But this cannot be entirely true, since Christ had emotions; God does, too.

But to return from the metaphysical, I have an example of debilitating *pathos*. The letter in the "Checkers" speech by Nixon is rather too sentimental for my taste, though we counted it as refutation by emotional appeal. Of course the lady was in a difficult situation, but she seemed to be trying to jerk tears from the audience. What need was there for her to speak of running a household on $80 a month? And, though regrettable that she is so young with a husband off to war and a child he has never seen, it seems hardly surprising. That sort of thing does happen if you marry a Marine.

This *pathos* and much other *pathos* seems too disgusting to me because it smacks of manipulation. I don't want to be made to cry or feel so strongly if reason forbids it. And with this piece of *pathos*, it seemed superfluous to Nixon's argument. I would classify it as *ad misericordiam*.

To me, the most moving and emotionally exciting elements in a discourse are forceful word choices, figures of speech, and flawless logic. I would much rather feel strongly about someone's perfect argument than cry about something not worth crying about. I think an excellent piece of *pathos* was Bush's "straight smooth highway to nowhere" ("On Democracy in Iraq and the Middle East"). This is clever, vivid, and convincing. It certainly captured my imagination and gave me a surge of joy. Burke's splendid metaphors do this too.

Some *pathos* as *pathos*, if done well, can be very convincing. I did like the "Lord Clive" discourse we read last year. It's written with much *pathos*, but it has a reason for being there. And the author has such a command of language that he knows how to wield the weapon without cheese. I believe that modern writers in general have less command of language, and they should probably steer clear of emotion. For the matter of that, I would recommend steering clear of reading many modern writers, at least until they have learned more logic.

[The following continues the discussion of emotional persuasion versus appeal to pity. A second student responds to the first student's thoughts.]

As I have thought about emotions and logic in some of my other classes, I must say that I personally see more of a need for logic than emotions. Below is the ending of an essay I wrote for another class:

I see many people today rely on outside stimuli in order to run their lives. Feelings become more important than fact. Emotions run deeper than truth. Opinions hold more weight than the logical arguments presented in any condition. From the quote, I received yet another push in the direction of making my own feelings rather than relying on outside situations to make my feelings. Further thought on the quote made me realize that one might also imply from it the bonds and oaths of marriage resting on those oaths and mutual assent to steer their opinions of their partner in the direction of love and acceptance.

God made the human mind as an organ of power and beauty. With it, we have the ability to feel, think, and reason. Without it we become mere animals. Instead of allowing our minds to focus on what the outside world demands and asks for, we should instead train ourselves to create opinions that further our development of God's goals. Our minds are an active, usable tool, not a recorder.

Emotions cause our bodies to simply record what the writer, speaker, or other wants us to feel.

However, I do agree that emotions have been as much a part of us as anything since our creation and they do serve their uses. In the CAP (Civil Air Patrol) as a commander and leader, I use emotion a lot; it is one of the few ways to motivate a cadet. By using this emotion I can reach where their minds and logical arguments could not. Although it might be considered manipulation, and in a way it is, I do it for their benefit because I have been through what they are going through before.

It seems to me that emotions are our most basic understanding of life. The newborn babe has emotions even if his logical faculties have not yet fully developed. The basic principles of emotion bring powerful motivation, strong friendships, loyal partisans, etc; but only for as long as the emotion last.

Complete Assignment 16.2 for this discourse.

In Summary, Lesson 16:

Analyze emotions from three angles:

1. Their _____
2. Their _____
3. Their _____

Terms to Remember:

- Unscrupulous
- Emphatic

Lesson Sixteen Assignments

Assignment 16.1

Earlier the text said that someone's will does not have direct control of one's emotions. As a Christian communicator, how then does one speak to unbelievers? Use scripture to answer this in 2-3 paragraphs.

Assignment 16.2

Read the discussion regarding *pathos* and *ad misericordiam* and answer the following questions: What's your opinion related to these thoughts? This student brought up *Julius Caesar* and other examples. What will you use to discuss this point? Where does *pathos* end and fallacy begin? Write three to four paragraphs.

Multimedia Focus 16.3

Find four commercials or ads (radio, television, newspaper, billboard, or magazine: YouTube will be a great resource for this) that use emotional appeal. Describe them in as much detail as possible. What kind of emotional appeal is used in each ad? What is the underlying message, if any? What are their theses (in your own words)? One paragraph per commercial.

Assignment 16.4

Take one of the advertisements from 16.3 and expand it into a presentation to the entire class. Show or display the advertisement to the class and explain it in great detail.

- Look at every aspect of the ad, in addition to the explicitly written message: performances, colors, music, movement, focus.
- Who is its audience and how does the commercial address it?
- Does the ad take the time to explain the *logos* and *ethos* in addition to the *pathos*? Is it well balanced?
- Is there a clear connection between the message (the product or point that the commercial tries to get across) and the means (the way that the commercial goes about selling the product–consider many car commercials, which often have little do actually do with cars).

Your presentation should be five to seven minutes in length.

Assignment 16.5

Read Cicero's "Catiline" speech. We will be analyzing this later. For now, describe the emotions you read in this speech. First, what emotions did Cicero express? What emotions did he try to arouse in his audience? From the editor's preface you have an idea how this affected his audience. Try to describe how this may have affected the outcome of Catiline's "trial." Two to three paragraphs.

Multimedia Focus 16.6

Search online for an advertisement for the ASPCA (American Society for the Prevention of Cruelty to Animals). Describe the ad, then comment on the use of *pathos*. Describe the visual images as well as the words used. Comment on how the ad uses *pathos* to persuade.

Assignment 16.7

US Presidential Candidate Barack Obama (two-term president from 2009 to 2017 used a popular "Yes we can!" slogan during his 2008 campaign. This is an emotionally-laden sentiment, but what exactly does it mean? Explore this in class or by researching it on the internet.

Assignment 16.8

Read President Roosevelt's "Day of Infamy" Speech from December 8, 1941. How does he use emotions throughout his discourse? What emotions does he want to elicit from his audience? What actions does he want them to take? Two to three paragraphs.

Assignment 16.9

Consider the Lung Cancer radio ad from this lesson. Discuss in an essay (two to three paragraphs) how well or how poorly emotion is used here. Think critically. Be ready to discuss in class.

Assignment 16.10

Read the brief passage from Macaulay called "Lord Clive." Note the very emotional language here. Look up any words that are unfamiliar to you. Be ready for a class discussion.

Multimedia Focus 16.11

Find a movie or TV show in which there is a great speech. Analyze the rhetoric of that speech. Who does the speaker address? How effective is it? What does the speaker use to persuade the audience (*ethos, pathos, logos*)? No ideas for great movie speeches? Here are a few options. You and your parents may need to agree that these are okay to watch.

Movies:

Independence Day, President's speech

Braveheart, Wallace's speech

Legend of Bagger Vance, Bagger's speech

The Blind Side, Charge of the Light Brigade speech

Secondhand Lions, Uncle Hub's speech

Great Dictator, Chaplin's speech

TV: *Sherlock*, Season 3, "The Sign of Three" episode, Best Man speech

(For more options, go to Filmsite.org/bestspeeches.html. Choose speeches that are 2 minutes or longer.)

Lesson Seventeen

Analysis of a Discourse

This next section of rhetoric involves the analysis of discourses. So far we have analyzed discourses according to what we have learned with regard to the Five Canons. Now we will put it all together and analyze our first discourse. Refer to the list below for questions we answer when writing an analysis. We will answer in full sentences and paragraphs, describing the hows and whys of each question. Answers must include examples (quotes) from the discourse as support.

Questions to Answer when Analyzing a discourse

1. What type of discourse is this?
2. What is the thesis?
3. Break into divisions by paragraph number.
4. Describe how each division supports the thesis.
5. What kind of introduction is it?
6. How does he persuade—ethically, emotionally, logically? Describe where each of these is used.
7. How does he conclude—what method(s) does he employ?
8. What fallacies do you find, and what kind?
9. What figures of speech do you find, and what kind? (Only if you have studied Figures in Lesson 21.)

How each Question should be answered

1. **What type of discourse is this?** As we learned in the first few days of rhetoric, a discourse is either epideictic (ceremonial), deliberative (in a legislative atmosphere), forensic (in a court of law), or propaganda (the use of a discourse in order to gain power by instilling fear). Give reasons.
2. **What is the thesis?** Most discourses contain the thesis in the first one or two sections. Sometimes it can be found farther down in the discourse. Remember that a thesis statement is one or two sentences that affirm or deny something about a particular subject. Tell why you chose that as the thesis.
3. **Break into divisions.** Using the divisions learned earlier in rhetoric, divide the discourse into these divisions. Not every discourse will have every division, and not every discourse will have the divisions in the same order they were presented earlier (except for the introduction and conclusion, hopefully!). The point of this exercise is to take a careful look at how the discourse is constructed. If you don't find the divisions, say so.
4. **Describe how each division supports the thesis.** It is important to learn how a writer or speaker supports his thesis. Sometimes one might not support his thesis well, and it is important to see that a discourse falls apart when it is not supported. When describing how the thesis is supported in each division, you should be able to provide quotes and examples from the discourse. ("He supports the thesis in paragraph 19 where he says, ...") This is also the place where the student will explain how the writer moves his topic along, and what it might mean.

5. **What kind of introduction is it?** We learned about the different kinds of introductions—narrative, inquisitive, preparatory, corrective, and paradoxical. Here you will explain what kind of introduction the writer uses and why.

6. **How does he persuade—ethically, emotionally, logically?** Find examples throughout the discourse where he uses these three types of appeal. Again, it is important to quote examples of these types of appeal. ("An example of emotional appeal is evident in paragraph 14, and it says...")

7. **How does he conclude—what method(s) does he employ?** Aristotle described four different methods for concluding. One can summarize his points, arouse emotions, make himself sound good and his opponent sound bad, and amplify his own points while extenuating his opponent's points.

8. **What fallacies do you find, and what kind?** Using your understanding of logic from the last section, students should find fallacies, if any. Some discourses will not contain any fallacies. It is still important for students to use their critical thinking skills in identifying the logical appeal (or lack thereof) of a writer or speaker. ("In paragraph 11 he commits the fallacy of *ad baculum* by saying, …")

9. **What figures of speech do you find, and what kind?** This required section only pertains to students in who have studied Figures of Speech in Lesson 21.

A complete, rhetorical analysis is written in paragraph form, in full sentences. Do not use the personal pronoun (I, me, my, mine) or the second person (you, your, we, our), so that you develop your analytical skills as a writer. **You must answer the questions WHY? HOW? and WHERE? as you write.**

Students usually choose one of two different methods for analyzing:

1. They might answer each question in order, or

2. They can answer the questions as they move chronologically through the discourse, from the introduction through the conclusion. That means that as they analyze the introduction they are also telling what kind of introduction it is, what kind of discourse it is, how this introduction supports the thesis (or if the thesis is in the introduction, say so here), how he persuades in the introduction, and so forth. Then the student moves on to discuss the rest of the discourse, in the order in which it is written. While this second method may seem more complicated, it actually uses higher-level thinking and organizational skills.

Regardless of the method you choose to use, you must have your own thesis statement that argues how the writer argues his or her thesis statement. For example, if you were to write an analysis of Winston Churchill's "Blood, Toil, Tears, and Sweat," you might use this thesis statement (for this example, assume the writer has already introduced the speaker and the speech):

> Churchill speaks to the British Parliament to assure them that he has formed a new government with the aim of preserving the British way of life through the defeat of Hitler's Germany.

Here, the analysis writer informs his reader of what Churchill aims to prove in the speech: that Churchill has formed a new government, will preserve British life, and defeat Hitler.

Your rhetorical analysis will break down every aspect that we have studied up until this point and explain it to your reader. You must use proof (properly quoted and cited) for each and every thing that you say throughout this essay.

In Summary, Lesson 17

Answer these questions when analyzing a discourse:

1. What type of _____
2. What is the _____
3. Break into _____ by _____
4. Describe how each _____ supports the _____
5. What kind of _____
6. How does he persuade: _____, _____ or _____
7. How does he _____; what methods does he employ?
8. What _____ do you find, and what kind?
9. What _____ of _____

Lesson Seventeen Assignments

Assignment 17.1

Read and annotate John F. Kennedy's "Inaugural Address." Answer the nine analysis questions for yourself, noting where you find evidence to support what you say.

Assignment 17.2

Using the notes you took for 17.1, write a rhetorical analysis of John F. Kennedy's "Inaugural Address." Thoroughly read the instructions in Lesson 17 to understand how to write a rhetorical analysis. This assignment does not have a specific length: it should be as long as it needs to be–the appropriate length to answer these questions in a cohesive form.

Assignment 17.3

Read and analyze Thomas Jefferson's "Inaugural Address." Complete the Full Analysis Worksheet and turn it in.

Lesson Eighteen

The Topics, an Aid to Invention

If [students'] subjects of discourse be improperly chosen; if they maintain extravagant or indecent topics; if they indulge themselves in loose and flimsy declamation, which has no foundation in good sense; or accustom themselves to speak pertly on all subjects without due preparation, they may improve one another in petulance, but in no other thing; and will infallibly form themselves to a very faulty and vicious taste in speaking. (Hugh Blair, *Lectures on Belles Lettres*)

As we know from Invention, the writer or orator must have a body of knowledge from which to draw, before beginning to write on any certain topic. One draws from his extensive knowledge on a subject, or researches a certain topic, before beginning to write. *Topics* (*topos*) falls under the category of "discovering what to write about." The subject of *Topics* is considered an aid to The First Canon: Invention.

Let me (Tyler) clarify a bit. Topics has long been an aspect of rhetoric that I have not fully grasped until recently, when I finally realized that our modern use of the word *Topics* does not follow Aristotle's definition. I believed that Aristotle meant *subject matter* when he used the word *Topics*. However, as George A. Kennedy clarifies, "*Topos* literally means 'place,' metaphorically that location of space in an art where a speaker can look for 'available means of persuasion.'"[79] So *Topics* is the place in writing where the rhetorician specifically seeks to persuade. More specifically, these *Topics* "are lines, or strategies, of argument, useful in treating many different subject matters" throughout a discourse.[80] Essentially, when we, today, use the word *Topics*, we mean subject matter. If we ask, "What's the topic of your paper?" we mean: "What's your paper about? What's it's subject matter?" However, when Aristotle says, "What's the topic of your paper?" he means: "How will your paper persuade?"

So, as Kennedy tells us, Topics refers to **your strategy for arguing in your discourse**. Therefore, as you read through the rest of this chapter, keep that in mind (and we'll try to clarify when possible).

This means that, as you approach the writing of your discourse, you need to actually plan what you're going to write, but not merely the content or the subject matter–the **method of argumentation**, the strategy you'll use to go about arguing. This goes *before* you actually begin writing–*Topics* is part of Invention, after all.

Steps for Moving from Invention to Arrangement

1. <u>Invent</u>: Come up with the subject matter about which you plan to write. This involves intense brainstorming and planning. You need to think ahead, do a little research, really consider where you plan to go with your topic.

---

[79] Kennedy, *On Rhetoric*, 45.

[80] Kennedy, *On Rhetoric*, 190

2. <u>Research</u>: This can be big or small depending on the size and scope of your discourse. If you have a research-based paper, you need to consider the scientific method and *hypothesize* or ask a Research Question ahead of time that you're researching the answer to. Starting with a thesis statement before doing any research will invariably result in biased information—due to confirmation bias. You may inadvertently only research that which matches your theory, disregarding what which may disagree with it.

   You need to have a significant bibliography, a well of knowledge from which you'll draw as you write your paper. This mean researching more information that you plan to write about. SEE: Lessons 25-26

   You may need to return to this step as you write your paper, because your arguments may require more support than you can predict. <u>This is normal.</u>

3. <u>Selecting a Thesis Statement</u>: After you've done your research, come up with a Thesis Statement, a statement which affirms or denies something about a particular subject, a statement which you can defend. SEE: Lesson 6.

4. <u>Topics</u>
   a. <u>Choosing a Persuasion Strategy (using Aristotle's *Topics*)</u>: Remember, you've not started writing yet. But you're almost there. You're planning *how* you will persuade. Look through the *Topics* and decide what approaches will work for you (or some combination thereof). Simply starting to write your paper without a plan will result in a mess of frustration. Before beginning to conquer the blank page, you need to plan how you'll start to wage that war.

   b. <u>Outline</u>. As you begin to construct your outline, transferring information from your notes to your outline, think about your strategy—place your soldiers and equipment where they need to go and how they will be best used. Think: how does one point flow into the next? Should I be writing from more general to specific? Do I need to compare multiple ideas and make a judgment call? Do I need to discuss causes and their effects or whether or not things are possible?

   Feel free to mix and match. These are *tools* for you to use as you plan and compose your essay. Doing this well means that you're moving from the First to the Second Canon.

There are three aids to invention: The common topics, the special topics, and external (research—see Lesson 25). Special topics involve certain discourses such as forensic (judicial matters as argued in courts of law). Rhetoricians of all ages have revered Cicero as the master of that craft.

With regard to special topics, ancient Greek and Roman rhetoricians agreed that rhetoric concerned itself with *declamation* (an exercise in oratory; the recitation of a classic speech), most especially in their courts and lawmaking bodies. The art of rhetoric as used in a court and among lawmakers fell into disuse until representative governmental bodies (parliaments or congresses) began to spread across the Western world. During the early Christian times and periodically through the Middle Ages, the practice of rhetoric was preserved, and even revered, as useful in sermons. Then with the development of universities across the west, and as the Renaissance spread, rhetoricians blew the dust off those great Greek and Roman ideas and began exploring how to employ declamation—how to persuade artfully—in their lawmaking and judicial bodies.

The Common Topics

The Common Topics provide rhetoricians with a stock of general lines of argument that can be used in the development of any subject. These might be for any sort of occasion, as Aristotle described. His list of types of Common Topics is extensive, and a few of them have been outlined as follows.

Division

Division lists the parts that go to make something up, in an effort to define it. Here one lays out the organization of the exposition or argument that is to follow. An argument then might elaborate on the list as stated in the division. One could think of Division as a simple list that elaborates on the parts of the discourse. When arguing, this can be used to establish the grounds for an argument by elimination: enumerate the alternatives, then eliminate each one to arrive at the conclusion you want.

The use of division follows in this manner: "The accused, Oliver Twist, could have been the one who overturned the fruit stand for any one of these reasons: A) he was ordered to steal fruit by that vagabond named Fagin, B) he wanted to cause mayhem in the market square, C) he was temporarily blinded by the sun and accidentally bumped into the cart, or D) he was angry at the owner of the fruit stand for selling him a bruised apple. We have shown that Oliver could not possibly have been interested in mayhem, because he is a kind young man, and he is not given to angry outbursts of any sort. Further, he did not see the sun because it was a rainy day. This young man was ordered to steal by Fagin; that is the only possible motive, and Oliver should not be prosecuted but rather protected from the crooked influence of that criminal, Fagin." This construction is not only useful in a court trial (Forensic); it is useful in expository writing and in argumentative discourse.

Comparison

Comparison is a common method for teaching, defining, or reasoning; holding up two or more things to examine them for their relationships or differences. Cicero says Comparison can be "used to embellish or prove or clarify or vilify" (Book 4).

Similarity, under the category of Comparison, is "the likeness of two or more things...the basic principle behind all inductive argument and all analogy. In induction: we note similarity among a number of instances and make an inference about a further unobserved or unconfirmed instance."[81] Analogy uses the similarities of similar topics (for example: if theft is a sin, so is carjacking). An analogy argues that if two things are alike in one or two characteristics, they are probably alike in another characteristic (argues from the similarities of dissimilar things). Analogy doesn't prove anything, but it has persuasive value.

Cicero comments on the circumstances in which Analogy might apply. In a legal case, if a specific crime does not violate any specific law, the court can draw an analogy from similar laws or cases, and apply them to the current case.[82][83]

---

[81]   Corbett, *Classical Rhetoric*, 93

[82]   *Ad Herennium* 1.13

[83]   ADDITIONAL NOTE: There were three main types of analogy. In the original Greek sense, analogy involved a comparison of two proportions or relations. Thus "principle" was said to be an analogical term when said of a point and a spring of water because a point is related to a line as a spring is related to a river. This type of analogy came to be called the analogy of proportionality. In the second sense, analogy involved a relation between two things, of

An excellent example of the use of analogy comes from Martin Luther King's "Letter from Birmingham Jail," in which King wants to force his opponents to see how their accusations of him make no sense.

> In your statement you assert that our actions, even though peaceful, must be condemned because they precipitate violence. But is this a logical assertion? Isn't this like condemning a robbed man because his possession of money precipitated the evil act of robbery? Isn't this like condemning Socrates because his unswerving commitment to truth and his philosophical inquiries precipitated the act by the misguided populace in which they made him drink hemlock? Isn't this like condemning Jesus because his unique God-consciousness and never-ceasing devotion to God's will precipitated the evil act of crucifixion? We must come to see that, as the federal courts have consistently affirmed, it is wrong to urge an individual to cease his efforts to gain his basic constitutional rights because the quest may precipitate violence. Society must protect the robbed and punish the robber.[84]

In this case, presenting these other unfair accusations of innocent men should stir his accusers and force them to either back down or hold steady. The latter option will deepen the divide between just and unjust causes.

Another example of analogy is found in "Birmingham:" "Like a boil that can never be cured so long as it is covered up but must be opened with all its ugliness to the natural medicines of air and light, injustice must be exposed with all the tension its exposure creates, to the light of human conscience and the air of national opinion, before it can be cured."[85] King's vivid wording here illustrates an evil that must be exposed and dealt with.

Difference

The Topic of Difference contrasts two or more things. It is used to gather arguments for confirmation or refutation.

The topic of difference can be turned into a defense of an ideology, as it is used here:

> The difference between working towards communism and "communism" itself is like the difference between building a house and living in a house. The Soviet Union, for example, never claimed to have achieved communism. In theory, what was taking place in the Soviet Union was an attempt to do the work needed to construct a communist society. Just as building a house is hard work, that has to be done in order to have a house to live in, the Stalinist system of the Soviet Union was seen as the hard work that was being done by everyone to build a communist system. It was never seen by any of the Communists as "communism" itself, any more than a construction foreman would think that the act of building a home is the same as lounging on the couch inside a home. In truth, most

---

which one is primary and the other secondary. Thus "healthy" was said to be an analogical term when said of a dog and its food because while the dog has health in the primary sense, its food is healthy only secondarily as contributing to or causing the health of the dog. This second type of analogy became known as the analogy of attribution, and its special mark was being said in a prior and a posterior sense (*per prius et posterius*). A third type of analogy, sometimes appealed to by theologians, appealed to a relation of likeness between God and creatures. Creatures are called good or just because their goodness or justice imitates or reflects the goodness or justice of God. This type of analogy was called the analogy of imitation or participation. (http://plato.stanford.edu/entries/analogy-medieval/ date accessed: 3-17-2003)

[84] Kingencyclopedia.stanford.edu

[85] Ibid.

Communists today recognize that the Soviet Union was mostly just a large, corrupt, top down bureaucracy that didn't represent the ideals of Marxism or Communism.[86]

The above example shows how the topic of Difference can sometimes be used to argue from the wrong side of an argument.

Trace the path of Difference in an excerpt from Martin Luther King's "Letter from Birmingham Jail."

> You express a great deal of anxiety over our willingness to break laws. This is certainly a legitimate concern. Since we so diligently urge people to obey the Supreme Court's decision of 1954 outlawing segregation in the public schools, at first glance it may seem rather paradoxical for us consciously to break laws. One may ask: "How can you advocate breaking some laws and obeying others?" The answer lies in the fact that there are two types of laws: just and unjust. I would be the first to advocate obeying just laws. One has not only a legal but a moral responsibility to obey just laws. Conversely, one has a moral responsibility to disobey unjust laws. I would agree with St. Augustine that "an unjust law is no law at all."
>
> Now, what is the difference between the two? How does one determine whether a law is just or unjust? A just law is a man-made code that squares with the moral law or the law of God. An unjust law is a code that is out of Harmony with the moral law. To put it in the terms of St. Thomas Aquinas: An unjust law is a human law that is not rooted in eternal law and natural law. Any law that uplifts human personality is just. Any law that degrades human personality is unjust. All segregation statutes are unjust because segregation distorts the soul and damages the personality. It gives the segregator a false sense of superiority and the segregated a false sense of inferiority. Segregation, to use the terminology of the Jewish philosopher Martin Buber, substitutes an "I-it" relationship for an "I-thou" relationship and ends up relegating persons to the status of things. Hence segregation is not only politically, economically and sociologically unsound, it is morally wrong and sinful. Paul Tillich has said that sin is separation. Is not segregation an existential expression of man's tragic separation, his awful estrangement, his terrible sinfulness? Thus is it that I can urge men to obey the 1954 decision of the Supreme Court, for it is morally right; and I can urge them to disobey segregation ordinances, for they are morally wrong.[87]

The discussion above progresses in the following manner:

- Just law: squares with the moral law of God. Unjust law: out of harmony with moral law.

- Just law: uplifts human personality. Unjust law: human law not rooted in eternal law.

- Just law becomes unjust: I/thou becomes I/it; relegates persons to the status of things.

- Segregation is separation (law on people): separation is sin; goes against the moral law of God.

- Integration is morally right—obey it. Segregation is morally wrong—disobey it.

Figure out the syllogism (one or more) you can find in here.

Remember that Topics concerns subjects that we can come up with or ways to put together an argument (Invention). We are continuing to look at methods of invention here—ways to persuade

---

[86]   http://www.rationalrevolution.net/war/communism_and_marxism.htm

[87]   Kingencyclopedia.stanford.edu

an audience. While you read through this list, think of ways that these methods would supply material for an argument.

Degree

Differences in Degree deal with *more or less*. Aristotle provided a list of topics of degree in his Book I, Chapter 7 of *Rhetoric*. Here are a few for discussion purposes.

1. "A greater number of things can be considered more desirable than a smaller number of the same things." This regards things of the same species. This is helpful only when all other things are equal. One student emphatically agreed with this statement when she replaced "things" with "chocolate chips."

2. "That which is an *end* is a greater good than that which is only a *means*." Does this idea work when considering that countless dictators considered it worthwhile to slaughter countless people (means) in pursuit of the perfect form of government (end)? How about when daily exercise (means) is in pursuit of good health (end)?

3. "What is scarce is greater than what is abundant." Can you think of examples?

4. "What men of practical wisdom would choose is a greater good than what ignorant men would choose." Take this line of reasoning to its logical conclusion. Who defines those of "practical wisdom"? Could this become a problem in society? How so? Talk through different examples and their outcomes.

5. "What the majority of men would choose is better than what the minority would choose." Follow this line of reasoning to its logical conclusion. As with Item 4 above, discuss whether it would become problematic.

6. "What men would really like to possess is a greater good than what men would merely like to give the impression of possessing." This one is intriguing. What do you suppose Aristotle was referencing here? Niccolo Machiavelli said that if a man who sought power was not virtuous, he should at least *seem* virtuous in order to get what he wants. This implies that power is a greater good than morals, because power is what the ruler really wants, and in order to get it he must *pretend* to be virtuous. In other words, *The end justifies the means.*

7. "If a thing does not exist where it is more likely to exist, it will not exist where it is less likely to exist." This is an *a fortiori* argument, meaning "from the stronger." It works from the greater to the lesser: "If a man lies to his wife, he will have no problem lying to his friends." This might also work from the lesser to the greater.

Cause and effect

Remember that a rhetorician's job is to persuade his audience of the *possibility* of something happening. Where in logic we arrived at absolutes by deduction and syllogistic reasoning, in rhetoric we want to *persuade*. So a cause might not be the absolute reason; what matters is whether we can *convince* our audience that this is *possible*.

An effect can have a number of possible causes (a fallen tree could have fallen because it is old and rotten, or it fell in a wind, or was cut down). Find *the* cause that works. There is then a progression of thought that we follow to find the cause for a certain effect.

1. The cause we assign for an effect must be capable of producing the effect. (If there is a strange puddle on the kitchen floor, we wonder what caused that effect. The refrigerator may have leaked, or the toddler may have tried to pour herself a cup of juice. But then, there is that new puppy…)

2. Once we think we have found sufficient cause for something, we must decide whether there might be other causes. (Yes, the toddler loves to drink juice, but the puppy hasn't been house-trained yet...)

3. Consider whether the potential causes could exist. (If the toddler was at her grandmother's house when the puddle was noticed, she is ruled out as a suspect.)

4. Consider whether the supposed cause would consistently produce an effect and whether it would without a doubt produce the same effect. (Does the puppy always make messes on the floor, or is he getting better at waiting to go outside?)

5. *Post hoc ergo propter hoc.* This fallacy says, "after this, therefore because of this," or in other words, "every time I wash my car it rains." This supposes that when two events occur near to each other in time, one has an effect on the other. (If the puppy walks through the room, there will always be a mess in that room.

In rhetoric we can argue from an effect back to a cause, or we can start with a cause and argue that it will produce a particular effect or effects. When you remember that a rhetorician does not have to prove something <u>absolutely</u>, just <u>possibly</u>, this Topic of cause and effect can be pretty useful.

Antecedent and Consequence

Antecedent and Consequence answers the following question: If A happens, does B follow? "Only if this man believes in Jesus Christ, he has eternal life in heaven." There is usually an enthymeme in this argument. Here, it is "all believers in Jesus Christ will have eternal life." Sometimes it is easy to refute an implied premise (see the section on enthymemes), so make sure to offer sufficient argumentation.

Identify the antecedent and consequence from this quote from King's "Birmingham Jail" discourse:

> So let him march; let him make prayer pilgrimages to the city hall; let him go on freedom rides—and try to understand why he must do so. If his repressed emotions are not released in nonviolent ways, they will seek expression through violence; this is not a threat but a fact of history. So I have not said to my people, "Get rid of your discontent." Rather, I have tried to say that this normal and healthy discontent can be channeled into the creative outlet of nonviolent direct action.[88]

This Topic can be an extremely persuasive method, given sufficient proof. A rhetorician can run into problems if he pushes the Antecedent/Consequence too far to be believable, but it's interesting to recall that a rhetorician concerns himself with persuasion, not absolute proof.

Aristotle, a pagan, made a very interesting correlation when describing cause/effect, antecedent/consequence: "that which is a beginning of other things is a greater good than that which is not, and that which is a cause is a greater good than that which is not; the reason being the same in each case, namely that without a cause and a beginning nothing can exist or come into existence."[89]

---

[88] Ibid.

[89] http://classics.mit.edu/Aristotle/rhetoric.1.i.html

Contradictions

The following argument is used in many ways and on many occasions. Think of how these arguments are useful. Go beyond the obvious. Where can these arguments be useful in the biblical worldview?

Remember the Law of Non-contradiction: *A thing cannot at the same time and in the same respect be and not be.* One cannot say "the light is shining" and "the light is not shining" at the same time. You either breathe or you don't breathe—you cannot do both at the same time. Aristotle's Laws of Truth have their origin here: "one cannot say of something <u>that it is</u> and <u>that it is not</u> in the same respect and at the same time." Students of logic will remember it stated simply, "A and Non-A cannot exist at the same time and place."

Circumstance

The Possible and the Impossible – An excellent way to prove that something is possible or impossible is to convince the audience that others have succeeded in doing similar things, or that what is proposed is not at all possible. It can be a powerful method of persuasion. Interestingly, one can argue Possible/Impossible as Similarity/Analogy, if the similarity rings true. Aristotle mentioned the use of the possible in this way:

> Since only possible actions, and not impossible ones, can ever have been done in the past or the present, and since things which have not occurred, or will not occur, also cannot have been done or be going to be done, it is necessary for the political, the forensic, and the ceremonial speaker alike to be able to have at their command propositions about the possible and the impossible, and about whether a thing has or has not occurred, will or will not occur. Further, all men, in giving praise or blame, in urging us to accept or reject proposals for action, in accusing others or defending themselves, attempt not only to prove the points mentioned but also to show that the good or the harm, the honour or disgrace, the justice or injustice, is great or small, either absolutely or relatively; and therefore it is plain that we must also have at our command propositions about greatness or smallness and the greater or the lesser–propositions both universal and particular. Thus, we must be able to say which is the greater or lesser good, the greater or lesser act of justice or injustice; and so on. (1.3)

Aristotle essentially makes clear the necessity of being widely read; how can we convince others, using a wide variety of resources, if we have not ourselves been diligent students?

Identify and discuss this example of Possible/Impossible from President Franklin Delano Roosevelt's First Inaugural Address:

> And yet our distress comes from no failure of substance. We are stricken by no plague of locusts. Compared with the perils which our forefathers conquered, because they believed and were not afraid, we have still much to be thankful for. Nature still offers her bounty and human efforts have multiplied it. Plenty is at our doorstep, but a generous use of it languishes in the very sight of the supply.[90]

Aristotle supposed some <u>Possible/Impossible</u> topics to consider. These may seem strange, or even ridiculous and useless, but studying these will aid the development of our own topics (and hopefully here you have just seen our attempt at a Possible/Impossible argument).

---

[90]   http://www.americanrhetoric.com/speeches/fdrfirstinaugural.html

Think of as many examples as possible for each one. Get realistic with your topic ideas. Think according to a biblical worldview. For a start, work on a creation/evolution argument.

This Possible/Impossible list below, also from Aristotle (2.19), may provide some material for your own Topics.

1. "If it is possible for one of a pair of contraries to be or happen, then it is possible for the other: e.g. if a man can be cured, he can also fall ill; for any two contraries are equally possible, in so far as they are contraries." For example, if you can get a kitchen (bathroom, bedroom, etc.) messy, you can also clean it up (an argument used by countless parents).

2. "If the harder of two things is possible, so is the easier." If it's possible for a person to write with a pencil, it's also possible he can write with a pen.

3. "If a thing can come into existence in a good and beautiful form, then it can come into existence generally; thus a house can exist more easily than a beautiful house."

4. "If the end is possible, so is the beginning; for all things that occur have a beginning." Does this help a creation/evolution discussion? Why or why not?

5. "Where the parts are possible, the whole is possible; and where the whole is possible, the parts are usually possible." The first leaders of the U.S. argued this, because they saw that separate confederations were possible, so a confederation of states was also possible.

6. "If a thing can be produced without art or preparation, it can be produced still more certainly by the careful application of art to it. Hence Agathon has said: To some things we by art must needs attain,/Others by destiny or luck we gain." In other words, if it can be done at midnight the night before, it can be done a few days in advance, with planning. (This is an argument used by teachers and parents alike.)

Past Fact and Future Fact

This topic deals with whether or not something has happened, and whether or not something would happen.

Past Fact is useful in court trials, dealing with whether or not something has occurred:

1. "If the less probable of two events has occurred, the more probable event is likely to have occurred, too." For example, "If the early believers found two disciples in Acts guilty of lying to God, couldn't it have been possible that they were also lying to their friends?" (This argument is also applicable in the topic of *Degree.*)

2. "If someone had the power and the desire and the opportunity to do something, then he or she has done it."

Future Fact supposes:

1. "If the power and the desire to do something are present, then that something will be done." In other words, if one possesses a gun, it is likely that it will be used.

2. "If the antecedents of something are present, then the natural consequences will occur." For example, if a drunk person has started his car, there will be an accident. (This one deals with chance and circumstances; it may not happen every time, but the likelihood is higher.)

3. "If the means are available, the end will be accomplished."

Abraham Lincoln, U.S President during the Civil War, spoke at the dedication of a cemetery in Gettysburg. His purpose was not only to honor the fallen soldiers, but also to urge the Union to complete their mission and win this brutal, bloody war. Take a look at his Past Fact/Future Fact argument in his Gettysburg Address.

Fourscore and seven years ago our forefathers brought forth on this continent a new nation, conceived in liberty and dedicated to the proposition that all men are created equal. Now we are engaged in a great civil war, testing whether that nation, or any nation so conceived and so dedicated, can long endure...The world will little note nor long remember what we say here, but it can never forget what they did here. It is for us, the living, rather, to be dedicated here to the unfinished work which they who fought here have thus far so nobly advanced. It is rather for us to be here dedicated to the great task remaining before us—that from these honored dead we take increased devotion to that cause for which they gave the last full measure of devotion; that we here highly resolve that these dead shall not have died in vain; that this nation, under God, shall have a new birth of freedom; and that government of the people, by the people, for the people, shall not perish from the earth.[91]

Note that he begins with a statement of fact from Americans' shared history, then he touches on the dire necessity of decisively ending the war.

Recall your studies of Greek philosophy. When Aristotle adds those Past Fact and Future Fact items, above, what is he saying about Fate, or inevitability? How does that contrast with the biblical worldview?

Testimony

Testimony, according to Aristotle, derives its material from outside sources. Following are different types of Testimony.

Authority is an informed opinion by someone in control. It carries less weight today than it once did. It is not infallible, but it has great persuasive force. A psychiatrist would have more authority when testifying about emotional side effects of abuse than an ordinary citizen. Sometimes experts offer conflicting testimony. Then we rely on other criteria to decide which opinion to accept. The rhetorician would need to select from conflicting authorities which ones he will emphasize to prove his points.

Cicero, in discussing the use of Testimony as opposed to Example, argues for the strength of Testimony, referring to Greek rhetoricians who have their own methods of persuasion. Here he not only defends Testimony but eloquently refutes his detractors:

"But," they say, "since examples correspond to testimony, it is proper that, like testimony, they should be taken from men of the highest reputation." First and foremost, examples are set forth, not to confirm or to bear witness, but to clarify. ... The difference between testimony and example is this: by example we clarify the nature of our statement, while by testimony we establish its truth. Furthermore, the testimony must accord with the proposition, for otherwise it cannot confirm the proposition. But the rhetoricians' performance does not accord with what they propose. How so? In that they promise to write a treatise of the art, and then mostly bring forward examples from authors who were ignorant of the art. Now who can give authority to his writings on the art unless he writes something in conformity with the art? Their performance is at variance with what they seem to promise; for when they undertake to write the rules of their art, they appear to say that they have themselves invented what they are teaching to others, but when they actually write, they show us what others have invented. (4.3)

Note his refutation, and discuss how he proves through refutation.

---

[91] http://www.americanrhetoric.com/speeches/gettysburgaddress.htm

Good questions for discussion are:

1. "Is there anything inconsistent, contradictory, or illogical in the expression of the opinion itself?"
2. "Do the experts harbor any prejudices that might influence or color the proffered opinion?"
3. "Do any of the experts have an axe to more grind? An advantage to gain? A score to settle?"
4. "Is one expert's opinion based on more recent, reliable information than the other's is?"
5. "Is one expert's opinion accepted by more experts? By the more authoritative experts?"
6. "What are the basic assumptions behind the expressions of opinion? Are any of these assumptions vulnerable? Does the exposure of these assumptions reveal that the conflict between the experts is more apparent than real because they are viewing the same matter from different points of view?"[92]

Testimonials were persuasive during Aristotle's time and can also be today. They can be remarkably persuasive in certain circumstances and with certain audiences, but they can also be vulnerable to refutation. Types of testimonials are as follows:

- personal recommendation
- advertising
- public announcement on the TV or radio
- blogs and other social media (but be very careful when using items on social media; they are only as reliable as the authors themselves, and you never know whether they have correctly quoted or cited a source)
- someone attesting to the character of another
- opinion poll
- best-seller list
- audience-rating

Statistics are authoritatively used to confirm statements, settle contrary and contradictory assertions, and discredit assertions.

Remember that when a poll is taken in order to gain statistics, the way a question is asked will likely affect the answer. Pollsters enter into their survey-taking after they have made assumptions. They have anticipated certain results, so their questions will be worded in such a way as to obtain those results. They assume the following: people always know their own mind on questions put to them, and people will give truthful answers to questions put to them. However, pollsters do not take into account other issues such as people who want to harm the results and give answers other than the ones they truly believe. Other factors which adversely affect results would be a polling of an inadequate cross-section of people, which would then make the results come out differently (for example, if pollsters wanted to get a statistic on the number of minorities in a city, but they wanted to inflate the numbers, they would do most of their surveying in parts of the city where more of those minorities reside).

---

[92]   Corbett, *Classical Rhetoric*, 113-114

Maxims are precepts, proverbs, or famous sayings. They could be clichés such as "The early bird catches the worm" or "It's always darkest before the dawn." They can also be general statements about human actions, or about things that are to be chosen or avoided in human action (you don't judge a book by its cover). One should avoid using maxims on which to base one's argument, because if it is challenged, one may be unprepared to defend its truth, and thus we have drawn attention from the focus of our discourse and onto the maxim.

Law - statutes, contracts, testaments, records, and documents that can be drawn on to substantiate or refute a claim. Documents are hard to refute. They provide excellent, convincing proof, unless one cannot prove that the author really wrote it, the document was not signed by witnesses, it was a photocopy, or appeared to have been tampered with.

The wording of documents is always open to interpretation. The U.S. Constitution is the document upon which our government is based, but the Supreme Court's main function is to interpret the wording of the Constitution.

Precedent - something that has happened before. Precedents bring to bear on a present case what has been done in a similar case in the past (this is done in court cases all the time). Often someone will refer to an incident or example that should serve to strengthen one's case or harm his opponent's case. For example, when arguing that a woman has the right to an abortion, a lawyer will always point to the U.S. Supreme Court case of Roe vs. Wade, which set a precedent on the rights of women to choose abortion and now is considered the law of the land.

As you write your thesis paper, use these methods above to aid your proving or arguing.

In Summary, Lesson 18

Topics is considered an aid to the First Canon: _____

Three aids to Invention: _____, _____, _____

Terms to Remember:
- Pert (pertly)
- Petulant (petulance)
- Infallible
- Maxim
- Precedent

Lesson Eighteen Assignments

Assignment 18.1

Give at least two examples from this Topic of Degree, item 5: "What the majority of men would choose is better than what the minority would choose." What kind of appeal does this Topic employ (*ethos, pathos, logos*)? What is the fallacy here? Sometimes what the majority wants is not always the best. Under what conditions would this be true? 250 words.

Assignment 18.2

Regarding Contradictions, this topic can be applied in many arguments. It's rather simple: You either breathe or you don't breathe—you cannot do both at the same time. God either exists or He doesn't. This type of argument agrees with the Laws of Thought from early Logic lessons. Which Law of Thought is this? Write an argument using this Law, proving either: God's existence, creation versus evolution, or life beginning upon conception. (5 paragraphs)

Assignment 18.3

Could you apply the argument of irreducible complexity to Possible/Impossible number 5 ("Where the parts are possible, the whole is possible; and where the whole is possible, the parts are usually possible")? This argument is used by proponents of Creationism. It can also be called the argument of the mousetrap. Spend time discussing this with your teacher or in a writing assignment.

Assignment 18.4

Regarding Possible/Impossible topic number 6 ("If a thing can be produced without art or preparation, it can be produced still more certainly by the careful application of art to it), how does this argument apply to the creation/evolution theory? Is this a benefit or a detriment to the creationist's argument? Is there another possible/impossible topic on this list that also could apply to the creation/evolution argument (either way)? If so, which one, and why?

Assignment 18.5

Read and study Abraham Lincoln's second Inaugural Address, called "With Malice Toward None." Discuss his use of Past/Future Fact. Be ready for classroom discussion.

Assignment 18.6

Does Future Fact item number 3, above ("If the means are available, the end will be accomplished"), mean that human nature is such that if the opportunity exists to take revenge, one will do so? Does this negate the power of the Holy Spirit to resist temptation? Either take the "devil's advocate" role or take the biblical argument against Aristotle. Explain your answer in five paragraphs.

Assignment 18.7a

To prepare for what's coming up, read and watch Martin Luther King Jr.'s "I Have a Dream" speech. Find the emotional and ethical language he uses. You'll notice quite a few. List them and tell what kind of emotional or ethical appeal you have found, and where it's from. List at least five of each in a bulleted list.

Assignment 18.7b
Read "A Call for Unity" found in *AFE* and answer the discussion questions in anticipation of reading King's "Letter from Birmingham Jail."

Assignment 18.7c
Analyze Martin Luther King Jr.'s "Letter From Birmingham Jail" online. Please note that this discourse does not follow the classic arrangement. Instead of pointing out the divisions, do the following: Find the three major questions the clergy asks him, and he answers. Then find the three grave disappointments he lists (what disappoints him?). The rest of your analysis should be the same (thesis, support, etc.). How does he employ Topics, aside from differentiae?

Assignment 18.7d
Read and analyze Frederick Douglass' "I Hear the Mournful Wail of Millions" from *AFE*.

Assignment 18.8a
Read Jonathan Swift's "A Modest Proposal." Answer the discussion questions found after the discourse in *AFE*.

Assignment 18.8b
After reading "A Modest Proposal," you can see how Swift uses satire to draw attention to a problem. His "solution" is so gruesome that it is ridiculous. Here is an opportunity to brainstorm for which social ill of the day you would most like to propose a modest solution. This would have to be profitable to society (or a portion thereof) and almost so ludicrous that it might actually be considered by society. 1) Describe the problem, 2) Provide a solution, and 3) Describe the benefit to society.

Assignment 18.8c
For your own "Modest Proposal" assignment, plan it out like a commercial, or like someone trying to market the idea to government officials. Record it as a video, lasting around three minutes. Be ready to share it.

Assignment 18.9
Read and analyze Cicero's "Against Catiline" speech. Complete the Full Analysis Worksheet and turn it in.

Assignment 18.10
Read the first two sections of "The Communist Manifesto." Feel free to read the whole thing; it is very informative for today's Christians. In five paragraphs discuss its use of definition and historical analysis as he goes to prove his point (and what is his point? Discuss this also).

Assignment 18.11
Read and analyze Franklin Delano Roosevelt's "Fear Itself" speech. Complete the Full Analysis Worksheet and turn it in.

Assignment 18.12

At this point in your education you have probably read some about government theory and philosophy. Now that you have read "Manifesto of the Communist Party" and some presidential speeches, have a class discussion about the role of government. What is the biblical view of government? Your teacher could assign some writing as a follow-up.

Assignment 18.13

Consider what would happen if/when humans decide to create a theocracy here on earth. What would be the benefits? What problems would arise? (Think about a Christian theocracy, as well as an Islamic theocracy.) First, what is true about humans, from a biblical worldview? Take into account what we know about humankind. This can be a classroom debate, a forum discussion, or an essay.

Assignment 18.14a

Read John F. Kennedy's "*Ich Bin Ein Berliner*" speech and answer the discussion questions.

Assignment 18.14b

Read and analyze Ronald Reagan's "Brandenburg Gate" speech. As you do, also address his use of the Possible/Impossible topic.

Assignment 18.14c

How are Reagan's and Kennedy's Berlin Wall addresses similar or different? What do they both attempt to accomplish, and how do they seek to accomplish those things differently?

Assignment 18.15a

Read Pericles' "Funeral Oration." To better understand it, outline this discourse by summing the main points paragraph by paragraph. (This can be done in outline form or in sentence form.) Next, address the following in 2-3 paragraphs: What is the main point of his oration (besides honoring the dead)? Discuss what he believes is the source of Athens' greatness.

Assignment 18.15b

Compare Pericles' "Funeral Oration" to Lincoln's "Gettysburg Address" and discuss the comparison/contrast between the two. At this point you should be able to compare not only the content, but the construction of the two discourses. Two to three paragraphs.

Assignment 18.16

Find four articles and opinion pieces (two news articles, two opinion pieces)* about environmentalism (i.e., global warming/climate change, etc.). Look for the use of statistics and other facts to support the point of the article or opinion.

Write a 750-1000 word essay that 1) compares/contrasts the use of data and facts, and 2) comments on the authors' use to support his or her thesis. For purposes of this essay, choose one that you have researched from which to quote specifically. Use the others in your Works Cited list.

*Note: be careful of the source for your information. You will find evenly balanced articles, and you will find shockingly biased articles. Simply be aware of the bias of certain sources and authors.

You may decide to quote from extremely biased sources on either side. It may turn out to be the point of your essay!

Assignment 18.17
Read Benjamin Netanyahu's speech to the United Nations on 9/29/2014, found in *AFE*. Break down how he compares and contrasts Israel's enemy, Hamas, to other Islamic terrorist groups in the Middle East (then known as ISIS, Khorasan, Al Qaeda, etc.). Pay attention to his use of logic as he builds his argument. How effective is his argument? (Find a video of this speech–it's very good!)

Lesson Nineteen

Invention: Opinion Pieces

Oh, dear, we are all like that. Each of us knows it all, and knows he knows it all–the rest, to a man, are fools and deluded. One man knows there is a hell, the next one knows there isn't; one man knows high tariff is right, the next man knows it isn't; one man knows monarchy is best, the next one knows it isn't; one age knows there are witches, the next one knows there aren't; one sect knows its religion is the only true one, there are sixty-four thousand five hundred million sects that know it isn't so. There is not a mind present among this multitude of verdict-deliverers that is the superior of the minds that persuade and represent the rest of the divisions of the multitude. Yet this sarcastic fact does not humble the arrogance nor diminish the know-it-all bulk of a single verdict-maker of the lot, by so much as a shade. Mind is plainly an ass, but it will be many ages before it finds it out, no doubt. Why do we respect the opinions of any man or any microbe that ever lived? I swear [I] don't know. Why do I respect my own? Well–that is different. (Mark Twain, "Three Thousand Years among the Microbes")

Another form of persuasive communication can be found in the Editorial section of the newspaper or news magazine: the Opinion Piece. This is a place where the dialogue is usually current and always strongly opinionated. This is a place where the voice of reason is badly needed, and where the voice of truth is often absent. This is the place where the Christian voice must be introduced.

Begin reading the opinion pages of the local newspaper. If you do not get a local paper, find one online from a major city.

Letters to the editor are shorter, generally from 100-200 words in length. Opinion pieces are the longer ones. Some are written by the newspaper's editorial staff, others are written by syndicated columnists, and still others may be written by members of the local community.

The age of the letter-to the-editor and the opinion column has greatly shifted in the 21st century. Now an "opinion piece" that was once chosen from among many submissions to be printed in one issue, to various forms of social media without any filters. This has been a blessing and a curse for the media world. Now all one has to do to get heard is to shout it out over one's chosen form of social media. Truth doesn't have to matter, nor does the level of taste or civility. It feeds humans' narcissistic need to be heard and validated.

There is no mistaking, though, that some opinion-sharing media have flourished and become valuable, serving as beacons of light in a dark world. As rhetoricians we want to study what has been done well, so we can imitate it, and what is poorly (or even evilly) executed or disseminated, so we can refute it.

Lesson Nineteen Assignments

Assignment 19.1

Bring three sample letters to the editor, found in your local or online paper, to class. Remember that letters to the editor are brief, somewhere around 100-200 words. Using your three letters to the editor, comment on each one in the following manner. Answer each question, for each point, with two or more sentences.

> What is the main point of the letter?
>
> Does the writer make his point well?
>
> Does he resolve the subject (come up with a good conclusion or answer to the issues.
>
> What fallacies do you find, if any? Or does the writer point out a fallacy? What is it?

Assignment 19.2

In light of what you have been reading, why should a Christian write letters to the editor? What could a Christian contribute? What does God promise about His Word being sent out into the world? Three paragraphs.

Assignment 19.3

Comment on three of your classmates' opinion pieces using the class forum. Use the standards that have been required all along.

Assignment 19.4

Time to write an opinion piece of 500-700 words relating to a current topic of concern to you. This time use a quote from another source in your opinion piece to support your view, or use it by way of refutation (refute the quote with logic). Post it according to class standards. If there's time, choose another opinion piece that you have written this year and rewrite it, taking your teacher's and classmates' comments into account.

Assignment 19.5

Write a second opinion piece. This time, apply scripture to the topic: inject a verse, or part of a verse, into your letter. This is how you skillfully weave God's truth into a current topic for readers to see. Make this 500-700 words, and post it to the class forum.

Assignment 19.6

Read Blair's passage "On Style" found in *AFE*. "Translate" what he says in your own words. Be ready to discuss this passage in class.

Lesson Twenty

The Third Canon:
Style in the Written Word

True eloquence is irresistible. It charms by its images of beauty, it enforces an argument by its vehement simplicity. Orators whose speeches are "full of sound and fury, signifying nothing," only prevail where truth is not understood, for knowledge and simplicity are the foundation of all true eloquence. Eloquence abounds in beautiful and natural images, sublime but simple conceptions, in passionate but plain words. Burning words appeal to the emotions as well as to the intellect; they stir the soul and touch the heart. (Attributed to Albert Ellery Bergh)

It should be observed that each kind of rhetoric has its own appropriate style. The style of written prose is not that of spoken oratory, nor are those of political and forensic speaking the same. Both written and spoken have to be known. (Aristotle, *The Rhetoric & The Poetics of Aristotle* 3.12)

Proper words in proper places, make the true definition of a style. (Jonathan Swift, "Letter to a Young Clergyman")

The right word may be effective, but no word was ever as effective as a rightly timed pause. (Mark Twain)

(I)f the practice of composition be useful, the laborious work of correcting is no less so; it is indeed absolutely necessary to our reaping any benefit from the habit of composition. What we have written, should be laid by for some little time, till the ardour of composition be past, till the fondness for the expressions we have used be worn off, and the expressions themselves be forgotten; and then, reviewing our work with a cool and critical eye, as if it were the performance of another, we shall discern many imperfections which at first escaped us. Then is the season for pruning redundancies; for weighing the arrangement of sentences; for attending to the juncture and connecting particles; and bring style into a regular, correct, and supported form. (Hugh Blair, *The Rhetoric of Blair, Campbell, and Whately*)

Now that we have covered Invention and Arrangement, we move on to Style, artfully using words to make our discourse appealing and beautiful. To that end, we will focus on what others say about excellence in writing before moving on to excellence in speaking (the Fifth Canon, Delivery; SEE: Lesson 24). We aim to depart our high school years speaking well, writing beautifully and convincingly.

Lexis is the Greek word for style, carrying the threefold meaning of thought, word, and speaking. In other words, the Greek idea of style in rhetoric was taking thoughts collected by invention and putting them into words for speaking out in delivery.

Precepts and Principles: An Overview of Style

Classical rhetoricians taught that a person acquired versatility of style in three ways:

- through a study of precepts or principles (*ars*)
- through practice in writing (*exercitato*), and
- through imitation of the practice of others (*imitatio*).

In his Third Book of Aristotle's *Rhetoric*, he identifies **Six Stylistic Principles:**[93]

1. **Correctness and Clarity of Language**
2. **Impressiveness**
3. **Appropriateness and Genuineness**
4. **Prosody**
5. **Periodic Style**
6. **Figurative Language & Figures of Speech**

Each one of these considerations builds on the next, attempting to cultivate an understanding and fluency of style that appeals to our audience and assists in the persuasion. Let's look deeper at each consideration.

I.   Correctness and clarity of language

If a person aims to persuade through rhetoric, the words he uses must actually and accurately communicate with his audience. Therefore, those words must be clear. Aristotle divides this category into "Five Heads:"

a. **Use proper connecting words:** Aristotle begins his discussion of style by addressing "the proper use of connecting words, and the arrangement of them in the natural sequence which some of them require."[94] When writing, we have lists of reasons built upon lists of support or phrases within clauses making compound and complex sentences–often things can get confusing.

   Aristotle argues that we should always make clear connections between parts so that we can logically make our case. "Thus" and "Therefore" and "So" indicate conclusions, telling your audience you are about to arrive at your points. However, conjunctions, while they link different clauses or parts of phrases, can also change the meaning. Saying: "I went to the store *and* bought ice cream" is conjoining those two actions. If you replace the *and* with *but*, you've altered the meaning of those actions, making them almost seem mutually exclusive.

b. **Use the correct word for the correct purpose–don't be vague.** Aristotle then advocates the correct use of names for objects, rather than vague titles or categories.

   Has your dad ever asked for the "clicker" when looking for the remote for the TV? There are many things that click in a house–might he mean the clock? A device for training dogs?

   Precision in diction: *Precise words* are exact, without adding anything extra that might convey different meanings. **Precision in writing** means to cut out all unnecessary words or phrases. This is also called *concision*, being *concise*. Say exactly what you mean, and no more, no less.

   Words may be considered imprecise (to borrow Blair's ideas found in Lesson 1):

---

[93]   http://classics.mit.edu/Aristotle/rhetoric.3.iii.html

[94]   Aristotle, *Rhetoric* 3.5 http://rhetoric.eserver.org/aristotle/rhet3-5.html

— when they do not express exactly what we intended to say

— when they express the idea but not quite fully

— when they express the idea but with something more than we intended.

c. **Avoid ambiguities**. Aristotle uses a bit of sarcasm when discussing what seems to be common sense: if you want to persuade, do not be ambiguous "unless, indeed, you definitely desire to be ambiguous, as those do who have nothing to say but are pretending to mean something."[95] If you are ambiguous, you just look like you have nothing to say and have just wasted your audience's time.

d. **Use the correct part of speech and the correct use of numbers (counting nouns)** - Again, Aristotle here advocates being precise and accurate in all language.[96] Interestingly, he uses an example about perception: When talking about sound and color, the same verb cannot be used for both. Do not use a visual word ("The red beam of light temporarily *blinded* me") when describing a sound ("The brass band blinded me"). Choose descriptive words that will work in the context in which you are writing.

e. **Above all, be clear**. "It is a general rule that a written composition should be easy to read and therefore easy to deliver. This cannot be so where there are many connecting words or clauses, or where punctuation is hard, as in the writings of Heracleitus."[97] Aristotle goes out of his way to emphasize, again and again, the need for clarity and accuracy, even going so far as to call out an earlier philosopher, Heracleitus, for breaking this cardinal rule.

Blair agrees with Aristotle, arguing for concision:

> One of the first and most obvious distinctions of the different kinds of Style, is what arises from an author's spreading out his thoughts more or less. This distinction forms, what are called the Diffuse and the Concise Styles. A concise writer compresses his thought into the fewest possible words; he seeks to employ none but such as are most expressive; he lops off, as redundant, every expression which does not add something material to the sense. Ornament he does not reject; he may be lively and figured; but his ornament is intended for the sake of force, rather than grace. He never gives you the same thought twice. He places it in the light which appears to him the most striking; but if you do not apprehend it well in that light, you need not expect to find it in any other. His sentences are arranged with compactness and strength, rather than with cadence and harmony. The utmost precision is studied in them; and they are commonly designed to suggest more to the reader's imagination than they directly express.[98]

Style in the Written Word vs. the Spoken Word

The student of rhetoric must remember that there is a difference between the written and the spoken word. An essay is not a speech, nor is a speech an essay–though one can be the basis for the

---

[95]   ibid

[96]   For this point, we have adapted and combined numbers 4 & 5 from Book 3, Chapter 5 of Aristotle's *Rhetoric*, because they're more specific to the Greek than to English. Moreover, we're adding a new 5th Head from 1407b in Book 5.

[97]   ibid

[98]   Lecture 18

other. Aristotle delineates the differences between the two, describing a formal, written discourse as "the more finished" while "the spoken better admits of dramatic delivery–like the kind of oratory that reflects character and the kind that reflects emotion."[99] Written discourses are more formal, for they are not delivered in a single setting, to a specific group of people, at a certain time. Also, because the writer is not necessarily physically present to clarify or amplify meaning, he must be as precise and clear as possible, relying on his words alone to convey his purposes. A speech can rely on much more than the words. In fact, if a speaker merely reads the words on the page, he can spurn his audience, driving them away. He must *deliver* his speech, using his whole body, as well as the rhetorical appeals of *ethos, pathos,* and *logos* to grab hold of his listeners and convince them. Again, this will be discussed later in Lesson 24: Delivery.

Writing Voice

In studying composition, we speak of a writer's *voice*: the style that the writer utilizes. This is daunting to think about, and it has certainly been over-thought. Voice encompasses everything from favorite words that an author uses again and again, to the types of words he uses, to the figures of speech he utilizes–it's personality, in written form.

> Voice is not style. It's not technique. It's not branding. It's not a decision to write in first or third person. So what is it? Your writer's voice is the expression of YOU on the page. It's that simple— and that complicated. Your voice is all about honesty. It's the unfettered, non-derivative, unique conglomeration of your thoughts, feelings, passions, dreams, beliefs, fears, and attitudes, coming through in every word you write. Voice is all about your originality and having the courage to express it.[100]

As we delve into style, we are about to give you many, many tools, so consider <u>which</u> ones you'll use and <u>how</u> you'll do so. Use the examples found in this lesson and throughout this entire text as sources of inspiration, but remember that *you* need to develop your own style as a writer, just as you need to figure out who you are as a person.

Excellence in Writing

In the written discourse, the onus rests upon the words, phrases, clauses, sentences, and paragraphs alone to do the deed of persuading. We must aim for excellence in every aspect of our writing.

A discussion of Style includes clear language. The writer and speaker needs not only to prove his point, he needs to do it compellingly, with appropriate language which conveys neither too much nor too little. That language should be keyed to both the audience and the situation. Often when writing persuasively, the writer or speaker needs to describe the problem, present possible causes, and then discuss the solution.

---

[99] Aristotle, *Rhetoric* 3.12

[100] Gardner, Rachelle. "What is Writer's Voice?" *Rachelle Gardner, Author Media*, 16 June 2011, www.rachellegardner.com/what-is-writers-voice/. Accessed 22 June 2017.

Some rhetoricians in Antiquity taught Style as technical writing. They broke down rhetoric into formulas and theories–imposed "rules, to regularize, and to codify–thus not to provide for subtlety or finesse… [Interestingly, they] traditionally viewed style as a set of qualities 'laid on' to the thoughts which invention had proved and disposition set out, rather than something integral to the whole speech."[101] In other words, two different ideas of Style came out of antiquity: those who could break arguments down and apply paint to beautify the discourse, and those who emphasize that the subject itself should be stylistic and beautiful, thus making the discourse compelling.

Categories of Style

There are three levels of style, each used for their own purposes and in their distinct situations. The occasion and the audience both must be assessed when making the decision of which style you'll avail yourself.

- <u>Low or plain style</u> (*attenuata, subtile*), for instructing–more often what rhetoricians declared to be fitting for uneducated audiences

- <u>Middle or forcible style</u> (*mediocris*) for moving the reader or listener, and often suitable for the average audience. This persuades, may be used in a deliberative or forensic discourse.

- <u>High or florid style</u> (*gravis, florida*) for charming; this would be used for higher classes, the intelligent and highly literate class. This might lend itself to an epideictic discourse.

This, therefore, involves both *diction* and *syntax*. Diction focuses on the choice of words, not using a word without thinking through both its *connotation* (its implied meaning) and its *denotation* (its dictionary definition). Words, however, cannot be chosen or used in a vacuum–they must be employed and arranged properly in a sentence: this is syntax. From there, sentences must be positioned properly within a paragraph, and paragraphs within a discourse (but this now relates more to Arrangement than to Style).

Style involves selecting words carefully, aiming for what Gustave Flaubert calls "*le mot juste*"–the precise word.[102] Here we study the *correct, pure, clear* words. We choose whether to be flowery or more simple, "demonstrating an economy of words."[103] We make choices about the way we order our words, putting them together to sound the best and most evocative. We take time to re-work sentences to see that the choices a writer makes truly do affect the way a sentence communicates, and subsequently the way an audience receives and believes the speaker or writer.

Grammatical Competence

Unlike grammar, rhetoric is not concerned with parts of words, but whole words and how they fit together.

In ascending order, grammar looks at the *phoneme, syllable, word, phrase*, and *clause*. Rhetoric considers the word, phrase, clause, paragraph, division, and the whole composition. Grammar concerns itself with correctness; rhetoric with effectiveness.

---

[101]   Kennedy, George A., *Classical Rhetoric and its Christian and Secular Thought from Ancient to Modern Times*, p. 106

[102]   Goodman, Richard, *The Soul of Creative Writing*. New Brunswick, NJ, Transaction Publishers, 2009.

[103]   Baldwin, *The Twelve Trademarks*, 25

An Ample Vocabulary

In order to develop a good style, students must have an ample vocabulary. How does one acquire the rich vocabulary he needs to develop a good style? Following is a list of ways one can increase one's vocabulary.

Read at every opportunity. The best writing is done by those who read the most. Not only do they have the most to say, their vocabulary is also wider than the non-reader's. As you read, *annotate* when possible. Underline, highlight, write in the margins (use sticky notes if you're unable to write in your book), but *engage* with the text so as to make use of the reading you do.

Look up the meanings of words to increase understanding of new and unfamiliar words. Studying lists of words will help with spelling and the acquisition of new words. Studying words in the context in which they are written is even better: the word's usage becomes much more clear and more easily remembered. Exposing yourself to unfamiliar words, becoming familiar with their meaning and usage, is vital to increasing your vocabulary. Aim to actually use these words in context in order to help cement the understanding of new words. Then, practice writing in different ways to improve a sentence.

Purity of diction means "Good Usage." According to George Campbell, who builds upon Aristotle's lessons on style, words must be *in reputable use, in national use,* and *in present use.*[104]

- *Reputable use* deals with the language that is appropriate to the occasion. A group of teenagers will not always understand the language of King James' English. A group of senior citizens will not appreciate being talked to in the language used by today's youths If we desire to communicate with a contemporary audience–let alone persuade them–we must use current words and idioms that are understood by people today.

- *National use* refers to the locally acceptable and understandable terms that are not overly technical for an audience, nor are they foreign terms that would not be commonly understood. Avoid dialectical words, technical words, coinages, and foreign words (though if you must use them, as we have used Latin or Greek words, italicize them to indicate that they are for a specific time). But remember that some situations call for the use of localisms, technical jargon, etc. Perhaps they can be used when speaking to a group of people of one ethnicity, regionality, nationality, or a particular religious affiliation, or when discussing a technical detail with a group of engineers. In other words, if you use a slang term that is understood in the southern states of the US, it might not be clearly understood, and might even be a source of confusion, in other regions of the US.

- *Present use* has varied meanings, especially today, when words and their meanings are subject to interpretations by their various audiences (as noted in *Postmodern Times* by Gene Edward Veith). However, by present, we mean current usage of a word. While a word might have had one meaning in its roots, using its current meaning will confuse fewer people. For example, the word "nice" once meant "ignorant." However, if a speaker decided to speak of the ignorance of his audience, he might want to prepare himself for a not-so-nice reaction from that crowd.
A word might be used in a certain way by members of mainstream pop culture or appropriated by different groups for different reasons. Thus, we rely on <u>reputable</u> reference

---

[104]   Campbell, *The Philosophy of Rhetoric*, 175

sources for our language: *Dictionary of Modern English Usage, Dictionary of Contemporary American Usage*, etc. They will include discussions of the purity of usage of a phrase or word.

II. Impressiveness - Description: Show, don't tell (Aristotle's *Rhetoric* 3.6)

The rhetorician does not merely provide information to his audience. Rather, he weaves an argument, using information to back him up. To accomplish this, a writer must utilize description to affect the audience, to draw them in with his words. This has bred a maxim that applies to writers of all types: "Show, don't tell."

Take these two examples, one from a famous speech by Winston Churchill and another from the opening lines of *The Hobbit* by J.R.R. Tolkien, and notice how they show rather than tell.

On June 4, 1940, Winston Churchill gives a rousing speech after the evacuation of the British forces from Dunkirk, hoping to assuage the wounds that the British people keenly felt after such a seeming defeat. Churchill takes the time to expound upon the cause for which the Allies are fighting. He could simply say: "The British and French will fight the evil Nazis until they are destroyed!" But he does not:

> The British Empire and the French Republic, linked together in their cause and in their need, will defend to the death their native soil, aiding each other like good comrades to the utmost of their strength. Even though large tracts of Europe and many old and famous States have fallen or may fall into the grip of the Gestapo and all the odious apparatus of Nazi rule, we shall not flag or fail. We shall go on to the end, we shall fight in France, we shall fight on the seas and oceans, we shall fight with growing confidence and growing strength in the air, we shall defend our Island, whatever the cost may be, we shall fight on the beaches, we shall fight on the landing grounds, we shall fight in the fields and in the streets, we shall fight in the hills; we shall never surrender, and even if, which I do not for a moment believe, this Island or a large part of it were subjugated and starving, then our Empire beyond the seas, armed and guarded by the British Fleet, would carry on the struggle, until, in God's good time, the New World, with all its power and might, steps forth to the rescue and the liberation of the old.[105]

He unifies the "good comrades," the French and British nations, who have been "linked together in their cause and in their need," fighting against the "grip of the Gestapo and all the odious apparatus of Nazi rule." This is not merely a war against an invader, but a timeless tale of good versus evil, right versus wrong. The cause for which they wage war is just, and his speech is almost Homeric in its elevated tone. Churchill utilizes figures of speech such as *anaphora* (repetition: "we shall fight") to demonstrate the push forward and onward, again and again, in every earthly location imaginable, leading to a climax (another figure of speech) of victory over the Germans. This section is peppered with alliterations, solidifying the epic Greek allusions–this is no mean squabble among mortals, but a mythic struggle for the destiny of man.

Churchill utilizes the elements of style to make his point, weaving together figures of speech, emotions, ethics, and logic all together. Style works significantly to differentiate the imparting of information from a persuasive discourse.[106]

---

[105] Churchill, Winston. "We Shall Fight on the Beaches." Churchill, The International Churchill Society, 13 Apr. 2017, www.winstonchurchill.org/resources/speeches/1940-the-finest-hour/we-shall-fight-on-the-beaches. Accessed 22 June 2017.

[106] Watch a dramatized depiction of events leading up to–and the development of–that speech in the movie *Darkest Hour* (2017).

This works just as well in fiction (though authors such as Ernest Hemingway might seemingly disagree). If we examine the opening lines of J.R.R. Tolkien's *The Hobbit*, he clearly seeks to depict Bilbo Baggins' home of Bag End and characterize good Mr. Baggins in one concise, fell swoop:

> In a hole in the ground there lived a hobbit. Not a nasty, dirty, wet hole, filled with the ends of worms and an oozy smell, nor yet a dry, bare, sandy hole with nothing in it to sit down on or to eat: it was a hobbit-hole, and that means comfort.[107]

Tolkien's language here is simple and direct, without difficult jargon that his readers must wade through–for his intended audience is children. Though Hobbits live in holes, make no mistake: they are comfortable above all else, as what follows in the book describes in even more detail.

Compare their voices

Try this same exercise for Churchill's "Blood, Toil, Tears, and Sweat" and for paragraph 22 of "Letter to a Noble Lord," found in *AFE*. How do the authors show, rather than tell? Try this yourself, too. Choose something you have written, a random sentence or paragraph, and ask: do I show, rather than tell?

SEE also: Lesson 16 (*pathos*) and Lesson 21 (figures of speech).

III.   Appropriateness and Genuineness

Aristotle desires for the rhetorician to use appropriate tools to draw his audience along with him, to persuade them rather than hit them over the head with words. Rhetoric is, after all, made up of discourses and discussions: we cannot discourse in a vacuum or in isolation. Relationship to the audience is inherently built-in. "Your language will be appropriate if it expresses emotion and character, and if it corresponds to its subject."[108] We aim to tailor our use of appeals. Aristotle especially hones in on *pathos* here, to the appropriate subject, audience, and circumstance.

Genuineness–or sincerity, or honesty–deals not only in style but also in *ethos*. Does the writer communicate with his audience in a tone of believability? Does he treat his audience with respect rather than "talking down" to them? Does his use of language relate to the audience of his time? (Edmund Burke's language may not be as easy to grasp today as it was in his time and to his audience in Parliament, but was it appropriate and genuine for his contemporaries?)

Propriety of diction refers to what is appropriate for the occasion. Diction changes according to the subject matter, our purpose, the occasion, and the audience. Aristotle teaches us to temper our language to the circumstance, and that it "will be appropriate if it expresses emotion and character, and if it corresponds to its subject. 'Correspondence to subject' means that we must neither speak casually about weighty matters, nor solemnly about trivial ones."[109] Experience (your success or failure, or instruction from your parents or teachers) will tell you what tone and style of speaking to adopt when speaking to your friends, as opposed to talking to the president of the college you wish to attend. You make adjustments as appropriate.

---

[107]   Tolkien, J.R.R. *The Hobbit, or, There and back again*. Boston, Houghton Mifflin Company, 1997. 9-10.

[108]   Aristotle 3.7

[109]   ibid

IV.   The Sound and Rhythm of Sentences: Euphony and Prosody

Sentence Euphony

The euphony (sounds like symphony), means pleasant to the ear, and refers to the rhythm of a phrase or line of writing. Aristotle notes: "[P]rose must be rhythmical, but not metrical, otherwise it will be a poem. Nor must this rhythm be rigorously carried out, but only up to a certain point."[110] Euphony and rhythm are largely a matter for the ear, and students would do just as well to read their prose aloud to catch awkward rhythms, clashing vowel and consonant combinations, and distracting jingles. Read the following sentence aloud. Does anything in particular disrupt the flow of reading?

> Progress is not proclamation nor palaver. It is not pretense nor play on prejudice. It is not of personal pronouns nor perennial pronouncement. It is not the perturbation of a people passion-wrought, nor a promise proposed. Progression is everlastingly lifting the standards that marked the end of the world's march yesterday and planting them on new and advanced heights today.[111]–Warren G. Harding

Notice the distracting repetition of the "p" sound throughout the sentence. Not only is it amusing here (and the audience will get positively perturbed), but the repeated sound can inhibit the flow of your sentence when overused. It will unnecessarily distract the audience from its main points. It is most important to read aloud to oneself when writing something for oral delivery, but many good writers also do this with writing that will be read silently. The sentence that is difficult to enunciate or halts on the tongue is often a problematic one. We always tell our students to read their writing aloud before handing it in.

Classical prosody

Prosody involves *meter, rhyme,* and *intonation.* Although rhetoric concerns itself with persuasive prose, it is helpful to see how some written lines have rhythm. These are mostly (almost exclusively) found in poetry, but sometimes they will appear in prose, and more formal speeches tend to include these things to make the discourse more pleasing to the audience. **Meter** is the pattern of stressed and unstressed syllables in writing, organized into sets of feet. **Feet** refer to the name of the individual unit of stressed and unstressed syllables before each starts to repeat.

- iamb (— /) (unstress, stress) - these feet are *iambic*
- trochee (/ —) (stress, unstress) - these feet are *trochaic*
- anapaest (— — /) (unstress, unstress, stress) - these feet are *anapestic*
- dactyl (/ — —) (stress, unstress, unstress) - these feet are *dactylic*
- spondee (/ /) (stress, stress) - these feet are *spondaic*

---

[110]   3.3

[111]   Dean, John W., *Warren G. Harding: The American Presidents Series.* Macmillan, 2004

We then consider the number of feet per line:

One foot	Monometer
Two feet	Dimeter
Three feet	Trimeter
Four feet	Tetrameter
Five feet	Pentameter
Six feet	Hexameter
Seven feet	Heptameter
Eight feet	Octameter

Meter refers to the type of foot plus the number of feet: *iambic pentameter* or *trochaic tetrameter*, for example.

Read "Sonnet 18" by William Shakespeare and see if you can identify the meter he uses.

> Shall I compare thee to a summer's day?
> Thou art more lovely and more temperate:
> Rough winds do shake the darling buds of May,
> And summer's lease hath all too short a date:
> Sometime too hot the eye of heaven shines,
> And often is his gold complexion dimm'd;
> And every fair from fair sometime declines,
> By chance, or nature's changing course, untrimm'd;
> But thy eternal summer shall not fade
> Nor lose possession of that fair thou ow'st;
> Nor shall Death brag thou wander'st in his shade,
> When in eternal lines to time thou grow'st;
> So long as men can breathe or eyes can see,
> So long lives this, and this gives life to thee.

Shakespeare uses *iambic pentameter*: five feet per line, as he considered *iambic pentameter* to be the closest to the way that the average person speaks.

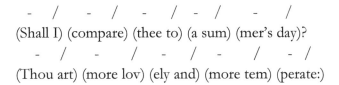

This does not mean that you need to constantly force meter into every single word you write or hope to speak, but often, when making a point, you want to consider the cadence, the rhythm that you employ. Aristotle maintains a bit of a delineation between prose and poetry but says that they can overlap to a point. "The form of a prose composition should be neither metrical nor destitute of rhythm. The metrical form destroys the hearer's trust by its artificial appearance, and at the same time it diverts his attention, making him watch for metrical recurrences...On the other hand, unrhythmical language is too unlimited; we do not want the limitations of metre, but some limitation we must have, or the effect will be vague and unsatisfactory."[112] Neither a speech nor an essay are conversations or information dumps. There must be at least some elevation in style. This has to do with speed as well as intensity–emotion will naturally follow as you aim to accentuate or emphasize certain words or parts of words, because you will need to de-emphasize some things in order to make sure that you are emphasizing others.

V.   Periodic Style

By periodic, Aristotle refers to the complexity of sentences. Your train of thought can be "either free-running, with its parts united by nothing except the connecting words...or compact" and to the point.[113] Are you long-winded, with maze-like sentences that go on forever, or do you write concisely?

Composition of the Sentence

By paying attention to the grammatical composition of the sentence, we can begin to add color to a simple sentence by adding more description. The rhetorician, even when trying to be persuasive and compelling, must always obey the rules of grammar and be aware of the patterns of the sentence in order to slightly vary them.

Abstract or Concrete word choice

Abstract: Theoretical, hard to understand, abstruse, conceptual terms that are difficult to describe in concrete terms. *Concrete*: Definite, easy to understand and pinpoint a definition. You could also use general or specific, formal or informal, academic or casual, Latinate (usually *polysyllabic*) or Anglo-Saxon (usually *monosyllabic*), common words or jargon.

The kind of diction that a writer habitually uses indicates the quality of his mind and style. A writer must be in command of several styles, so that he can accommodate his manner to various subject matters, occasions, purposes, and audiences. But even though a writer's style may vary, one can still associate him with a particular range of styles.

A writer's style is "weighty" if his words and sentences are long; it is "light" if his words and sentences are shorter and simpler. The "tone" of a writer's style is measured in part by the texture of the words—their phonic values, their abstractness or concreteness, their level of usage. A writer's style can be considered formal or informal based on the level of diction he uses.

---

[112]   Aristotle, *Rhetoric* 3.8

[113]   Aristotle, *Rhetoric* 3.9

Length of sentences

Rhetoricians determined the style and tone of a writer by counting words in his sentences and determining the average length of sentences. If a writer, for example, used more wordy sentences, his style was heavier. Modern writing is characterized by sentences that are generally shorter than those of earlier centuries.

Paragraphing

Paragraphing is a style just as sentence structure is a style. What denotes a paragraph is a typographical device indicating a separation of thought or movement from one thought to the next. In other words, the paragraph should be considered a complete thought, set apart from other components of thought. The indenting of the paragraph indicates a visual break. One best-seller of the late 1990s (*Blindness*) was written with no dialogue or paragraph breaks. Although it seems to be an artistic expression, it is difficult to read and keep up with the progression of thought.

Paragraphing is considered according to the following:

* length (measured in number of words and number of sentences)

* kind of movement or development in paragraphs (obviously, thought should move in building from one idea to another)

* use of transitional devices (insert a one- or two-sentence paragraph as a transition when needed)

Each of these many, varied aspects of style come together to form your own personal style of writing. It is certainly quite a lot to absorb, and it will not all come together overnight. This will take a lot of practice, both in writing and in reading. Look at what good authors do and contrast that with what poor authors attempt. Examine your own writing critically; try to weave in some of these tactics into things you've already written. The lesson on Figures of Speech (Lesson 21) will give you even more practical steps to amplify your writing, bringing it to the next level. Before moving on, go through the assignments and practice–then practice some more.

In-Class Activity:

<u>Vocab and Sentence Building</u>

Look at the two simply-worded sentences provided. Notice how we were able to improve upon the *style* of the sentences with a few simple diction and syntax choice.

Example 1a: *At lunch, the ladies came into the parlor wearing jewelry.*

Example 1b: *The ladies' luncheon crowd paraded into the parlor, glittering with diamonds, pearls and emeralds.*

Discuss: What choices in wording (diction) and arrangement (syntax) did we make? Why do you think we made those choice?

Rewrite each of the following sentence in two ways: 1) say it in as few words as possible, and 2) say it in an overdone ($10-word) manner, as in the sentence above.

Try this for yourself with these sentences:

1. It was hot outside so they went to the store for ice cream.
2. On the last day of school, the children excitedly left the building.
3. On the first day of school, the children excitedly entered the building.
4. The man asked for a glass of water.
5. Excited young fans met the baseball player and asked him for an autograph.
6. When they were ready, two coconuts dropped off the tall tree and bounced off the roof.
7. With a gushing sound, the swimmers watched the water flow out the side of their wading pool.
8. "I need your help," cried the young man.
9. The girl did not want to clean her room, so she argued with her mother.

In Summary, Lesson 20

Considerations for Style

1. Correctness and clarity
2. Impressiveness
3. Appropriateness and genuineness
4. The sound and rhythm of sentences
5. Periodic style

Terms to Remember:

- Onus
- Codify
- Strata
- Connotation
- Denotation
- Syntax
- Phoneme
- Assuage
- Propriety
- Euphony
- Prosody
- Polysyllabic
- Monosyllabic

Lesson Twenty Assignments

Assignment 20.1

Looking at each of the discourses you have read, what style of writing (low/plain, middle/forcible, or high/florid) would you give to each of them? Why? One or two sentences per discourse would be sufficient. We read:

- "Hitler's speech to Germany on February 20, 1938"
- Winston Churchill's "This was their finest hour"
- Queen Elizabeth's "I have the heart and stomach of a king"
- "The Gettysburg Address"
- "They're Smiling in Heaven"
- Churchill's "Blood Toil, Tears and Sweat"
- Paul's two speeches in Acts 13.16-41 and 26.1-31
- Plato's "Apology of Socrates"

Assignment 20.2

Read Edmund Burke's "Letter to a Noble Lord." How does he use his particular style to eviscerate the Duke of Bedford? Using the elements of this lesson on Style, write a Stylistic Analysis of "Letter to a Noble Lord." This includes: diction (remember there's a lot on this!), syntax, impressiveness, appropriateness and genuineness, euphony and prosody, and periodic style. Where and how is he effective? Are there places he's not effective? Think: what is his thesis statement and how does he prove it by utilizing style. You can certainly still talk about the other elements of analysis (arrangement, appeals, etc), but focus here on style.

This should be as long as it needs to be. Use quotes to support what you say.

Worldview Focus 20.3

Analyze Elizabeth Cady Stanton's Address, "The Destructive Male." This is a very good time to begin discussing "isms" such as feminism, communism, atheism, and more (late in the high school years), so this is a good place to start. What underlying presuppositions does she have? Against what underlying presuppositions does she argue? Contrast her view of women with her view of men. What descriptive words does she use when referring to each gender?

Assignment 20.4

Read "Ain't I A Woman" by Sojourner Truth. Compare Truth's argument with Stanton's, which is clearly more refined–what is Truth's style? Observe and comment on her diction. Prepare for a class discussion.

Worldview Focus 20.5

Read the article "Selflessness or Self-Obsession" by Mark Earley. Write a five-paragraph essay with a clear thesis in which you give sensible, biblical worldview reasons and examples as to how this problem might be solved, and why it exists in the first place. Be ready to discuss this in class.

Assignment 20.6

Your teacher will assign two speeches to watch or listen to online. They might be appropriately drawn from a current political campaign, or they might come from a stock of 20th century speeches. Take notes on the effectiveness of the speeches and the speakers. What are their techniques? What works? What was their main point? How did they prove it? This will be a graded discussion next week.

Assignment 20.7

Another way to increase your vocabulary is to rewrite something in your own words. Rewrite these passages in your own words: Ephesians 2.1-9 and 1 Corinthians 15.58.

Assignment 20.8

In his writings Paul used many different phrases to encourage believers. Rewrite in your own words some of his loving, encouraging passages, below. Answer the following questions in one paragraph total: Which of his phrases most spoke to you about loving encouragement? What word choices were most effective? Why?

2 Corinthians 7.3   Galatians 4.19   1 Thessalonians 2.8-11
1 Thessalonians 2.19-20   1 Thessalonians 3.8

Assignment 20.9

Read Mark Twain's "My Childhood on a Missouri Farm" and write your own version of it, but from your own childhood memory. Choose a strong memory you have from your childhood–it doesn't matter what it is, but it should be a fond memory–and recreate it. Notice that Twain does not simply recall an individual situation or instance, but a location and all the associated memories that go along with it. Think: where did you go? What did you do there? Who went with you? What happened to you there? What mischief did you get into? What did you eat? What did you play? etc. Start by brainstorming and then building from there.

This is more than just making a list: your aim here is to recreate, in vivid detail and with luminous language, that place and time. Really examine Twain's choice of language throughout his piece: he utilizes every sense and expertly chooses the exact right word for the moment and impact he intends.

Assignment 20.10

Take a paragraph from Mark Twain's essay, "My Childhood on a Missouri Farm" and find the average number of words per sentence. Then find the average number of words per sentence in Hemingway's excerpt in Imitation Exercises. What conclusions, if any, can you make about this?

Assignment 20.11

Read E.M. Forster's essay "My Wood" and answer the discussion questions. Your teacher may choose to have you imitate a paragraph or two so you can immerse yourself in his writing.

Lesson Twenty-One

The Third Canon:
Style–Figures of Speech

In writing are the roots, in writing are the foundations of eloquence; by writing resources are stored up, as it were, in a sacred repository, when they may be drawn forth for sudden emergencies, or as circumstances require. (Marcus Fabius Quintilianus)

Thought can be lofty without being elegant, but to the extent it lacks elegance it will have less effect on others. Force without finesse is mere mass. (Fernando Pessoa, *The Book of Disquiet*)

When [Winston Churchill] came to power in the spring of 1940, he brooked no recrimination about the past, lest the future thereby be lost. He mobilized the English language and sent it into battle to steady his fellow countrymen and hearten those Europeans upon whom the long dark night of tyranny had descended. (Edward R. Murrow, November 30, 1954)[114]

All through the ages, great communicators have paid attention to their use of language to persuade. They "dressed-up" their language to fit the audience and the occasion. The more creative ones employed Figures of Speech, which–either subtly or overtly–painted pictures in the minds of their audiences.

Hugh Blair uses his own Figures to describe their use and importance in the study of rhetoric: "[Figures] give us the pleasure of enjoying two objects presented together to our view, without confusion; the principal idea, which is the subject of the discourse, along with its accessory, which gives it the figurative dress."[115]

The use of Figures to embellish or decorate our writing are not an end themselves. First we compose our thoughts and plan our arguments, and then we take a second (or third or fourth) look to see how we can best beautify what we are trying to prove. "Because figures can render our thoughts vividly concrete, they help us to communicate with our audience clearly and effectively; because they stir emotional responses, they can carry truth, in Wordsworth's phrase, 'alive into the heart by passion'; and because they elicit admiration for the eloquence of the speaker or writer, they can exert a powerful ethical appeal."[116] We want our audience to believe and understand our arguments and to appreciate the illuminations we have woven into our discourse.

Watch how writers have embellished speech to make their point. Why say "the sun rises," when you can invoke word pictures in your audience's minds by saying, as James Thompson says, "But

---

[114]   Take a moment to pause on this quote and notice what he has written so beautifully in so few words!

[115]   Corbett, *The Rhetoric of Blair, Campbell, and Whately*, 80.

[116]   Corbett, *Classical Rhetoric for the Modern Student*, 377-378.

yonder comes the king of the day/Rejoicing in the east." Or perhaps it is better described as "Rosy-fingered dawn," as Homer does in *The Iliad* and *The Odyssey*. We can identify with the word "rosy," and we each get a picture in our minds of a red-pink dawn.

Most of these Figures are found in prose, and others in poetry. We will study some of the Figures in prose, then we will complete some exercises to familiarize ourselves with the Figures. As we move forward from here, we will employ our understanding of the Figures to our analysis of discourses. Implicit in this is that we will also expand our ability to write and speak well, beautifully, and compellingly.

Some authors will use the terms "scheme" and "trope" when discussing Figures. We will not do so, but it's helpful to understand that "schemes" appeal to the senses (alliteration, rhyme, onomatopoeia). Tropes appeal to the mind (metaphor, hyperbole).

We have listed the most common Figures of Speech, first in their classification, and second in alphabetical order. Classification can be considered as "The Six Rs": Rearrangement, Reinforcement, Removal, Repetition, and Replacement, and Repartees (also known as puns).

Rearrangement:
Anastrophe

Apposition

Climax

Isocolon

Parallelism

Paraprosdokian

Parenthesis

Reinforcement:
Allusion

Antithesis

Apostrophe

Hyperbole

Irony

Litotes

Metaphor

Paradox

Polysyndeton

Rhetorical Question

Simile

Removal:
Asyndeton

Ellipsis

Repetition:
Alliteration

Anadiplosis
Anaphora
Antimetabole
Antistrophe
Assonance
Epanalepsis
Polyptoton

Replacement:
Anthimeria
Metonymy
Onomatopoeia
Oxymoron
Personification
Synecdoche

Repartees (Puns):
Antanaclasis
Paronomasia
Syllepsis

Figures of Speech

Alliteration [Repetition]—Repetition of initial or medial consonants in two or more adjacent words. Examples:

"I have a dream that my four children will one day live in a nation where they will not be judged by the color of their skin but by the content of their character" (Martin Luther King Jr., "I Have a Dream").

"Like almost all dissidents of my generation, I was a protester without a plan and a visionary without a vision" (Michael Baumann, "The Chronicle of an Undeception").

"Here lies one who neither flattered nor feared any flesh" (Attributed to James Douglas, 4th Earl of Morton, at the grave of John Knox).

Allusion [Reinforcement]–The writer or speaker makes reference to an event, person, place, or literary work. It serves to aid the audience's grasp of the topic and enrich the discourse itself. It may not be a direct quote; it may be subtle. The writer or speaker should be sure that their audience will understand and appreciate the allusion. Examples:

"O, my offense is rank, it smells to heaven;/ It hath the primal eldest curse upon't, a brother's murder" (Shakespeare, *Hamlet*, 3.3.36-38). In a subtle allusion, Claudius refers to his act of murdering his brother the king in terms of that first murder of brother upon brother, Cain and Abel.

"Let both sides unite to heed in all corners of the earth the command of Isaiah–to 'undo the heavy burdens...and to let the oppressed go free'" (John F. Kennedy, Inaugural Address).

Anadiplosis [Repetition]—Repetition of the last word of one clause at the beginning of the following clause. Examples:

"In the beginning God created the heaven and the earth. And the earth was without form, and void" (*KJV*, Genesis 1.1-2).

"Human institutions arise from human action; human action arises from human nature; and human nature is notoriously intractable" (Michael Bauman, "The Chronicle of an Undeception").

"Fear is the path to the dark side. Fear leads to anger. Anger leads to hate. Hate leads to suffering" (Yoda, in *Star Wars*).

Anaphora [Repetition]—Repetition of the same word or group of words at the beginnings of successive clauses. Examples:

"Indifference elicits no response. Indifference is not a response. Indifference is not a beginning; it is an end" (Elie Wiesel, "The Perils of Indifference").

"We shall go on to the end, we shall fight in France, we shall fight on the seas and oceans, we shall fight with growing confidence and growing strength in the air, we shall defend our Island, whatever the cost may be, we shall fight on the beaches, we shall fight on the landing grounds, we shall fight in the fields and in the streets, we shall fight in the hills, we shall never surrender" (Winston Churchill, speech in the House of Commons, June 4, 1940).

"Love is patient and kind; love does not envy or boast; it is not arrogant or rude. It does not insist on its own way; it is not irritable or resentful; it does not rejoice at wrongdoing, but rejoices with the truth. Love bears all things, believes all things, hopes all things, endures all things. Love never ends" (*ESV*, 1 Corinthians 13.4-8a).

Anastrophe [Rearrangement]—Inversion of the natural or usual word order (also thought of as "Yoda-speak"). Examples:

"All hail the pow'r of Jesus' name, let angels prostrate fall" (Hymn by Edward Perronet).

"All to Jesus I surrender, all to Him I freely give; I will ever love and trust Him, In His presence daily live" (Hymn by Judson W. Van de Venter).

"Powerful you have become; the dark side I sense in you" (Yoda, in *Star Wars: Attack of the Clones*).

Antanaclasis [Repetition, Repartee]–Repetition of a word in two different senses. Examples:

"If we don't hang together, we'll hang separately" (Benjamin Franklin).

"Put down your arms, or we'll tear off his!" (*The Hobbit: An Unexpected Journey*. Directed by Peter Jackson, 2012).

"This fellow might be in 's time a great buyer of land, with his statutes, his recognizances, his fines, his double vouchers, his recoveries. Is this the fine of his fines and the recovery of his recoveries, to have his fine pate full of fine dirt? Will his vouchers vouch him no more of his purchases, and double ones too, than the length and breadth of a pair of indentures?" (Shakespeare, *Hamlet*, 5.1.96-102).

"I pray thee, good Mercutio, let's retire. / The day is hot, the Capulets abroad. / And, if we meet, we shall not 'scape a brawl, / For now, these hot days, is the mad blood stirring" (Shakespeare, *Romeo and Juliet* 3.1.1-4).

Anthimeria [Replacement]—The substitution of one part of speech for another. Examples:

"Send me a text message" has become "Text me." "Add me as a friend on [name your favorite social media]" has evolved to "Friend me." *These are not artful examples of Figures of Speech, but they show how language can change with the rearrangement of parts of speech.*

"Verbing weirds language" (Attributed to Bill Watterson's *Calvin and Hobbes* cartoon).

"We glassed the valley to spot an elk." (Hunters sometimes refer to looking through their binoculars as "glassing.")

"Her parents summered at the Jersey shore."

"They shall all of them be left to the birds of prey of the mountains and to the beasts of the earth. And the birds of prey will summer on them, and all the beasts of the earth will winter on them" (*ESV*, Isaiah 18.6).

Antimetabole [Repetition]—Repetition of words, in successive clauses, in reverse grammatical order. Examples:

"We didn't land on Plymouth Rock; Plymouth Rock landed on us" (Malcolm X).

"The problem of the human heart is at the heart of the human problem" (Michael Baumann, "Chronicle of an Undeception).

"Mankind must put an end to war, or war will put an end to mankind" (John F. Kennedy, address to the U.N. General Assembly, September 25, 1961).

Antistrophe (also called Epistrophe) [Repetition]—Repetition of the same word or phrase at the end of successive clauses. Example:

"In 1931, ten years ago, Japan invaded Manchuko–without warning. In 1935, Italy invaded Ethiopia–without warning. In 1938, Hitler occupied Austria–without warning. In 1939, Hitler invaded Czechoslovakia–without warning. Later in 1939, Hitler invaded Poland–without warning. And now Japan has attacked Malaya and Thailand–and the United States–without warning" (Franklin D. Roosevelt).

"We have not come this far without a struggle, and I assure you we cannot go further without a struggle" (Winston Churchill, November 1936).

Antithesis [Rearrangement/Reinforcement]—the juxtaposition of contrasting ideas, often in parallel structure. Examples:

"Not that I loved Caesar less, but that I love Rome more" (Shakespeare, *Julius Caesar*, 3.2.22).

"I am a young man with very old pensions; he is an old man with very young pensions–that's all" (Edmund Burke, "Letter to a Noble Lord").

"A just law is a man-made code that squares with the moral law or the law of God. An unjust law is a code that is out of harmony with the moral law" (Martin Luther King Jr., "Letter from Birmingham Jail").

"I am under obligation both to Greeks and to barbarians, both to the wise and to the foolish" (*ESV*, Romans 1.14).

Apposition [Rearrangement]—Placing side by side two coordinate elements, the second of which serves as an explanation or modification of the first. (Similar to parenthesis.) Examples:

"I believe in God the Father, maker of heaven and earth, and in Jesus Christ His only Son, our Lord" (Apostle's Creed).

"I, John, your brother and partner in the tribulation and the kingdom and the patient endurance that are in Jesus, was on the island called Patmos on account of the word of God and the testimony of Jesus" (*ESV*, Revelation 1.9).

Apostrophe [Reinforcement]—A sudden turn from the general audience to address a specific group or person, or personified abstraction, absent or present. Example:

"For Brutus, as you know, was Caesar's angel./Judge, O you gods, how dearly Caesar loved him" (Shakespeare, *Julius Caesar*, 3.2.181-182).

"Is this a dagger which I see before me,/ The handle toward my hand?/Come, let me clutch thee!/I have thee not, and yet I see thee still" (Shakespeare, *Macbeth*, 2.1.33).

Assonance [Repetition]—The repetition of similar vowel sounds, preceded and followed by different consonants, in the stressed syllables of adjacent words. Examples:

"And, sir, when we think of eternity, and of the future consequences of all human conduct, what is there in this life that should make any man contradict the dictates of his conscience, the principles of justice, the laws of religion, and of God?" (William Wilberforce, "On the Horrors of the Slave Trade"). (Also Antimetabole)

"[So] far, we fail to see any guarantee of peace. We do not see any guarantee of the freedoms that were promised to the nations in the Atlantic Charter" (Albert Einstein, The Fifth Nobel Anniversary Dinner, December, 1945).

Asyndeton [Removal]—Deliberate omission of conjunctions between a series of related clauses. Examples:

"[We] shall pay any price, bear any burden, meet any hardships, support any friend, oppose any foe to assure the survival and the success of liberty" (John F. Kennedy, Inaugural Address, 1961).

"But, in a larger sense, we cannot dedicate, we cannot consecrate, we cannot hallow this ground" (Abraham Lincoln, "Gettysburg Address").

Climax [Rearrangement]—Arrangement of words, phrases, or clauses in an order of increasing importance. Examples:

"And only slowly did I come to understand that to destroy is easy, that to build is hard, and that to preserve is hardest of all" (Michael Baumann, "Chronicle of an Undeception").

"In the beginning was the Word, and the Word was with God, and the Word was God" (*ESV*, John 1.1).

Ellipsis [Removal]—Deliberate omission of a word or of words which are readily implied by the context. Examples:

"Render to all what is due them: tax to whom tax is due; custom to whom custom; fear to whom fear; honor to whom honor" (*NASB*, Romans 13.7).

"I became unpopular in England for the one, and in Ireland for the other" (Edmund Burke, "Speech in the Electors of Bristol").

"The wage of the righteous leads to life, the gain of the wicked to sin" (*ESV*, Proverbs 10:16).

Epanalepsis [Repetition]—Repetition at the end of a clause of the word that occurred at the beginning of the clause. Examples:

"In times like these, it is helpful to remember that there have always been times like these" (Paul Harvey).

"I have said these things to you, that in me you may have peace. In the world you will have tribulation. But take heart; I have overcome the world" (*ESV*, John 16.33).

Hyperbole [Reinforcement]—The use of exaggerated terms for the purpose of emphasis or heightened effect. Examples:

"I have told you a million times to stop exaggerating!" (Moms everywhere have said this, about two million times.)

"The apathy of the people is enough to make every statue leap from its pedestal and to hasten the resurrection of the dead" (William Lloyd Garrison, "For Immediate Abolition").

"You blind guides! You strain out a gnat but swallow a camel" (*NIV*, Matthew 23.24).

Irony [Reinforcement]—Use of a word in such a way as to convey a meaning opposite to the literal meaning of the word. Examples:

<u>Verbal irony</u>: "For Brutus is an honourable man;/So are they all, honourable men" (Shakespeare, *Julius Caesar*, 3.2.82-83).

<u>Situational irony</u>: When the CIA hired an in-house expert to discover the mole who had turned over secrets to the Russian government, they discovered the one they'd hired was the one for whom they were looking.

Another example of situational irony in literature: A prophecy in *Oedipus Rex* foretold that he would kill his father and marry his mother. His parents did all they could to prevent that from occurring, but as a grown man he unwittingly did that very thing.

Isocolon [Rearrangement]—Any parallel structure, that is, similarity of structure in a pair or series of related words. (Similar to **Parallelism**.) Examples:

"<u>You ask, what is our policy? I will say</u>: It is to wage war, by sea, land and air, with all our might and with all the strength that God can give us; to wage war against a monstrous tyranny, never surpassed in the dark and lamentable catalogue of human crime. That is our policy. <u>You ask, what is our aim? I can answer</u> in one word: victory; victory at all costs, victory in spite of all terror, victory, however long and hard the road may be; for without victory, there is no survival" (Winston Churchill, "Blood, Toil, Tears, and Sweat").

"I returned and saw under the sun that the race is not to the swift, nor the battle to the strong, neither yet bread to the wise, nor yet riches to men of understanding, nor yet favor to men of skill; but time and chance happeneth to all" (*KJV*, Ecclesiastes 9.11).

Litotes [Reinforcement]—Deliberate use of understatement, not to deceive someone but to enhance the impressiveness of what we say. Often it is expressed in the negative to stress a concept or idea. It might help to think of Litotes as the opposite of Hyperbole. Examples:

Benvolio: What, art thou hurt?

Mercutio: Ay, ay, a scratch, a scratch; marry, 'tis enough./ Where is my page? Go, villain, fetch a surgeon.

Romeo: Courage, man; the hurt cannot be much.

Mercutio: *No, 'tis not so deep as a well, nor so wide as a/ church door; but 'tis enough,'twill serve.* Ask for me/tomorrow, and you shall find me a grave man (Shakespeare, *Romeo and Juliet*, III, i, 92-98). (Also **Paronomasia**)

"Out of them shall come songs of thanksgiving, and the voices of those who celebrate. I will multiply them, and they shall not be few; I will make them honored, and they shall not be small" (*ESV*, Jeremiah 30.19).

Metaphor [Reinforcement]—an implied comparison between two things of unlike nature that yet have something in common. Examples:

"The Duke of Bedford is the leviathan among all the creatures of the Crown. He tumbles about his unwieldy bulk; he plays and frolics in the ocean of the royal bounty. Huge as he is, and whilst 'he lies floating many a rood,' he is still a creature. His ribs, his fins, his whalebone, his blubber, the very spiracles through which he spouts a torrent of brine against his origin and covers me all over with the spray–everything of him and about him is from the throne. Is it for him to question the dispensation of the royal favour?" (Edmund Burke, "Letter to a Noble Lord").

"Let me not to the marriage of true minds/Admit impediments. Love is not love/Which alters when it alteration finds,/Or bends with the remover to remove:/O no; it is an ever-fixed mark, /That looks on tempests, and is never shaken;/It is the star to every wandering bark,/Whose worth's unknown, although his height be taken./Love's not Time's fool, though rosy lips and cheeks /Within his bending sickle's compass come; /Love alters not with his brief hours and weeks, /But bears it out even to the edge of doom./If this be error and upon me proved,/I never writ, nor no man ever loved" (Shakespeare, Sonnet 116).

Metonymy [Replacement]—Substitution of some attributive or suggestive word for what is actually meant. Examples:

House for the members of Parliament, *boots on the ground* for soldiers, *the saints* or *believers* for Christians, *arms* for guns, *East* or *West* referring to Western Civilization or Eastern Civilization, *Crown* or *throne* for royalty, *White House* for the executive branch of the US Government, or the US President.

"A well regulated Militia, being necessary to the security of a free State, the right of the people to keep and bear Arms, shall not be infringed" (Second Amendment to the US Constitution).

"The sin of Judah is written with a pen of iron; with a point of diamond it is engraved on the tablet of their heart, and on the horns of their altars" (*ESV*, Jeremiah 17.1).

"I have been so greatly disappointed with the white church and its leadership" (Martin Luther King Jr., "Letter from Birmingham Jail").

Onomatopoeia [Replacement]—Use of words whose sound echoes the sense. Examples:

"Clang, clang, clang went the trolley/ Ding, ding, ding went the bell/ Zing, zing, zing went my heartstrings/ For the moment I saw him I fell/ Chug, chug, chug went the motor/ Bump, bump, bump went the brake/ Thump, thump, thump went my heartstrings/ When he smiled, I could feel the car shake" (From *Meet Me in St. Louis*).

"Be not afeard; the isle is full of noises,/ Sounds and sweet airs, that give delight and hurt not./ Sometimes a thousand twangling instruments/ Will hum about mine ears, and sometime voices" (Shakespeare, *The Tempest*, 3.2135-138).

Oxymoron [Replacement. *Can also be categorized as Reinforcement and Rearrangement.*]—The yoking of two terms that are ordinarily contradictory. Examples:

Anarchist organization, clean coal, jumbo shrimp

"So [the Government goes] on in strange paradox, decided only to be undecided, resolved to be irresolute, adamant for drift, solid for fluidity, all-powerful to be impotent" (Winston Churchill, November 1936). (Also Polyptoton)

"Here's much to do with hate, but more with love./Why then, O brawling love! O loving hate!/O anything of nothing first create!/O heavy lightness, serious vanity!/Misshapen chaos of well-seeming forms!/Feather of lead, bright smoke, cold fire, sick health!/Still-waking sleep, that is not what it is!/This love I feel, that feel no love in this" (Shakespeare, *Romeo and Juliet*, 1.1.173-180).

Paradox [Reinforcement]—An assertion seemingly opposed to common sense, but that may yet have some truth in it. Example:

"What a pity that youth must be wasted on the young" (George Bernard Shaw).

"And therefore, since I cannot prove a lover/To entertain these fair well-spoken days,/I am determined to prove a villain/And hate the idle pleasures of these days" (Shakespeare, *Richard III*, I, i).

Parallelism [Rearrangement]—Similarity of structure in a pair or series of related words, phrases, or clauses. (Similar to Isocolon.) Examples:

"When we consider the vastness of the continent of Africa; when we reflect how all other countries have for some centuries past been advancing in happiness and civilization; when we think how in this same period all improvement in Africa has been defeated by her intercourse with Britain; when we reflect that it is we ourselves that have degraded them to that wretched brutishness and barbarity which we now plead as the justification of our guilt; how the slave trade has enslaved their minds, blackened their character, and sunk them so low in the scale of animal beings that some think the apes are of a higher class, and fancy the orang-outang has given them the go-by" (William Wilberforce, "On the Horrors of the Slave Trade").

"For my life is spent with sorrow, and my years with sighing; my strength has failed because of my iniquity, and my body has wasted away" (*ESV*, Psalm 31.10). (Also **Ellipsis**)

Paraprosdokian [Rearrangement]—Surprise or unexpected ending of a phrase or series. Examples:

"He was at his best when the going was good" (Alistair Cooke on the Duke of Windsor).

"You wouldn't trust the man who made the mess to clean it up. That is Truman. And by the same token you can't trust the man who was picked by the man who made the mess to clean it up and that's Stevenson" (Richard M. Nixon, "Checkers Speech").

"A bear in his natural habitat: a Studebaker." (Fozzie Bear, *The Muppet Movie*, 1979.)

Parenthesis [Rearrangement]—Insertion of some verbal unit in a position that interrupts the normal syntactical flow of the sentence. Examples:

"In the air–often at serious odds, often at odds hitherto thought overwhelming–we have been clawing down three or four to one of our enemies; and the relative balance of the British and German Air Forces is now considerably more favorable to us than at the beginning of the battle" (Winston Churchill, "Be Ye Men of Valour").

"If they do this,–/As, if God please, they shall,–my ransom then/Will soon be levied" (Shakespeare, *King Henry V*, 4.3.119-121).

"But whatever anyone else dares to boast of—I am speaking as a fool—I also dare to boast of that" (*ESV* 2 Cor. 11.21b).

Paronomasia [Replacement]—(Pun) Use of words alike in sound but different in meaning. (Similar to Antanaclasis.) Examples:

Mercutio: Nay, gentle Romeo, we must have you dance.

Romeo: Not I, believe me. You have dancing shoes/With nimble <u>soles</u>, I have a <u>soul</u> of lead/ So stakes me to the ground I cannot move (Shakespeare, *Romeo and Juliet*, 1.4.13-16).

Benvolio: What, art thou hurt?

Mercutio: Ay, ay, a scratch, a scratch; marry, 'tis enough./ Where is my page? Go, villain, fetch a surgeon.

Romeo: Courage, man; the hurt cannot be much.

Mercutio: No, 'tis not so deep as a well, nor so wide as a/ church door; but 'tis enough,'twill serve. Ask for me/tomorrow, and you shall find me a *grave* man. (Shakespeare, *Romeo and Juliet*, 3.1.92-98) (Also **Litotes**)

Personification or **Prosopopoeia** [Replacement]—Investing abstractions or inanimate objects with human qualities or abilities. Examples:

"...the moon gazed on my midnight labours, while, with unrelaxed and breathless eagerness, I pursued nature to her hiding-places" (Mary Wollstonecraft Shelley, *Frankenstein*).

"And let every other power know that this Hemisphere intends to remain the master of its own house" (John F. Kennedy, Inaugural Address).

Polyptoton [Repetition]—Repetition of words derived from the same root. Examples:

"We know through painful experience that freedom is never voluntarily given by the oppressor, it must be demanded by the oppressed" (Martin Luther King Jr., "Letter from Birmingham Jail").

"This command I entrust to you, Timothy, my son, in accordance with the prophecies previously made concerning you, that by them you may fight the good fight" (*NASB*, 1 Timothy 1.18).

"Love is not love/Which alters when it alteration finds,/Or bends with the remover to remove" (Shakespeare, Sonnet 116).

Polysyndeton [Reinforcement]—Deliberate use of many conjunctions. Example:

"And God made the beasts of the earth according to their kinds and the cattle according to their kinds and everything that creeps upon the ground according to its kind. And God saw that it was good" (*ESV*, Genesis 1.25).

"By the world, / I think my wife be honest and think she is not. / I think that thou art just and think thou art not. / I'll have some proof! Her name, that was as fresh / As Dian's visage, is now begrimed and black / As mine own face. If there be cords, or knives, / Poison, or fire, or suffocating streams, / I'll not endure it. Would I were satisfied! (Shakespeare, *Othello*, 3.3.441-445).

Rhetorical Question [Reinforcement]—Asking a question, not for the purpose of eliciting an answer but for the purpose of asserting or denying something obliquely. Examples:

"Did this in Caesar seem ambitious?/When that the poor have cried, Caesar hath wept:/Ambition should be made of sterner stuff:/Yet Brutus says he was ambitious;/And Brutus is an honourable man./You all did see that on the Lupercal/I thrice presented him a kingly crown,/Which he did thrice refuse: was this ambition?" (Shakespeare, *Julius Caesar*, 3.2.91-98).

"[Why] does it need a war to bring out our qualities and reassert our pride? Why do we have to be invaded before we throw aside our selfish aims and begin to work together as only we can work, and achieve as only we can achieve?" (Margaret Thatcher, July 1982).

Simile [Reinforcement]—an explicit comparison between two things of unlike nature that yet have something in common. Examples:

"Woe to you, scribes and Pharisees, hypocrites! For you are like whitewashed tombs, which outwardly appear beautiful, but within are full of dead people's bones and all uncleanness" (*ESV*, Matthew 23.27).

"O, she doth teach the torches to burn bright!/ It seems she hangs upon the cheek of night/ Like a rich jewel in an Ethiope's ear " (Shakespeare, *Romeo and Juliet*, 1.5.44-46).

Syllepsis [Reinforcement]—(Repartee) Use of a word understood differently in relation to two or more other words, which it modifies or governs. Examples:

"In an instant both boys were rolling and tumbling in the dirt, gripped together like cats; and for the space of a minute they tugged and tore at each other's hair and clothes, punched and scratched each other's nose, and covered themselves with dust and glory" (Mark Twain, *The Adventures of Tom Sawyer*).

"Oh, flowers are as common here, Miss Fairfax, as people are in London" (Oscar Wilde, *The Importance of Being Ernest)*. Note that even the title of Wilde's book is itself a syllepsis, as it is important to be earnest—and the book proves that point.

Synecdoche [Replacement]—A figure of speech in which a part stands for the whole. Similar to **Metonymy**. Examples:

General term replaces specific term: *vessel* for *ship, weapon* for *sword, creature* for *man, arms* for *rifles, vehicle* for *bicycle*

Specific term replaces the general term: *bread* for *food, cutthroat* for *assassin, White House* for *officials who work there*

Part for the whole: *sail* for *ship, hands* for *helpers, roofs* for *houses, boots* for *soldiers*

Matter for what is made from it: *silver* for *money, canvas* for *sail, steel* for *sword*

"She sets a nice table."

"Beware Ephraim" Hosea 5, where Ephraim is a person, but it is used to refer to Israel as a whole.

Lesson Twenty-One Assignments

Assignment 21.1

Figures of Speech Exercise 1.

Assignment 21.2

What Figures of Speech can you detect in the following quote by Dietrich Bonhoeffer? "Cheap grace is preaching forgiveness without requiring repentance, baptism without church discipline, Communion without confession. … Cheap grace is grace without discipleship, grace without the cross, grace without Jesus Christ, living and incarnate."

Assignment 21.3

Analyze JFK's "Inaugural Address" for Figures of Speech. Choose three sentences (or paragraphs or just phrases) that stand out to you and write a short essay discussing how he uses them to prove his thesis. Five paragraphs.

Assignment 21.4

Figures of Speech Exercise 2.

Assignment 21.5

Figures of Speech Exercise 3

Assignment 21.6

Take the Figures of Speech Test.

Lesson Twenty-Two

Progymnasmata

Progymnasmata[117] was the name given to writing and speaking exercises in ancient rhetoric schools. Teachers instructed them in eloquence through imitation at first. The exercises in forms of good writing increased in difficulty as the students progressed, beginning with simple rewrites of common fables and memorization of simple stories. Easy little fables and stories communicated some brief lesson for children to focus on. Some schools required more advanced students to translate fables and stories from one language to another and back again. (For our purposes, we will stick with English!)

Typically students learned 14 types of progymnasmata exercises, each more difficult than the last:

- Fable
- Narrative
- Chreia
- Proverb
- Refutation
- Confirmation
- Commonplace
- Encomium
- Vituperation
- Comparison
- Impersonation
- Description
- Thesis or Theme
- Defend / Attack a Law

The form, the careful arrangement, of each exercise was vitally important, just as it is in the discourses we read and write in rhetoric. Pay attention to the arrangement of each example we provide here.

---

[117] For additional information regarding progymnasmata, see the list of suggested reading in Appendix I, Works Cited.

Fables

The fables below will be used by rhetoric students in writing exercises. Try rewriting one in a shorter version, retaining the meaning and sense of the fable, and then expand it, adding detail, description, and perhaps dialogue.

For example, take the first fable, "The Fox and the Crow," which is 168 words, and rewrite it in just 75 words but retaining the main points. Then in your own words, add more description and dialogue to reach 300 words. This exercise at the Rhetoric level helps students edit concisely. If you can say it at 300 words, can you also cut out half the words (or more) and still make sense?

Also "The Crow and the Pitcher" contains many repetitions. It might be easy to cut down this fable, but what can you do to embellish upon the fable to 300 words WITHOUT repeating yourself?

The Fox and the Crow

A Fox once saw a Crow fly off with a piece of cheese in its beak and settle on a branch of a tree.

"That's for me, as I am a Fox," said Master Reynard, and he walked up to the foot of the tree. "Good-day, Mistress Crow," he cried. "How well you are looking to-day; how glossy your feathers; how bright your eye. I feel sure your voice must surpass that of other birds, just as your figure does; let me hear but one song from you that I may greet you as the Queen of Birds."

The Crow lifted up her head and began to caw her best, but the moment she opened her mouth the piece of cheese fell to the ground, only to be snapped up by Master Fox.

"That will do," said he. "That was all I wanted. In exchange for your cheese I will give you a piece of advice for the future. Do not trust flatterers."

Lesson: Do not trust flatterers.

Word count: 168

The Lion and the Mouse

Once when a Lion was asleep a little Mouse began running up and down upon him. This soon wakened the Lion, who placed his huge paw upon him, and opened his big jaws to swallow him.

"Pardon, O King," cried the little Mouse. "Forgive me this time, and I shall never forget it! Who knows but what I may be able to do you a turn some of these days?"

The Lion was so tickled at the idea of the Mouse being able to help him, that he lifted up his paw and let him go.

Some time after the Lion was caught in a trap, and the hunters who desired to carry him alive to the King, tied him to a tree while they went in search of a wagon to carry him on.

Just then the little Mouse happened to pass by, and seeing the sad plight in which the Lion was, went up to him and soon gnawed away the ropes that bound the King of the Beasts.

"Was I not right?" said the little Mouse.

Lesson: Little friends may prove great friends.

Word count: 186

The Fox and the Stork

At one time the Fox and the Stork were on visiting terms and seemed very good friends. So the Fox invited the Stork to dinner, and for a joke put nothing before her but some soup in a very shallow dish. This the Fox could easily lap up, but the Stork could only wet the end of her long bill in it, and left the meal as hungry as when she began.

"I am sorry," said the Fox, "that the soup is not to your liking."

"Pray do not apologise," said the Stork. "I hope you will return this visit, and come and dine with me soon."

So a day was appointed when the Fox should visit the Stork; but when they were seated at table all that was for their dinner was contained in a very long-necked jar with a narrow mouth, in which the Fox could not insert his snout, so all he could manage to do was to lick the outside of the jar.

"I will not apologise for the dinner," said the Stork.

Lesson: One bad turn deserves another.

Word count: 183

The Fox and the Grapes

One hot summer's day a Fox was strolling through an orchard until he came to a bunch of Grapes just ripening on a vine which had been trained over a lofty branch.

"Just the thing to quench my thirst," quoth he. Drawing back a few paces, he took a run and a jump, and just missed the bunch. Turning round again with a One, Two, Three, he jumped up, but with no greater success.

Again and again he tried after the tempting morsel, but at last had to give it up, and walked away with his nose in the air, saying: "I am sure they are sour."

Lesson: It is easy to despise what you cannot get.

Word count: 117

The Crow and the Pitcher

A Crow, half-dead with thirst, came upon a Pitcher which had once been full of water; but when the Crow put its beak into the mouth of the Pitcher he found that only very little water was left in it, and that he could not reach far enough down to get at it. He tried, and he tried, but at last had to give up in despair.

Then a thought came to him, and he took a pebble and dropped it into the Pitcher. Then he took another pebble and dropped it into the Pitcher. Then he took another pebble and dropped that into the Pitcher. Then he took another pebble and dropped that into the Pitcher. Then he took another pebble and dropped that into the Pitcher. Then he took another pebble and dropped that into the Pitcher.

At last, at last, he saw the water mount up near him, and after casting in a few more pebbles he was able to quench his thirst and save his life.

Lesson: Little by little without stopping does the trick.

Word count: 179

The Bundle of Sticks

An old man on the point of death summoned his sons around him to give them some parting advice. He ordered his servants to bring in a bundle of sticks, and said to his eldest son: "Break it."

The son strained and strained, but with all his efforts was unable to break the bundle. The other sons also tried, but none of them was successful.

"Untie the bundle," said the father, "and each of you take a stick." When they had done so, he called out to them: "Now, break," and each stick was easily broken. "You see my meaning," said their father.

Lesson: Together you are strong; separated you are weak.

Word count: 112

The Goose With the Golden Eggs

One day a countryman going to the nest of his Goose found there an egg all yellow and glittering. When he took it up it was as heavy as lead and he was going to throw it away, because he thought a trick had been played upon him. But on second thought he took it home and showed it to his wife. Soon they found to their delight that it was an egg of pure gold.

Every morning the same thing occurred, and he soon became rich by selling his eggs. As he grew rich he grew greedy; and thinking to get at once all the gold the Goose could give, he killed it and opened it only to find nothing.

Lesson: By wanting too much, too fast, you may do something wrong and lose what you have.

Word count: 138

The Chreia, to be imitated

Chreia is a short, witty description of someone's wise saying. It is covered in eight simple steps. Not every scholar agrees with the elements listed below, but we have provided the more commonly known steps, below.

1. Praise the sayer or doer, or praise the chreia itself (*Encomium*)
2. Give a paraphrase of the theme
3. Say why this was said or done
4. Provide a contrast
5. Provide a comparison
6. Give an example of the meaning
7. Support the saying or action with testimony
8. Conclude with a brief epilogue

The material for chreia comes from wise (or ridiculous) sayings. Once students know the form, they can write their own chreias (and other forms of progymnasmata) with ease.

The obvious practical application is for those times when a student is asked to write an essay about a person or a saying. Once this formula is learned, the student should easily be able to write one any time, on any given subject.

This textbook will not teach all forms of progymnasmata. However, students of this text will learn three forms (chreia, commonplace, and vituperation) and write their own. Later they will also imitate the writing of great thinkers, word for word, so they can observe by doing (see Imitation below in this Lesson).

Aphthonius of Antioch (ca 4th century AD), is known for his development of standard progymnasmata. His Chreia, laid out below, is often used by students today. He praises the following wisdom attributed to Isocrates: "The root of education is bitter, but sweet are its fruits."

Praise the Sayer, or Encomium

It is fitting that Isocrates should be admired for his art, which gained for him an illustrious reputation. Just what it was, he demonstrated by practice and he made the art famous; he was not made famous by it. It would take too long a time to go into all the ways in which he benefited humanity, whether he was phrasing laws for rulers on the one hand or advising individuals on the other, but we may examine his wise remark on education.

Paraphrase of the Theme

The lover of learning, he says, is beset with difficulties at the beginning, but these eventually end as advantages. That is what he so wisely said, and we shall wonder at it as follows.

Why this was Said or Done

The lovers of learning search out the leaders in education, to approach whom is fearful and to desert whom is folly. Fear waits upon the boys, both in the present and in the future. After the teachers come the attendants, fearful to look at and dreadful when angered. Further, the fear is as swift as the misdeed and, after fear, comes the punishment. Indeed, they punish the faults of the boys, but they consider the good qualities only fit and proper. The fathers are even more harsh than the attendants in choosing the streets, enjoining the boys to go straight along them, and being suspicious of the marketplace. If there has been need of punishment, however, they do not understand the true nature of it, but the youth approaching manhood is invested with good character through these trials.

Provide a Contrast

If anyone, on the other hand, should flee from the teachers out of fear of these things, or if he should run away from his parents, or if he should turn away from the attendants, he has completely deprived himself of their teaching and he has lost an education along with the fear. All these considerations influence the saying of Isocrates that the root of learning is bitter.

Provide a Comparison

For just as the tillers of the soil throw down the seeds to the earth with hardship and then gather in a greater harvest, in like manner those seeking after an education finally win by toil the subsequent reknown.

Give an Example of the Meaning

Let me call to mind the life of Demosthenes; in one respect, it was more beset with hardships than that of any other rhetor but, from another point of view, his life came to be more glorious than any other. For he was so preeminent in his zeal that the adornment was often taken from his head, since the best adornment stems from virtue. Moreover, he devoted to his labors those energies that others squander on pleasures.

Support the Saying or Action with a Testimony

Consequently, there is reason to marvel at Hesiod's saying that the road to virtue is hard, but easy it is to traverse the heights. For that which Hesiod terms a road, Isocrates calls a root; in different terms, both are conveying the same idea.

Conclude with a Brief Epilogue

In regard to these things, there is reason for those looking back on Isocrates to marvel at him for having expressed himself so beautifully on the subject of education.

The Commonplace

Commonplace, the next type of progymnasmata exercise, either attacks a negative saying or trait, or praises what is virtuous or honorable. In his *Ad Herennium* Cicero makes it clear how a Commonplace can be used in court cases, and then outlines ten types of commonplace:

> [T]he prosecutor will use the commonplace against one who has preferred the disadvantageous to the advantageous when he lacked the right of decision. The defendant's counsel, on his part, will use a commonplace in the form of complaint against those who deem it equitable to prefer the ruinous to the advantageous; and at the same time let him ask the accusers, and the jurors themselves, what they would have done had they been in the

defendant's place, and he will set before their eyes the time, the place, the circumstances, and the defendant's deliberations...

Amplification is the principle of using Commonplaces to stir the hearers. To amplify an accusation it will be most advantageous to draw commonplaces from ten formulae.

(1) The first commonplace is taken from authority, when we call to mind of what great concern the matter under discussion has been to the immortal gods, or to our ancestors, or kings, states, barbarous nations, sages, the Senate; and again, especially how sanction has been provided in these matters by laws.

(2) The second commonplace is used when we consider who are affected by these acts on which our charge rest; whether all men, which is a most shocking thing; or our superiors, such as are those from whom the commonplace of authority is taken; or our peers, those in the same situation as we with respect to qualities of character, physical attributes, and external circumstances; or our inferiors, whom in all these respects we excel.

(3) By means of the third commonplace we ask what would happen if the same indulgence should be granted to all culprits, and show what perils and disadvantages would ensue from indifference to this crime.

(4) By means of the fourth commonplace we show that if we indulge this man, many others will be the more emboldened to commit crimes — something which the anticipation of a judicial sentence has hitherto checked.

(5) By the fifth commonplace we show that if once judgement is pronounced otherwise than as we urge, there will be nothing which can remedy the harm or correct the jurors' error. Here it will be in point for us to make a comparison with other mistakes, so as to show that other mistakes can either be moderated by time or corrected designedly, but that so far as the present mistake is concerned, nothing will serve either to alleviate or to amend it.

(6) By means of the sixth commonplace we show that the act was done with premeditation, and declare that for an intentional crime there is no excuse, although a rightful plea of mercy is provided for an unpremeditated act.

(7) By means of the seventh commonplace we show it is a foul crime, cruel, sacrilegious, and tyrannical; such a crime as the outraging of women, or one of those crimes that incite wars and life-and-death struggles with enemies of the state.

(8) By means of the eighth commonplace we show that it is not a common but a unique crime, base, nefarious, and unheard-of, and therefore must be the more promptly and drastically avenged.

(9) The ninth commonplace consists of comparison of wrongs, as when we shall say it is a more heinous crime to debauch a free-born person than to steal a sacred object, because the one is done from unbridled licentiousness and the other from need.

(10) By the tenth commonplace we shall examine sharply, incriminatingly, and precisely, everything that took place in the actual execution of the deed and all the circumstances that usually attend such an act, so that by the enumeration of the attendant circumstances the crime may seem to be taking place and the action to unfold before our eyes.[118]

---

[118]   http://penelope.uchicago.edu/Thayer/E/Roman/Texts/Rhetorica_ad_Herennium/2*.html#note168

The Commonplace will address not a person's specific qualities, but general qualities. Its arrangement generally follows this outline. Take time to discuss this outline and use what we have supplied in parentheses to write your own Commonplace.

The subject for this Commonplace is the Proverbs discussion of the fool. Remember that here we are talking in general terms, describing a fool who has departed from the wisdom of his father.

- Begin with the contrary or a contradiction ("A fool despises his father's instruction"–from Proverbs 15.5a). Introduce this by describing how this might happen. In other words, describe the fool and what he says to his father that shows his folly.

- Compare something better ("Whoever heeds reproof is prudent"–from Proverbs 15:5b).

- Introduce a proverb that rebukes the negative quality ("Leave the presence of a fool, for there you do not meet words of knowledge"–Proverbs 14.7).

- Use a side story to imagine the past life of the person accused. (Consider using the parable of the prodigal son to show what this fool has done when he despised the teaching of his father. Or perhaps focus on the other son who was outraged by his father's feast to welcome back the prodigal.)

- Scorn the idea of taking pity on such a fool. ("Do not feel sorry for the fool who has departed from the ways of his father, for he has been taught, and warned, from his earliest days.")

- Consider the following items in discussing this virtue or vice: legality, justice, expediency, practicability, decency, consequences. (In other words, choose one or more of these considerations, such as legality. Describe how the foolish son's behavior could lead to his being tossed into jail. Or perhaps a consequence can be clearly shown when the prodigal son lost all his money and even sank so low as to consider eating the scraps that had been tossed to the pigs.)

We have supplied ideas for consideration. Where we have added just a few words, you will "flesh out" with several sentences for each element.

The Invective

Vituperation or invective compares to the Commonplace exercise but speaks not against <u>general</u> vices or types of persons, but a <u>specific</u> individual. This is not petty or base, but always done with "a certain portion of grace and wit, learning worthy of a well-bred man, and quickness and brevity in replying as well as attacking, accompanied with a refined decorum and urbanity."[119] At all times, maintain propriety, not stooping to a straw man or *ad hominem* attack, but using proper reason and logic.

Directions for Composition

Attack a specific person or thing for being vicious or mean.

1. Compose an exordium (introduction)
2. Describe the stock a person comes from: his people, his country, his ancestors, his parents. For a thing, describe the background that developed that thing. *Do not use this as an opportunity to attack the person's race. Rather, you could describe how being raised in a crime-ridden neighborhood contributed to the person's lawless behavior, or being raised in a privileged home taught him to expect privilege all through life.*
3. Describe the person's upbringing: education, instruction in art, training in laws. For a thing, describe the ideas contained therein.
4. Describe the person's deeds, which should be described as the results of: his/her evils of mind (such as weakness or indiscretion); his/her evils of body (such as plainness, lethargy, or lack of vigor); his/her evils of fortune (as lack of or corruption of high position, power, wealth, friends). For a thing, describe its evil effects upon the world.
5. Make a disfavorable comparison to someone (or something) else to escalate your vituperation.
6. Conclude with an epilogue including either an exhortation to your hearers not to emulate this person (or thing), or a prayer. [120]

An excellent example of a vituperative can be seen in Demosthenes' "Invective Against Philip of Macedon" in *AFE*. Perhaps the greatest invective, however, is Edmund Burke's "Letter to a Noble Lord."

---

[119]   Cicero, *De Oratore* 1.4.17 http://pages.pomona.edu/~cmc24747/sources/cic_web/de_or_1.htm

[120]   Adapted from "Silva Rhetoricae," rhetoric.byu.edu.

Imitation

After the first couple of Imitation exercises the sheet will include a Writer's Workshop Exercise. This is a practice in rewriting a sentence from the imitation passage, using your own words but keeping the grammatical flow intact. Writers often pattern their sentences after those of the masters in writing so they can see how the sentence flows.

Before we start Writer's Workshop exercises, first we must begin with simple imitation: copying by hand a passage from a well-known writer. We have included passages beginning with some of the earliest English writers and moving to modern. Each writer has a distinct "voice," which you will hopefully recognize and appreciate.

When Michelangelo first began his career as an artist, he joined the prominent artistic studio in his city. The master did not tell him to begin painting whatever he liked. First, the master set a well-known painting in front of him and ordered him to copy it, brush-stroke by brush-stroke. The master did not order Michelangelo to become a forger; instead, this was the first step in observing the techniques of the great artists who had gone before him. Legend says that Michelangelo's goal was to copy a painting so perfectly that his master couldn't tell the difference, and he even snuck his copy into the place of the real painting, to see how long it would take his master to notice.

If Michelangelo can begin his career as a brilliant artist by imitating great artists so he could observe their techniques, then you can improve your writing by imitating great writers.

Follow these guidelines for each of your imitation assignments.

- First, read the excerpt. Pay careful attention to how the author uses language: his adjectives and adverbs, even how he sets the scene.

- Take just twenty minutes on the imitation at any one time. Your attention on the assignment should be fresh so that this isn't merely an automatic exercise.

- Copy the passage using a pen, instead of typing it. Just as in the directions above, spending more than twenty minutes at a time, and typing it instead of writing, becomes a mindless chore. Focus on what you are writing. Take note of the writer's "voice." A mechanical way of insuring accuracy and the proper pace is to make your handwriting as legible as you can.

- When you encounter an unfamiliar word, do not just copy it. Underline it, look it up in the dictionary and, if necessary, note its definition in the margin.

- As instructed above, your handwriting must be legible. If your handwriting is large, double space your lines. Leave a 1" margin on the right and left of your page. As always, your name and the date must appear at the top of the page. The author's name and (when available) the title of the work, must both appear below your name and the date.

A word about the Writer's Workshop found at the bottom of later passages: See Assignment 23.2. There you are given some passages to imitate not by copying word for word, but by using the writer's grammatical structure and replacing your own words.

Passages for Imitation

King James Version: **Job 2.1-10**

Again there was a day when the sons of God came to present themselves before the LORD, and Satan came also among them to present himself before the LORD. And the LORD said unto Satan, From whence comest thou? And Satan answered the LORD, and said, From going to and fro in the earth, and from walking up and down in it. And the LORD said unto Satan, Hast thou considered my servant Job, that there is none like him in the earth, a perfect and an upright man, one that feareth God, and escheweth evil? and still he holdeth fast his integrity, although thou movedst me against him, to destroy him without cause. And Satan answered the LORD, and said, Skin for skin, yea, all that a man hath will he give for his life. But put forth thine hand now, and touch his bone and his flesh, and he will curse thee to thy face. And the LORD said unto Satan, Behold, he is in thine hand; but save his life. So went Satan forth from the presence of the LORD, and smote Job with sore boils from the sole of his foot unto his crown. And he took him a potsherd to scrape himself withal; and he sat down among the ashes. Then said his wife unto him, Dost thou still retain thine integrity? curse God, and die. But he said unto her, Thou speakest as one of the foolish women speaketh. What? shall we receive good at the hand of God, and shall we not receive evil? In all this did not Job sin with his lips.

> **Writer's Workshop:** Copy this down, by hand, twice as follows: first, word for word. Second, "translate" this into today's English. Do not simply copy a more modern version or translation; in fact, do not use one. Translate it on your own.

Joseph Conrad, *Heart of Darkness*

We penetrated deeper and deeper into the heart of darkness. It was very quiet there. At night sometimes the roll of drums behind the curtain of trees would run up the river and remain sustained faintly, as if hovering in the air high over our heads, till the first break of day. Whether it meant war, peace, or prayer we could not tell. The dawns were heralded by the descent of a chill stillness; the wood-cutters slept, their fires burned low; the snapping of a twig would make you start. We were wanderers on a prehistoric earth, on an earth that wore the aspect of an unknown planet. We could have fancied ourselves the first of men taking possession of an accursed inheritance, to be subdued at the cost of profound anguish and of excessive toil. But suddenly, as we struggled round a bend, there would be a glimpse of rush walls, of peaked grass-roofs, a burst of yells, a whirl of black limbs, a mass of hands clapping of feet stamping, of bodies swaying, of eyes rolling, under the droop of heavy and motionless foliage. The steamer toiled along slowly on the edge of a black and incomprehensible frenzy. The prehistoric man was cursing us, praying to us, welcoming us—who could tell? We were cut off from the comprehension of our surroundings; we glided past like phantoms, wondering and secretly appalled, as sane men would be before an enthusiastic outbreak in a madhouse. We could not understand because we were too far and could not remember because we were travelling in the night of first ages, of those ages that are gone, leaving hardly a sign—and no memories."[121]

> **Writer's Workshop:** First, copy word for word. Second, imitate the following sentence in your own words, only retaining the same grammatical structure. For example, look at a rewording of the following passage: "The prehistoric man was cursing us, praying to us,

---

[121]   Conrad, Joseph. *Heart of Darkness: and, The Secret Sharer.* New York, Penguin Group, 1997., 108

welcoming us—who could tell?" Rewrite of the passage, keeping the grammatical structure the same: "The angry mountain lion was snarling at us, threatening us, warning us–who could tell?"

<u>Your passage for imitation</u>: Whether it meant war, peace, or prayer we could not tell.

Zora Neale Hurston, *Their Eyes Were Watching God*

So Janie began to think of Death. Death, that strange being with the huge square toes who lived way in the West. The great one who lived in the straight house like a platform without sides to it, and without a roof. What need has Death for a cover, and what winds can blow against him? He stands in his high house that overlooks the world. Stands watchful and motionless all day with his sword drawn back, waiting for the messenger to bid him come. Been standing there before there was a where or a when or a then. She was liable to find a feather from his wings lying in her yard any day now. She was sad and afraid too.[122]

Writer's Workshop: First, copy word for word. Second, imitate the following sentence in your own words, only retaining the same grammatical structure, just as you did for the passage above.

<u>Your passage for imitation</u>: She was liable to find a feather from his wings lying in her yard any day now. She was sad and afraid too.

Ernest Hemingway, "Big Two-Hearted River: Part 1"

Nick looked at the burned-over stretch of hillside, where he had expected to find the scattered houses of the town and then walked down the railroad track to the bridge over the river. The river was there. It swirled against the log spires of the bridge. Nick looked down into the clear, brown water, colored from the pebbly bottom, and watched the trout keeping themselves steady in the current with wavering fins. As he watched them they changed their positions by quick angles, only to hold steady in the fast water again. Nick watched them a long time."[123]

Writer's Workshop: First, copy word for word. Second, imitate the entire passage in your own words, only retaining the same grammatical structure, just as you did for the passage above.

Harper Lee, *To Kill a Mockingbird*

Maycomb was an old town, but it was a tired old town when I first knew it. In rainy weather the streets turned to red slop; grass grew on the sidewalks, the courthouse sagged in the square. Somehow, it was hotter then: a black dog suffered on a summer's day; bony mules hitched to Hoover carts flicked flies in the sweltering shade of the live oaks on the square. Men's stiff collars wilted by nine in the morning. Ladies bathed before noon, after their three-o'clock naps, and by nightfall were like soft teacakes with frostings of sweat and sweet talcum.[124]

Writer's Workshop: First, copy word for word. Second, imitate the following sentence in your own words, only retaining the same grammatical structure, just as you did for the

---

[122]   Hurston, Zora Neale. *Their Eyes Were Watching God: a novel*. New York, HarperPerennial, 1999., 84

[123]   Hemingway, Ernest. "Big Two-Hearted River: Part 1." *In Our Time*. New York, Scribner, 2003., 133

[124]   Lee, Harper. *To Kill a Mockingbird*. New York, Fawcett Popular Library, 1962., 9

passage above: *In rainy weather the streets turned to red slop; grass grew on the sidewalks, the courthouse sagged in the square.*

William Shakespeare, *Henry V*, 4.3.18-67

What's he that wishes so?
My cousin, Westmorland? No, my fair cousin;
If we are mark'd to die, we are enow
To do our country loss; and if to live,
The fewer men, the greater share of honour.
God's will! I pray thee, wish not one man more.
By Jove, I am not covetous for gold,
Nor care I who doth feed upon my cost;
It yearns me not if men my garments wear;
Such outward things dwell not in my desires.
But if it be a sin to covet honour,
I am the most offending soul alive.
No, faith, my coz, wish not a man from England.
God's peace! I would not lose so great an honour
As one man more methinks would share from me
For the best hope I have. O, do not wish one more!
Rather proclaim it, Westmorland, through my host,
That he which hath no stomach to this fight,
Let him depart; his passport shall be made,
And crowns for convoy put into his purse;
We would not die in that man's company
That fears his fellowship to die with us.
This day is call'd the feast of Crispian.
He that outlives this day, and comes safe home,
Will stand a tip-toe when this day is nam'd,
And rouse him at the name of Crispian.
He that shall see this day, and live old age,
Will yearly on the vigil feast his neighbours,
And say "To-morrow is Saint Crispian."
Then will he strip his sleeve and show his scars,
And say "These wounds I had on Crispin's day."
Old men forget; yet all shall be forgot,
But he'll remember, with advantages,
What feats he did that day. Then shall our names,
Familiar in his mouth as household words—
Harry the King, Bedford and Exeter,
Warwick and Talbot, Salisbury and Gloucester—

Be in their flowing cups freshly rememb'red.
This story shall the good man teach his son;
And Crispin Crispian shall ne'er go by,
From this day to the ending of the world,
But we in it shall be rememberèd-
We few, we happy few, we band of brothers;
For he to-day that sheds his blood with me
Shall be my brother; be he ne'er so vile,
This day shall gentle his condition;
And gentlemen in England now a-bed
Shall think themselves accurs'd they were not here,
And hold their manhoods cheap whiles any speaks
That fought with us upon Saint Crispin's day.[125]

> **Writer's Workshop:** First, copy word for word. Second, "translate" the passage into today's English. Do not use any outside sources for this.

Mary Shelley, *Frankenstein*

"Be calm! I entreat you to hear me, before you give vent to your hatred on my devoted head. Have I not suffered enough that you seek to increase my misery? Life, although it may only be an accumulation of anguish, is dear to me, and I will defend it. Remember thou hast made me more powerful than thyself; my height is superior to thine; my joints more supple. But I will not be tempted to set myself in opposition to thee. I am thy creature, and I will be even mild and docile to my natural lord and king, if thou wilt also perform thy part, the which thou owest me. Oh, Frankenstein, be not equitable to every other, and trample upon me along, to whom thy justice, and even thy clemency and affection, is most due. Remember, that I am thy creature; I ought to be thy Adam; but I am rather the fallen angel, whom thou drivest from joy for no misdeed. Everywhere I see bliss, from which I alone am irrevocably excluded. I was benevolent and good; misery made me a fiend. Make me happy, and I shall again be virtuous."[126]

> **Writer's Workshop:** First, copy word for word. Second, imitate the following sentences, just as you have done for other passages above. *I was benevolent and good; misery made me a fiend. Make me happy, and I shall again be virtuous.*

John Milton, *Paradise Lost*

Thus Eve with count'nance blithe her story told;
But in her cheek distemper flushing glowed.
On th'other side, Adam, soon as he heard
The fatal trespass done by Eve, amazed,
Astonied stood and blank, while horror chill

---

[125] http://shakespeare.mit.edu/henryv/full.html

[126]   Shelley, Mary. *Frankenstein*. Dallas, The Worldview Library, 2007., 115

Ran through his veins, and all his joints relaxed;

From his slack hand the garland wreathed for Eve

Down dropped, and all the faded roses shed:

Speechless he stood and pale, till thus at length

First to himself he inward silence broke.

"O fairest of Creation, last and best

Of all God's works, creature in whom excelled

Whatever can to sight or thought be formed,

Holy, divine, good, amiable or sweet!

How art thou lost, how on a sudden lost,

Defaced, deflow'red, and now to death devote?"[127]

> **Writer's Workshop:** First, copy once, word for word. Then "translate" this passage into today's language. Do not worry about keeping the rhyme or rhythm in your translation, and do not use outside sources for help.

Charles Dickens, *A Tale of Two Cities*

A large cask of wine had been dropped and broken in the street. The accident had happened in getting it out of a cart; the cask had tumbled out with a run, the hoops had burst, and it lay on the stones just outside the door of the wine-shop, shattered like a walnut-shell.

All the people within reach had suspended their business, or their idleness, to run to the spot and drink the wine. The rough, irregular stones of the street, pointing every way, and designed, one might have thought, expressly to lame all living creatures that approached them, had dammed it into little pools; these were surrounded, each by its own jostling group or crowd, according to its size. Some men kneeled down, made scoops of their two hands joined, and sipped, or tried to help women, who bent over their shoulders, to sip, before the wine had all run out between their fingers. Others, men and women, dipped in the puddles with little mugs of mutilated earthenware, or even with handkerchiefs from women's heads, which were squeezed dry into infants' mouths; others made small mud embankments, to stem the wine as it ran; others, directed by lookers-on up at high windows, darted here and there, to cut off little streams of wine that started away in new directions; others devoted themselves to the sodden and lee-dyed pieces of the cask, licking, and even champing the moister wine-rotted fragments with eager relish. There was no drainage to carry off the wine, and not only did it all get taken up, but so much mud got taken up along with it, that there might have been a scavenger in the street, if anybody acquainted with it could have believed in such a miraculous presence.[128]

> **Writer's Workshop:** First, copy word for word. Second, imitate the following sentence, just as you have done for other passages above. *The accident had happened in getting it out of a cart; the cask had tumbled out with a run, the hoops had burst, and it lay on the stones just outside the door of the wine-shop, shattered like a walnut-shell.*

---

[127]   Milton, John. *Paradise Lost*. England, Clays Ltd., 2000., Book IX, 866-901

[128]   Dickens, Charles. *A Tale of Two Cities*. New York, Penguin, 1960., 36-37.

Jane Austen, *Pride and Prejudice*

"My reasons for marrying are, first, that I think it a right thing for every clergyman in easy circumstances (like myself) to set the example of matrimony in his parish; secondly, that I am convinced it will add very greatly to my happiness; and thirdly–which perhaps I ought to have mentioned earlier, that it is the particular advice and recommendation of the very noble lady whom I have the honor of calling patroness. Twice has she condescended to give me her opinion (unasked too!) on this subject; and it was but the very Saturday night before I left Hunsford–between our pools at quadrille, while Mrs. Jenkinson was arranging Miss de Bourgh's footstool, that she said, 'Mr. Collins, you must marry. A clergyman like you must marry. Choose properly, choose a gentlewoman for *my* sake; and for your own, let her be an active, useful sort of person, not brought up high, but able to make a small income go a good way. This is my advice. Find such a woman as soon as you can, bring her to Hunsford, and I will visit her.' Allow me, by the way, to observe, my fair cousin, that I do not reckon the notice and kindness of Lady Catherine de Bourgh as among the least of the advantages in my power to offer. You will find her manners beyond anything I can describe; and your wit and vivacity, I think, must be acceptable to her, especially when tempered with the silence and respect which her rank will inevitably excite."[129]

> **Writer's Workshop:** First, copy word for word. Second, imitate the following sentence, just as you have done for other passages above. *My reasons for marrying are, first, that I think it a right thing for every clergyman in easy circumstances (like myself) to set the example of matrimony in his parish; secondly, that I am convinced it will add very greatly to my happiness; and thirdly–which perhaps I ought to have mentioned earlier, that it is the particular advice and recommendation of the very noble lady whom I have the honor of calling patroness.*

---

[129]   Austen, Jane. *Pride and Prejudice*. New Jersey, Watermill Press, 1981., 143-144

In Summary, Lesson 22

Terms to Remember:
- Invective
- Vituperation
- Exordium

Lesson Twenty-Two Assignments

Assignment 22.1

Read Psalms 29 and 110. Then write your own psalm of at least 10 verses. It could be a praise of some aspect of His creation, or a statement of your faith. If you do not think you are imaginative enough to make up your own, then rewrite one of those Psalms in your own words.

Assignment 22.2

Take the fable "The Goose that Laid the Golden Egg," and rewrite it in 50 words. Make sure your story retains all the main points of the fable. Then rewrite the fable to 500 words. Add character and dialogue whenever necessary. Retain the main sense of the fable.

Assignment 22.3

Read and rewrite the fable, "A Bundle of Sticks." First write it in 55-60 words, retaining the original sense of the fable. Then rewrite it to be 500-700 words, adding character and dialogue but retaining the sense of the original.

Assignment 22.4

Read and rewrite the story, "A Dissertation Upon Roast Pig," by Charles Lamb (found in *AFE*). This is a spoof about how cooked meat was discovered. Tell the story in 150 words, retaining the sense of the original story. Then write your own story (300-600 words) about how something that is now commonplace came about. Some ideas are (suggested; you may come up with your own): the napkin, waving a hand to say hello or goodbye; the use of forks, knives and spoons to eat; the invention of popcorn or some other food; and so forth.

Assignment 22.5

Rewrite the following sentences in your own words. Rewrite them using your own words to make totally new sentences, but retaining the grammatical flow of the sentences. (Note: this is the nature of the Writer's Workshop we will do during Imitation exercises.)

Rewrite 1: The skyline in all directions is close at hand, the high wall of the woods and deep cleavages of shade. There is a perfect freedom in the mountains, but it belongs to the eagle and the elk, the badger and the bear.

    Example: The store in every corner is well laid out, the tall stacks of groceries and dusty corners of shelves. There is a wonderful smell in the aisles, but it belongs to the clerk and the cashier, the baker and the butcher.

    Rewrite 2: The evening wore on. The sun went down, the sounds of darkness came, the chirp, creak and flap of unseen creatures. All too soon it was time for bed.

    Example: The school day wore on. The bell rang, the cries of children resounded, the slam, bang and clang of lockers. All too soon came the time for second period.

Assignment 22.6
Write a biblical defense for or against one of the following: income taxation, socialism, a one world government. Two to three pages. Be ready to discuss in class.

Assignment 22.7
Choose one of the following *chreia* to write:

1. From John F. Kennedy's Inaugural Address: "And so, my fellow Americans: ask not what your country can do for you—ask what you can do for your country."

2. Proverbs 1.7 "The fear of the LORD is the beginning of knowledge, but fools despise wisdom and discipline."

3. Luke 3.10-14 "And the crowds asked him, 'What then shall we do?'And he answered them, 'Whoever has two tunics is to share with him who has none, and whoever has food is to do likewise.' Tax collectors also came to be baptized and said to him, 'Teacher, what shall we do?' And he said to them, 'Collect no more than you are authorized to do.' Soldiers also asked him, 'And we, what shall we do?' And he said to them, 'Do not extort money from anyone by threats or by false accusation, and be content with your wages.'"

Assignment 22.8
Choose one of the *chreia* above (Assignment 22.5) that you did not do last time.

Assignment 22.9
Make up your own saying, or a biblical saying, or find a saying that you like, and write a *chreia* for it. ("My momma always said, 'Life is like a box of chocolates. You never know what you're going to get.'")

Assignment 22.10
Write a Commonplace using the same style of writing. The first Commonplace will be "The life of the student is better than that of the uneducated."

Assignment 22.11
Write a second Commonplace on the following saying: "The king is not above the law."

Assignment 22.12
Compose an Invective on one or more of the following people or situations:
—Karl Marx
—Adolf Hitler
—Socialism
—Secular Humanism (naturalism)
—Evolution

Assignment 22.13
Read Edmund Burke's "Letter to a Noble Lord." How does it exemplify the qualities of invective?

Assignment 22.14

Read Robert Kennedy's speech "On the Assassination of Martin Luther King, Jr." How it is an example of *encomium*? How does he accomplish this? What rhetorical techniques does he employ? Two to three paragraphs.

Assignment 22.15

Using Kennedy's speech "On the Assassination of Martin Luther King, Jr.," write your own *encomium* of someone you admire who has passed away. It can be someone you know or someone from history. Three to five paragraphs.

Lesson Twenty-Three

The Fourth Canon: Memory

Further—good parts, strong memory, receptiveness, quickness of intuition, and the like, for all such faculties are productive of what is good. (Aristotle, *The Rhetoric & The Poetics of Aristotle* 1.1)

Now let me turn to the treasure-house of the ideas supplied by Invention, to the guardian of all the parts of rhetoric, the Memory. (Cicero, *Ad Herennium* 3.16)

It is only the young and callow and ignorant that admire rashness. Think before you speak. Know your subject. (Cass Gilbert)[130]

Memory, a highly lauded skill of the Greeks, is the fourth of Aristotle's Five Canons of Rhetoric, and is intricately tied to Delivery, the fifth canon. Cicero extolled memory as "that repository for all things...the keeper of the matter and words that are the fruits of thought and invention" and that, without this canon, "all the talents of the orator...though they be of the highest degree of excellence, will be of no avail."[131] The rhetorician must *know* what he speaks about, otherwise nothing else matters.

Students tend to find memory the most daunting of the Five Canons, perhaps vying with Delivery, depending on the student. Yet, this seems to stem from a misunderstanding of memory—or at least an over-zealous emphasis on the *memorization* aspect of this canon. Yes, Cicero and others follow the traditional definition of the word, saying that the memory "is also to be exercised, by learning accurately by heart as many of our own writings, and those of others, as we can."[132] This is rote memory, which he does advocate. However, Cicero does not aim for rote memorization as the be-all, end-all of this Canon. Cicero champions the deeper understanding of a subject, which he calls *memory of matter*. Rote memorization is an important stepping stone toward that goal.

> Now, lest you should perchance regard the memorizing of words either as too difficult or as of too little use, and so rest content with the memorizing of matter, as being easier and more useful, I must advise you why I do not disapprove of memorizing words. I believe that they who wish to do easy things without trouble and toil must previously have been trained in more difficult things. Nor have I included memorization of words to enable us to get verse by rote, but rather as an exercise whereby to strengthen that other kind of memory, the memory of matter, which is of practical use. Thus we may without effort pass from this difficult training to ease in that other memory...So, since a ready memory is a useful thing, you see clearly with what great pains we must strive to acquire so useful a faculty. Once you know its uses you will be able to appreciate this advice. To exhort you further in the matter

---

[130] Gilbert, Cass. *Inventing the skyline: the architecture of Cass Gilbert.* Edited by Margaret Heilbrun, New York, Columbia University Press, 2000. 1

[131] Cicero, *De Oratore* 1.4.18 http://pages.pomona.edu/~cmc24747/sources/cic_web/de_or_1.htm

[132] Cicero, *De Oratore* 1.34.157 http://pages.pomona.edu/~cmc24747/sources/cic_web/de_or_1.htm

of memory is not my intention, for I should appear either to have lacked confidence in your zeal or to have discussed the subject less fully than it demands.[133]

Just as we learned grammar, times tables, states and their capitals, and many other pieces of knowledge by rote when we were children, they are but the foundation of deeper knowledge.

Thus, while this Canon rests upon the practice of word-for-word memorization, its end goal is not the ability to gorge and regurgitate information. The goal is *memory of matter*.

Memory of matter is about depth of knowledge, knowing your subject. Going back to the Latin, *materia* means a physical substance, as well as the substance or topic of discourse.[134] Cicero, who would have used the Latin here, is cutting to the heart of things: know the substance of which you speak, down to the bone.

When we tell our students about the Thesis project (SEE: Lesson 26), which not only contains a significant written portion, but also a delivery and defense aspect, they balk at the notion that they should memorize their entire fifteen- to twenty-minute speech. However, this is a project that we assign them before they begin their last year of high school, and they know that they will deliver it as a speech toward the end of that year. They have nearly nine months to work on it. This admonishment is not a sly way for us to ensure that they're writing their paper over the summer so that they have from September to May to memorize it. Rather, it is a reminder that they will be working on the project as a whole, from Invention (including a significant amount of research) to Delivery, for those nine months. By the time that their Thesis Defense date arrives, they should know their material backward and forward, upside-down and rightside-up, and every way in-between.

At its heart, the Thesis Defense tests the Canon of Memory, much more than the Canon of Delivery. The panel of Thesis judges then begin to question the student not on his recall of the information he has just presented (no one is asking what the third word of the sixth paragraph on the fifteenth page of his thesis was), but on his depth of knowledge: did you think through this aspect? Did you predict the effect that your theory or idea might have? or Did you consider how the secular world might react when you propose this Christian idea? The prepared student then must go deeper, beneath the words he wrote and spoke, discussing the philosophical or theological underpinnings of why and how he explored and came to the conclusions that he did. This is memory of matter, not merely memorization by rote.

All that being said, Cicero does clearly prescribe the practice of memorization as a prerequisite to memory of matter. And so, we shall begin to put the Canon of Memory into action through practicing memory. You'll notice that this will quickly transition us into the Fifth Canon: Delivery. We hone our memory so that we can deliver.

As to the technique of memorization, everyone who does so has a favorite method of committing words to memory. What works for some may not work for all. But those who memorize passages of scripture find it a rich, fulfilling exercise, because the Word of God is alive: "For the word of God is living and active, sharper than any two-edged sword, piercing to the division of soul and of spirit, of joints and of marrow, and discerning the thoughts and intentions of the heart" (*ESV*, Heb 4.12). The prophet Jeremiah praises God for his holy word: Your words were found, and I ate them, and your words became to me a joy and the delight of my heart, for I am called by

---

[133] Cicero, *Ad Herennium* 3.24
http://penelope.uchicago.edu/Thayer/E/Roman/Texts/Rhetorica_ad_Herennium/3*.html

[134] "Matter." Oxford Living Dictionaries, Oxford University Press, 2017, en.oxforddictionaries.com/definition/matter. Accessed 23 June 2017.

your name, O Lord, God of hosts (*ESV*, Jer 15.16). The act of eating God's word was prescribed by God himself when Jeremiah says in 1.9 "the Lord put out his hand and touched my mouth. And the Lord said to me, 'Behold, I have put my words in your mouth.'" (Jer 1.9) It's a beautiful depiction.

Psalm 119 praises God for His word. Verses 11 and 16 commend the act of committing it to heart: "I have stored up your word in my heart, that I might not sin against you…I will delight in your statutes; I will not forget your word" (*ESV* Ps 119.11, 16).

Some memorization techniques commonly used, not just for scripture:

- Memorize a few words at a time, adding more once you have begun to be comfortable with them.

- Write down the words by hand, then write them several more times, paying careful attention to each word.

- Say them out loud, over and over.

- Post them on your bathroom mirror and your refrigerator, next to your desk or bed (but not the windshield of your car!).

- Some find it useful to walk around while memorizing out loud.

- Ask someone to help you. Tell them to prompt you only when you ask for help, since you might just be pausing to let the rest of the words come to you.

Ten Tips for Memorizing Bible Verses[135]

[The main purpose of this article is to encourage memorization of Bible verses, but the principles are worthy regardless of what is memorized.]

Fix these words of mine in your hearts and minds; tie them as symbols on your hands and bind them on your foreheads. –Deuteronomy 11.18 (*NIV*)

What does it mean to fix God's words in your heart and mind? Among other things, it means to be continually conscious of the Bible's teachings as you go through your daily routine. And one practical way to make sure that God's words are always close at hand is to memorize verses and passages from the Bible.

At first glance, memorizing Bible verses might seem a strange activity. For many Christians, Bible verse memorization is something kids do in Sunday school, not something that serious adults do. And if you didn't grow up reciting memorized Bible verses to your Sunday school teacher, the idea of intentionally memorizing parts of a book–even the Book–might seem odd.

But there's power in the act of memorizing–of becoming so familiar with a word, phrase, or verse that it springs to mind instantly when something happens to trigger the memory. When you've truly internalized something, it can stay with you all your life–consider how easy it is to recall the lyrics to pop songs from your youth. And if you can still remember the lyrics to a Bon Jovi album from the '80s, you're quite capable of committing a few Bible verses to memory!

---

[135]   By Andy Rau, https://www.biblegateway.com/blog/2013/03/ten-tips-for-memorizing-bible-verses/
Reprinted with permission of Bible Gateway.

Ten Tips for Memorizing Bible Verses

1. Choose a verse to memorize that speaks to something in your life right now. A Bible verse that's relevant to what you're going through is easier to memorize than one that speaks to a topic that's abstract to you.

2. Start small. Choose a short verse to start with… and make it even shorter by breaking it down into pieces. Memorize the first five words in the verse first, and when you've got them down, add the next five. As you become more confident, you can add more words, sentences, and even entire verses—but don't add anything new until you've got the previous words down pat.

3. Write it down. A vast majority of Bible Gateway fans suggested this simple strategy: write the verse you're memorizing down on paper. But don't just write it once; write it many times—five or ten times is a good start (and some people write out their memory verses up to 50 times!). Physically writing the words out is an extremely useful tactile memory aid.

4. Say it out loud. Just as writing a verse out can help in memorizing it, so speaking the words aloud is an excellent way to burn them into your memory. One person suggested turning the radio off during your commute to work or school each day and reciting your memory verse out loud instead!

5. Incorporate the verse into your prayers. When you pray, include elements of the verse in your words to God. Pray that God will help you understand and apply the verse to your life. Pray for God's help in fixing the verse in your heart and mind.

6. Put it everywhere. Many people suggested writing your memory verse out on multiple index cards or sticky notes (combine this with tip number 3 above!) and putting them all over the place, so that you'll see the verse many times throughout your day. Tape the verse to your bathroom mirror or computer monitor. Tuck it into your purse, lunch sack, car glove compartment, school textbook, pockets… anywhere you'll see it. One person suggested making the verse your computer desktop background, and another goes so far as to laminate the verse and hang it in the shower!

7. Use music to help. Do you find it much easier to remember lyrics than spoken words? Try setting the Bible verse to a simple tune (perhaps repurposing a song you already know well) that you can sing to yourself. (If this sounds like a strange suggestion, consider that many famous hymns and worship songs use Bible verses as their lyrics, and were written specifically as aids for Bible verse memorization.)

8. Make it a game. Turn the act of memorizing into a personal challenge! You might write the verse out on flashcards, leaving key words blank, and quiz yourself. Get some friends or family members to help quiz you, or even to memorize the verse along with you and encourage/challenge you.

9. Translate the verse into a different language. This tip isn't for everyone, obviously, but several Bible Gateway fans suggested that if you're comfortable in more than one language, try translating your verse into a different language. Translation requires an intense focus on the meaning and language of a verse—an obvious help for memorization.

10. Repeat, repeat, repeat! Whatever strategy you follow in memorizing a Bible verse, do it repeatedly. Write it down, speak it out loud, sing it out, pray it—but whatever you do, do it over and over until it's a natural, reflexive action. The goal isn't to reduce it to a mindless, repeated activity, but to slowly press the verse into your memory through repetition. Repeat your memorization activity over the course of several hours, days, or even weeks to pace yourself—there's no prize for memorizing a Bible verse fastest; the point is to

internalize it over time. And that means you shouldn't be discouraged if it takes a while for the verse to "stick"—keep at it, and it will take root!

If you've never tried memorizing a Bible verse before, it's much easier than you think! Pick one or two of the strategies above and give them a try, adapting your strategy as you figure out what does and doesn't work for you. One thing is certain: you'll never regret spending more time focusing intently on God's Word. And there's nothing quite so wonderful as an encouraging Bible verse springing forth from memory at just the time you need to hear it.

Lesson Twenty-Three Assignments

Assignment 23.1

Select a passage of scripture to memorize. It should be 10-12 verses long. Print out the passage and turn it in to your teacher, who can read along as you speak. You will use this passage again later when we cover the Fifth Canon: Delivery.

Assignment 23.2

Select a speech, discourse, or other classical passage of literature. Practice it until it can be well done in front of an audience (3 to 5 minutes), with expression and interpretation (given meaning through the delivery of the words). Historic speeches and proclamations abound. Deliver something inspiring and classical.

Lesson Twenty-Four

The Fifth Canon:
Delivery–Style in the Spoken Word

These are the three things—volume of sound, modulation of pitch, and rhythm—that a speaker bears in mind. (Aristotle, *The Rhetoric & The Poetics of Aristotle*)

To avoid prolixity, I shall now begin my discussion of the subject, as soon as I have given you this one injunction: Theory without continuous practice in speaking is of little avail; from this you may understand that the precepts of theory offered ought to be applied in practice. (Cicero, *Ad Herennium*, Intro to Book I)

For skilful invention, elegant style, the artistic management of the parts comprising the case, and the careful memory of all these will be of no more value without delivery, than delivery alone and independent of these. (Cicero, ibid., 3.11)

The wise of heart is called discerning, and sweetness of speech increases persuasiveness...The heart of the wise makes his speech judicious and adds persuasiveness to his lips. (*ESV*, Proverbs 16.21, 23)

When an orator begins to speak aloud to his audience, he must consider that his or her words, as well as body language, must exude confidence, authority, and compassion. That compassion for the subject and for the audience must be evident throughout. Cicero asserts that delivery must be "impressive and graceful,"[136] and this is the point where speaking diverges from writing. The written word can, of course, be impressive, but even Shakespeare loses something when the words are trapped on the stage, not expressed as he intended. There is a reason that, on Inauguration Day, the president delivers an address rather than writing a blog post or taking out an ad in the newspaper. Delivery matters.

When delivering a speech, we build upon the written word. To once again recall Shakespeare, the inimitable Bard himself can be reduced to a cringe-worthy occasion when an apathetic 10th grader decides he or she does not want to deliver his words properly. How many times have you heard young children recite John 3.16 or Genesis 1.1 in Sunday school, speaking God's word without passion or anything resembling eloquence?

Grammar students at one school prepared all year for the Ephesians Chapel each May. They practiced and practiced memorizing a chapter of Ephesians–the first graders memorized chapter 1, the second graders did chapter 2, and so on, so that in sixth grade they had the entire book of Ephesians memorized, building year after year. The headmaster walked through the grammar school

---

[136]   Cicero, *Ad Herennium* 4.56

and, especially toward the end of the school year, as Ephesians Chapel drew closer, they all stood outside, reciting the verses in unison. It drove the headmaster, an actor, a bit crazy because he said they sounded like adorable little robots.

Delivery involves much more than simply speaking words aloud, or even memorizing them, much like writing involves much more than putting words on a page. There is a style that the rhetorician must employ, a voice he must utilize. What's more, just as your voice possesses a unique sound and quality that identifies you in the midst of others, your writing and speaking voices are unique as well.

Let's begin looking at the way a person conducts himself before an audience.

The Five Elements of Speaking: Voice, Contact with the Audience, Posture, Gesture, and Movement

I. Voice

There are many, varied aspects to Voice, for it is far more than simply reciting words aloud. Consider these **Six Aspects of Voice**:

- **Volume**
  First and foremost, you're giving a speech–this means you need to be heard. Do not always depend on a microphone and sound system to work; sometimes that will not always be available. Consider how to use your voice both to a room of noisy people, such as at an awards dinner or in a very large auditorium, and to a mid-sized room with an attentive audience. Maybe you need a microphone, but maybe it's not available. Look at the back row and address your listeners there.

- **Pitch**
  This is the general sound of your voice: high or low. As you no doubt know, this is as unique to each individual as a fingerprint, with as many ranges and pitches as there are people. A person has a natural pitch to his voice, yet he must imbue his pitch with tone to convey meaning.

- **Tone**
  The tone of your voice is important as well. Tone is the emotion you add into your words. You need to consider this as you prepare for and practice your speech. Listen for tone in everyday life; watch movies and listen to audiobooks. Pay attention to what people do (usually unconsciously) as they inject emotion into their voices.

- **Intonation**
  To avoid sounding monotone (the tone of your voice never varies up or down), vary your tone. Listen to how a voice goes up slightly at the end of a question, or drops slightly at the end of a thought. Also, think about when making a list of things, your tone tends to go up slightly as you introduce each element. After the word "but" in a compound sentence, we tend to lower our intonation (Ex: Billy thought he passed the test, but he actually failed).

- **Enunciation**
  Enunciation is the key to defeating mumbling. Younger people naturally speak faster, and when you're nervous, you're almost guaranteed to speak with even more speed. Know this as you prepare: time yourself speaking quickly and know if you're going to need to compensate for either time or clarity. Read aloud through your speech and make sure you

haven't used words you cannot pronounce reliably. Find yourself a synonym if you keep stumbling over the same word. Over-articulate your words: pronounce words as clearly as you can. And LISTEN to yourself. (See the box below: Eloquence.)

- **Pace**
  Speak at a speed which does not tire or overburden (or bore) your readers. You will tend to speak quickly, due to nerves, when in front of an audience–compensate for this. Pay attention to punctuation marks and pause properly with each (a two-beat count for periods and one for others).
  Exercise self-reflection as you practice speaking regularly in this class and others. Know yourself and be deliberate in each of these aspects of speaking.

Eloquence, Enunciation, and Elocution

Enunciation, as described above, is only part of eloquent speech. Your audience needs to know that you care about your subject, and also that you take care in the way that they hear you. That means listening to yourself in all the bulleted items above, but also paying attention to other vocal mishaps.

Think back to the last time you took part in a classroom discussion (or even in mealtime conversation with friends or family around a table). Can you recall how many times the word "like" was used by everyone? (And we're not talking about the verb "like"!) "I mean, like, I went to meet her and she said, like, 'I've been waiting here for, like, forever!'" Sadly, for some, that's probably not an exaggeration.

Admit it: sometimes your conversations go exactly that way. One group of students had such a problem using "like" that we set up a penalty of 5 cents for every misuse of "like." One student, in just one class period of a round table discussion, owed $2.50! (We used that money to have a party with donuts at the end of the speech unit, and we bought a LOT of donuts with all the penalties.) Another student admitted later that her boss, at her after-school job at the front desk of a fitness gym, told her to clean up her problem with "like" or she was fired. She was grateful that we had begun to work on it.

Go a little further, though. "Like" is not the only problem we have. Count the usage of "like" and also the following discussion fillers:

- Um
- Uh
- I mean
- I know, right?
- Ya know

Is there more? Ask your teachers and parents what they notice. Think of what your audience hears, and think very carefully about what impression they get from listening to your discussion fillers. Do you sound like you know what you're saying? How about the girl whose boss told her to stop the repetition of "like"? She admitted that it made her sound uneducated.

Also pay careful attention to your enunciation so that your audience can clearly understand what you say. Ask your teacher, classmates, or parents to listen to you read aloud (see the Psalm exercise below). Some frequently mispronounced words and phrases will make themselves known:

Phrase:	**Sometimes sounds like:**
From the end of the heavens	"From th'end o'the heavens"
The law of the Lord is perfect	"The law-o-th-Lor' is perfeck"

One student's speech included the term "human being" several times. We wondered what she meant when all we heard was "human bean." In this case, like the examples above, think about enunciating the final consonants of words instead of slurring them all together.

Practice out loud. Perhaps even record yourself speaking and listen to your enunciation. Print out the passage you will be reading aloud, hand a copy to someone (a friend or parent), and have them circle the parts where you are not enunciating well, or rushing through. Then use that printout to practice again.

II.   Contact with the Audience–more than just eye contact

Make the audience feel like you are talking to them–a speech without an audience is just a person standing alone in a room, talking to himself. Look directly at your audience. Look at one person, then at another randomly but not roving back and forth. If you think that looking at their eyes will make you lose your concentration, look at their foreheads. They will still think you are looking at them! Be interested in their reactions and emotions.

Don't apologize before you even begin. ("I was sick last night and didn't get a chance to work on this, so..." Or "This may not be very good, but oh well.") What does a pre-speech apology tell your audience? *Lower your expectations.* Some among you probably hope to do exactly that so that your audience is pleasantly surprised, or at least not disappointed. Your teacher should mark you down for this!

Concentrating on your notes reduces the effectiveness of the speech. This means you must know the content of your speech so well that you don't have to spend so much mental energy on remembering your speech (think back to the fourth Canon, Memory). You can still refer to notes from time to time; reading longer direct quotes so that you don't misquote them is good academic practice. However, keeping your eyes glued to your script tells the audience that they aren't worth your time.

A speech is a two-way interaction between the speaker and the audience. Use what they're giving you; feed off the audience. If you make a particularly impressive point, they may applaud–let them! They may laugh (hopefully appropriately: with you, not at you)–pause for a moment. Bowling over them will make both you and your audience feel awkward.

Watch Geraldine Ferraro's speech at the Democratic National Convention in 1984 (found on YouTube) and watch how she interacts with her audience, not only explicitly (actually verbally responding to them) but implicitly as well, pausing, laughing, smiling as they react to her.

III.   Posture

You should stand comfortably, not slouching; upright but not stiff. Stand with weight on both feet, not rocking back and forth or side to side, or up and down, which might make your audience seasick. Avoid keeping your hands in your pockets but comfortable at your sides or on the podium. It's entirely acceptable to rest your hands on your podium, which will allow for a good place upon which to build your gestures.

IV.   Gesture

We gesture in a speech to emphasize a point. Refrain from fidgeting with a pen or your paper, pushing your hair behind your ear continuously, adjusting your clothing, jingling coins in your pocket, and so forth. A good rule is to have one hand guide your eyes down the margin of the page so you do not lose track of where you are. The audience cannot see you do this, and it is a handy way to keep track.

Flipping papers during your speech is distracting. Make simple gestures to shift your papers: slide one over to the side instead of picking them all up to stack the used one in back, which is distracting.

Gestures do not need to be forced. Don't decide ahead of time to point during a certain part of your speech; your gestures should arise from the topic. Planning gestures will likely distract you, as you may be thinking more about gesturing during the speech than what you're about to say. A former student planned to emphatically pound his podium as he made a particular point during his Thesis Defense. He forgot to do it as he actually spoke the point, missing his mark by about two seconds, which made it seem as though he was having a fit, for he also was in the middle of pausing between sentences when he remembered to strike the podium with his fist. Thus, his action immediately informed his audience that he had missed something and remembered it at the wrong time, distracting them from the point he was, actually, eloquently making. It took everyone out of the moment.

Gestures have three benefits: they increase the speaker's energy and self-confidence; they assist in the communication of ideas; and they help hold the audience's attention. Facial expressions are important: a smile, a frown of concern. Look at your expressions in the mirror or record yourself as you practice speaking. Then go back and analyze what you do.

Watch good speakers, such as John F. Kennedy, Martin Luther King Jr., Bill Clinton, Franklin Delano Roosevelt, Ronald Reagan, and take note of their gestures. They don't need to animate every moment of their speech with gyrating hand motions (which would be distracting, in itself), but they punctuate specific moments with clear gestures: a closed fist, a pointed finger, an open palm. Similarly, look at a video of Adolf Hitler speaking. He practiced vehemently gesturing, and he looks like the madman he actually was. Winston Churchill could have made huge gestures to drive home his points, but instead he minimized his movements, and often even tucked his thumbs into his suspenders. Take some time to consider how (given the times and the content of his speeches) this impacted his audience.

V.   Movement

Just like gestures can communicate and draw your audience in (or be off-putting), so can movement. Think body language: if you stand up in the front with your arms folded across your chest, you're projecting an air of standoffishness. If you wiggle and squirm, fiddle with your hair or a piece of jewelry (or even a watch), your audience knows you're nervous. Girls, wear a barrette or hair tie to help you avoid playing with your hair; guys, maybe get a haircut before the big day.

Stand fairly still. Do not weave or pace. You can shift from one foot to another when making a new point, lean forward or step back occasionally for emphasis. Approach the podium confidently, not slouching or acting silly or as though to a gallows. Walk self-assuredly but not arrogantly. Make a good impression on your audience: if your audience knows you're about to begin speaking, whether you've just been announced or a program says so, their eyes are on you before you take the stage.

Don't rush into your speech. Take a moment to get comfortable, take a deep breath, look out over the audience, and smile.

In-Class Activity

Psalm 19 Read-Aloud

The purpose of this activity is to allow you to practice your physical presence in the room, as well as work on your diction and enunciation.

Take about 5-10 minutes to familiarize yourself with the text of the Psalm. For consistency in critique, all students should read from the same version of the Bible. We recommend the English Standard Version, but the New King James Versions also contains beautiful, poetic language that lends itself to this assignment. Sometimes students find the language difficult.

Each student will, in turn, walk to the front of the classroom and stand, preferably behind a podium, to deliver a recitation of this Psalm. Each recitation will be followed by a brief class critique.

Interpretation is important anytime we deliver a speech or read out loud. Here we do not mean translation of language; rather, we mean presenting the passage with appropriate emotion. If you read "The heavens declare the glory of God" with a monotone voice with your face a lifeless mask, your audience will receive it apathetically. But if you say it like it was meant to be said—with the joy with which the Psalmist wrote it—how much more will your audience get out of it?

As a class, listen closely for the *Six Aspects of Voice* from this lesson. Is the student speaking too quickly, too quietly, pausing at the wrong moments (or not pausing where punctuation occurs), reading in a monotone, stumbling over difficult words?

This is an excellent opportunity to practice *constructive criticism* and *self-reflection* as a class. The comments each student makes should build-up while still critiquing. The classroom should be a safe place for putting yourself out there and learning. Speaking is learned by doing, and the class must purposefully (respectfully) build one another up.

The class must also be *self-aware* and self-reflective, meaning that they can critique all they like, but they must also introspectively consider what they say to one another, recognizing that they must apply these things to their own speaking. For example, when reading verses 12-13 of Psalm 19, if students regularly provide critique about reading the question mark and exclamation points with the proper emotional emphasis and then do not apply this when it's their turn, they've only taken the opportunity to point out the speck in their peers' eyes, while ignoring the log in their own.

In-Class Activity

Poetry Read-aloud

Look at the instructions for the Psalm Read-aloud and apply those same rules to this exercise. Lewis Carroll's "Jabberwocky" is a poem comprised largely of gibberish (though some of these words–like "chortle"–have been incorporated into the English language). This will actually allow you to practice each of the five Elements of Speaking without necessarily being distracted by meaning: you can play with the effects of the poem and the words.

Jabberwocky
(from *Through the Looking Glass* by Lewis Carroll)

'Twas brillig, and the slithy toves
Did gyre and gimble in the wabe;
All mimsey were the borogroves,
And the mome raths outgrabe.

"Beware the Jabberwock, my son!
The jaws that bite, the claws that catch!
Beware the Jubjub bird, and shun
The frumious Bandersnatch!"

He took his vorpal sword in hand:
Long time the manxome foe he sought—
So rested he by the Tumtum tree,
And stood awhile in thought.

And as in uffish thought he stood,
The Jabberwock, with eyes of flame,
Came whiffling through the tulgey wood,
And burbled as it came!

One, two! One, two! And through and through
The vorpal blade went snicker-snack!
He left it dead, and with its head
He went galumphing back.

"And hast thou slain the Jabberwock?
Come to my arms, my beamish boy!
O frabjous day! Callooh! Callay!"
He chortled in his joy.

'Twas brillig, and the slithy toves
Did gyre and gimble in the wabe;
All mimsy were the borogroves,
And the mome raths outgrabe.

As you read "Father William"–also by Lewis Carroll–aloud, have fun with the pacing and the humor of it. It's also got a bit of nonsense (though not through the use of fake words, as in "Jabberwocky," but through this light, airy strange encounter). In this story, focus on both your interpretation and in the enunciation. And when you have rhymes and rhythms, there is a tendency to become rather sing-song when reading aloud. Instead, find words to emphasize in each stanza.

Father William
(from *Alice in Wonderland* by Lewis Carroll)

"You are old, Father William," the young man said
"And your hair has become very white;
And yet you incessantly stand on your head—
Do you think, at your age, it is right?"

"In my youth," Father William replied to his son,
"I feared I would injure the brain;
But now I'm perfectly sure I have none,
Why, I do it again and again."

"You are old," said the youth, "as I mentioned before,
And have grown most uncommonly fat;
Yet you turned a back somersault in at the door—
Pray, what is the reason of that?"

"In my youth" said the sage, as he shook his gray locks.

"I kept all my limbs very supple

By the use of this ointment—one shilling the box—

Allow me to sell you a couple."

"You are old," said the youth, "and your jaws are too weak

For anything tougher than suet;

Yet you finished the goose, with the bones and the beak—

Pray, how did you manage to do it?"

"In my youth," said his father, "I took to the law,

And argued each case with my wife;

And the muscular strength, which it gave to my jaw,

Has lasted the rest of my life."

"You are old," said the youth, "one would hardly suppose

That your eye was as steady as ever;

Yet you balanced an eel on the end of your nose;

What made you so awfully clever?"

"I have answered three questions, and that is enough."

Said his father; "don't give yourself airs!

Do you think I can listen all day to such stuff?

Be off, or I'll kick you downstairs!"

Fluency of Speech: Where Memory meets Delivery

When an orator begins preparing his speech for delivery, he must consider at what level of fluency he aims for when he delivers the speech. Does he hope to (or is he required to) speak fully from memory? Few speakers have the need to do so. Even when the president delivers an address, he utilizes the teleprompter or has his speech before him. More often, speakers have their notes in front of themselves and speak from an outline.

Before you begin speaking, you need to decide how you will deliver the speech. Remember that the delivery criteria (Posture, Movement, Gestures, Voice, Contact with the Audience) still apply. There are Four Types of Delivery:

1. Reading from a manuscript
2. Reciting from memory
3. Speaking impromptu
4. Speaking from notes or an outline

Each has its own benefits and drawbacks. You need to choose the right method for the right occasion (of course, your teacher may choose the method for you, as the situation or assignment warrants).

1. Reading from a manuscript

Some speeches must be delivered word for word, exactly as written. A full script is required for this. A political (deliberative) address is typically read verbatim from a manuscript. Consider why this is. What does a politician or a pastor (though not all pastors do this) want to get specifically right, and why?

Benefits:

Accuracy & Precision
Ensuring figures of speech and direct quotations

Drawbacks:

Tends to sound like "reading to" rather than "talking with" (meaning that you need to practice more before speaking).
Difficulty in establishing rapport with your audience because you have the manuscript wall between you and them–and they know it.

2. Reciting from Memory

This is the most impressive–if you can manage it. What speeches are memorized nowadays? How often does this occur?

Benefits:

This allows for a rapport between you and your audience as well as maintaining accuracy and precision of language.

Drawbacks:

Demands intense preparation.
Messing up is awkward, especially if you *really* forget your place.
This can lead to sounding like reading or reciting, rather than speaking or persuasion.

3. Speaking Impromptu

This can happen in class, at parties (especially weddings). Little or no immediate preparation or notes is given.

Benefits:

Tailored to the situation in a way that would be difficult to prepare for.
Connecting with the audience.

Drawbacks:

Nervousness leads to talking too fast which leads to awkwardness (maybe lots of 'uhs').
Lack of prep may lead to lack of depth

4. Speaking from notes or an outline

This is the most common speaking style today, which combines the Full Manuscript, Memorized, and Impromptu styles.

If you're adapting an essay into a speech (as our Thesis students must do), start this process by making a new outline based on the finished product. Break down the essay itself into sections, with topic sentences, quotes, intentionally-worded sentences. Think: what do I want to preserve word-for-word and what can I speak about off-the-cuff?

A former student called this the Treasure Map method (which is more fun than the Bullet Point or Outline method). You're planning the speech, point by point, but not memorizing it word-by-word or sentence-by-sentence, allowing yourself to utilize Cicero's advice about *memorizing the matter*–demonstrating that you know your topic incredibly well. This allows you to maintain the progression of the main points and arguments of your speech, while giving you the freedom (which can be scary, in itself) to connect with your audience a bit more.

Benefits:

More precise than impromptu
Allows for spontaneity and directness
Adaptable to the situation
Conversational because of minimal notes
More connection with the audience!

Drawbacks:

You need to <u>prepare</u> for your presentation with practice!

Speechwriting Tip: Number of words per minute

An average ten-minute speech contains from 1400 to 1600 words. This means a minute is around 150 words. Keep in mind that this is just an average!

Qualities of a Good Speaker, according to Scripture

In an earlier lesson we discussed the qualities of *Ethos*: ethical persuasion. The content of our discourse–what we write and what we speak–must reflect uprightness of character. Where can our standards be found? In scripture we find the source for all godly and upright speech.

The writer and speaker who loves the Lord our God, we believe, must aspire to please the Lord and speak truth to others, as Moses did with beautiful metaphor in Deuteronomy 32.1-3:

> Give ear, O heavens, and I will speak, and let the earth hear the words of my mouth. May my teaching drop as the rain, my speech distill as the dew, like gentle rain upon the tender grass, and like showers upon the herb. For I will proclaim the name of the Lord; ascribe greatness to our God! The Rock, his work is perfect, for all his ways are justice. A God of faithfulness and without iniquity, just and upright is he. (*ESV*)

Remember from the lesson in *Ethos* that the writer/speaker will jeopardize his credibility when he comes across as irritated, sarcastic, and peevish. So let's explore what Scripture has to say about speaking the truth in love.

Other qualities of a speaker:

1. Extend kindness to your audience:

- He has told you, O man, what is good; and what does the Lord require of you but to do justice, and to love kindness, and to walk humbly with your God? (*ESV*, Micah 6.8)

- Put on then, as God's chosen ones, holy and beloved, compassion, kindness, humility, meekness, and patience, bearing with one another and, if one has a complaint against another, forgiving each other; as the Lord has forgiven you, so you also must forgive. And above all these put on love, which binds everything together in perfect harmony. And let the peace of Christ rule in your hearts, to which indeed you were called in one body. And be thankful. Let the word of Christ dwell in you richly, teaching and admonishing one another in all wisdom, singing psalms and hymns and spiritual songs, with thankfulness in your hearts to God. And whatever you do, in word or deed, do everything in the name of the Lord Jesus, giving thanks to God the Father through him. (*ESV*, Col 3.12-17)

2. Humble, not boastful:

- Likewise, you who are younger, be subject to the elders. Clothe yourselves, all of you, with humility toward one another, for "God opposes the proud but gives grace to the humble." Humble yourselves, therefore, under the mighty hand of God so that at the proper time he may exalt you, casting all your anxieties on him, because he cares for you. (*ESV*, 1 Peter 5.5-7)

- It is better to be humble in spirit with the lowly than to divide the spoil with the proud. He who gives attention to the word will find good, and blessed is he who trusts in the Lord. The wise in heart will be called understanding, and sweetness of speech increases persuasiveness. (*NASV*, Pr 16.19-21)

3. Submit your speech to the Lord

- My son, give attention to my words; incline your ear to my sayings. Do not let them depart from your sight; keep them in the midst of your heart. For they are life to those who find them and health to all their body. Watch over your heart with all diligence, for from it flow the springs of life. Put away from you a deceitful mouth and put devious speech far from you. Let your eyes look directly ahead and let your gaze be fixed straight in front of you. Watch the path of your feet and all your ways will be established. Do not turn to the right nor to the left; turn your foot from evil. (*NASV*, Pr 4.20-27)

4. Be pleasant in manner

- Righteous lips are the delight of kings, and he who speaks right is loved. (*NASV*, Pr 16.13)
- The heart of the wise instructs his mouth And adds persuasiveness to his lips. Pleasant words are a honeycomb, Sweet to the soul and healing to the bones. (*NASV*, Pr 16.23-24)

5. Be ready with a defense of your faith (1 Peter 3.15):

This does not necessarily mean ONLY when you witness to or debate with an unbeliever. When you are a believer, what you say and do reflects God's grace.

- Continue steadfastly in prayer, being watchful in it with thanksgiving. At the same time, pray also for us, that God may open to us a door for the word, to declare the mystery of Christ, on account of which I am in prison—that I may make it clear, which is how I ought to speak. Walk in wisdom toward outsiders, making the best use of the time. Let your speech always be gracious, seasoned with salt, so that you may know how you ought to answer each person. (*ESV*, Col 4.2-6)

Speak the truth in love:

- And he gave the apostles, the prophets, the evangelists, the pastors and teachers, to equip the saints for the work of ministry, for building up the body of Christ, until we all attain to the unity of the faith and of the knowledge of the Son of God, to mature manhood, to the measure of the stature of the fullness of Christ, so that we may no longer be children, tossed to and fro by the waves and carried about by every wind of doctrine, by human cunning, by craftiness in deceitful schemes. Rather, speaking the truth in love, we are to grow up in every way into him who is the head, into Christ, from whom the whole body, joined and held together by every joint with which it is equipped, when each part is working properly, makes the body grow so that it builds itself up in love. (*ESV*, Eph 4.1-16)
- Put away falsehoods and speak the truth. (*ESV*, Eph 4.17-32)

Persuasive Speech

<u>The Persuasive Speech contains a number of components:</u>

1. Attention-getter: Presentation of Problem
   a. Examples
   b. Thesis (proposal of solution)
2. Examples to Ponder
   a. Outcome (the effects this problem can have)
   b. Additional example to impact your audience
3. Explanation of Proposal
   a. Restatement of thesis
   b. Facts to prove your point
   c. Effects, consequences of solution
4. Refutation of the opposition
5. Closing
   a. Move your audience to action

The time allowed can vary. Remember that the proportion should be similar to a classical

---

rhetorical discourse. Use the following for a ten-minute speech; adjust if your teacher wants a different time allotment.

1. 1.5 minute
2. 2 minutes
3. 3 minutes
4. 2 minutes
5. 1.5 minute

Look at the list of possible persuasive speech topics for ideas, below. These can just get you started. If you have other ideas, go ahead and use them.

- Human rights violations justify a national sovereignty violation
- Animals have rights, too
- Even hate speech is protected free speech (racial, religious, homosexual, etc.)
- Christians should not vote for a non-Christian candidate
- What are the moral implications of human cloning?
- Can the assassination of a dictator be justified?
- How should Christians be involved in the arts and entertainment? (see *Roaring Lambs* by Bob Briner)
- Living within your means, and the problem with spending (government and individual)
- Should governments negotiate with terrorists?
- Is physical force justified in punishing children?
- Is China taking over America?
- Gun companies should be held responsible for gun crimes
- Gambling should be outlawed
- The best way to stop terrorism
- Should governments censor material on the internet?

Impromptu Speech

As mentioned above, the need to speak off the cuff (impromptu) may not arise regularly, but it almost certainly will come up. Remember the benefits of an impromptu speech: connecting with your audience in the moment. Sometimes you're given the opportunity to briefly prepare your remarks ahead of time.

Practice for this eventuality here, with these prompts. Choose two of these topics and write speeches for them.

1. You have been asked to stand up and speak at a reception. Beforehand, the master of ceremonies has asked you to speak for 30 seconds. He has asked you to talk about your faith in Jesus Christ: how you met the Lord and what He means to you today.

2. You are competing for a grant that would pay for a year of college or training at the institution of your choice. You must speak for 30 seconds about your life-goals, your reasons for your goal and perhaps how you plan to meet these goals.

3. You are at a banquet in heaven and a new group of people has joined you. You have 30 seconds to describe the guest of honor: Jesus Christ.

4. A panel of teachers and politicians has gathered to decide whether to outlaw private Christian schools and home schools. You have been given 45 seconds to defend your side (what is your side?).

5. You must stand before a panel of pastors and elders and convince them that you should be allowed to go overseas on a mission trip (you can invent the place and purpose) for which they will be providing the funds. They have given you 45 seconds.

6. Describe your strongest asset which you think would be a benefit to this program (academic or missionary). What benefit does your particular asset have over other contestants? 45 seconds

7. Address the atheist who says, "Show me evidence of God and I will believe. Have Him do a miracle; let me hear Him speak. So far I see nothing." 1 minute

8. From a Christian perspective, how would you solve the problem of hunger in India? 45 seconds[137]

---

[137] Adapted from Henry Lee Ewbank, *Discussion and Debate.* New York: F.S. Crofts & Co., 1946.

Lesson Twenty-Four Assignments

Assignment 24.1

Remember that Psalms are meant to be read aloud. Look up two different translations of Psalm 19 (we recommend the *ESV*, the *NKJV*, the *NASB*, and the *Amplified*). Take a careful look at the entire Psalm and in two to three paragraphs answer the following questions: What is the purpose of this Psalm? How is it constructed (in other words, what happens from section to section)? Comment on the psalmist's use of language to carry out his intent. What effect does this kind of psalm have on the audience—the reader or the listener? How can *you* apply this to your speaking style?

Assignment 24.2

Find another Psalm of a similar length (up to 24 verses, perhaps) that has an entirely different purpose. Look up two different versions. Answer the very same questions about this Psalm that you see in assignment 24.1.

Assignment 24.3

Write a persuasive speech to present in class. Use the suggested format from this lesson.

Assignment 24.4

Read Mark Twain's essay "My Childhood on a Missouri Farm," found in *AFE*. Answer the questions found at the end of the essay. Then write an essay of your own (as described in the Mark Twain questions), using descriptive phrases to appeal to the senses. Be creative, use sensory words, but be realistic. Two to three pages. These can be read aloud to one another in class.

Assignment 24.5

Read Robert Kennedy's speech "On the Assassination of Martin Luther King, Jr." Also, watch the speech (it can easily be found online). Note that this is an impromptu speech. Analyze it for its rhetorical qualities. How does he still follow the rhetorical structure, and what does he do that is impressive for it being an unplanned speech? Five paragraphs (this is not a full analysis, though it can be turned into one).

Assignment 24.6

Watch another pair of videos of speeches, as directed by your teacher, or select two more TED talks (as allowed by your teacher). Take notes on the effectiveness of the speeches and the speakers. What are their techniques? What works? What was their main point? How did they prove it? This will be a graded discussion next week.

Assignment 24.7

Look at the qualities of a good speaker according to scripture toward the end of this lesson. Choose one of the following discourses and set it against the qualities presented here. How does the speaker demonstrate the qualities of a good speaker? Or does he not?

- "*Challenger* Speech" by Ronald Reagan
- "A Contaminated Moral Environment" by Vaclav Havel

- "We Shall Fight on the Beaches" by Winston Churchill
- "Axis of Evil" by George W. Bush
- "We Shall Overcome" by Lyndon B. Johnson
- "Address on the German Invasion of Poland" by Neville Chamberlain
- "On the Horrors of the Slave Trade" by William Wilberforce

Assignment 24.8

Write your own problem and solution. Think of this as preparation for a persuasive speech, which you will soon present. Once you write this you can decide whether it will work as a speech. Use a similar format to the discourse above (what portion of it you have read). Present a problem, give examples of this problem, bring up an outside source to affirm your ideas, then conclude. Be sure to have a thesis. Length: Five paragraphs.

Invention: Research

"Google" is not a synonym for "research." (Dan Brown, *The Lost Symbol*)

Research is formalized curiosity. It is poking and prying with a purpose. (Zora Neale Hurston)

At this point the teacher may be ready to assign a research paper project for the class. It could come at this time, or the teacher could wish to move it to an earlier time in the school year.

Resources

Since most students have done research projects in the past, this will mostly be review. However, students must all be up to speed on their research (and research paper-writing) skills so that not a lot of time must be spent teaching the "grammar" of writing a research paper.

Much research today is done on the Internet. While this is a handy source, two problems might arise if this is the only source used. First, not all Internet sites are reliable sources of information. You will not be able to rely on "Dave's World War Two Page" as readily as you could on a university or museum website. Remember, too, that some unreliable sources will not contain the full text of a document, or it might be full of transcription errors, or just plain factually wrong.

Second, some very reliable, informative sources have not yet made it to the Internet. You may be missing out on some important facts or fascinating sources from books or old magazines if you rely solely on the Internet.

Methods

As rapidly as technology changes, any methods of research and note-gathering may become outdated after this textbook is published, but the principles will remain largely the same. Of utmost importance, we emphasize that you MUST go to the library (if you live in the US or some country in which you have access to a good library). The librarians there will know and be able to instruct you in the latest research tools.

Notes

When we refer to "note," we mean the medium you choose, or your teacher instructs, for the purpose of gathering research. We suggest either an organized Word document, a spreadsheet, or 3x5 notecards. For the purposes of this textbook, we will refer to your notes—electronic or on paper—as "cards."

Every bit of information that is obtained for research must be kept on note cards, either electronic or paper. Even the list of sources themselves must be listed on note cards. Use a separate card for each source. A source card must have the same information on it that you will use on your bibliography: Author or editor, title of article or book, publication title, publishing company, city, and year. **(See below, Standard Format. Also refer to MLA in Writing Tips Lesson 1 of this book.)** The page numbers that you use may be placed here, but they most certainly must be placed on the card on which you write the information from that page! Obviously if it is an internet source, you will need to provide other information, such as URL, etc.

Give each source a code: A, B, C, etc.

Every card should contain the source code. Place the code you have assigned for that source. (For instance, if your first source is a book by John Smith, assign code A to that book and make sure that every card containing information from this book has the A.) This way you will never lose track of where you got the information.

Each card must also contain a topic word or phrase. If your paper is to discuss Civil War armaments, you will want to break down your paper into smaller subjects, such as cannons, sidearms, bayonets, rapid-fire guns, etc. The card should have one of these topic words written at the top for easier organization.

Each card should also contain the page number(s) used. Number the card (A1, A2, A3, etc., for the source and the number of the cards from that source).

Outline

A topical outline is necessary for organizing all the information into a paper that progresses well, makes sense, and flows logically. Different teachers require different formats. Some prefer topical outlines rather than full sentences, as the outline is a tool for the student. Items in Roman numerals should be major sections of the paper (Introduction, Body, Conclusion). Capital letters should indicate paragraphs. Think of the organization of this paper to follow the Arrangement we have learned in rhetoric. What kind of introduction will you use? Where is the thesis? How are you supporting the thesis?

Thesis-Driven

Since this is something we have spent time learning in rhetoric, a thesis statement must be included. Remember that a thesis statement is one or two sentences that affirm or deny something about a particular subject. Your research and the paper you write must support your thesis statement. This is a major portion of your grade. If you cannot come up with a thesis statement, it might mean that you are writing an historical report rather than a thesis paper. You may need to go back and try again.

Standard Format (MLA, APA, Turabian)

Every paper must adhere to a particular style format. Understanding this basic fact is the first step to formatting a solid paper with a bibliography.

Many schools use the MLA style, as this is what most colleges and universities require. Several different style manuals are accepted and required by various institutions. The MLA (Modern Language Association of America) is the generally accepted English Department style, though others, particularly APA (American Psychological Association) and Turabian, are becoming popular. This textbook will require MLA, while other teachers in other situations may require another form. Learning HOW to learn about this is more important than memorizing and regurgitating a specific style.

In-text Citations and Works Cited Pages

Every paper must contain a bibliography (now called "Works Cited"). See a style book (such as MLA) for the format for a Works Cited page. Parenthetical, in-text citations are the most accepted way to refer to your sources (as opposed to footnotes). Refer to a style book for use of endnotes.

Lesson Twenty-Five Assignments

Assignment 25.1

Select an element of pop culture (film, television, music, video games) that you love, and brainstorm what you love about it. Then, dig deeper: research that element and discuss how it came to be and how it became part of the larger pop culture whole. Why is that element so significant to pop culture? Why is it important to you? Follow the structure of a rhetorical discourse here.

Assignment 25.2

Go to debate.org and choose a topic (in consultation with your teacher) found there. Research both sides of the topic, then argue which side you believe is right, and find the refutations for why the other side is wrong. Make sure you're giving both sides their due. Follow the structure of a rhetorical discourse here.

Assignment 25.3

Choose debate teams and a topic. Spend one week planning your debate, then you will have your debate in a timed session during class. Do your research and be prepared!

Lesson Twenty-Six

The Thesis Project:
The Culmination of Rhetoric

The Thesis Project is the culmination of your study of rhetoric. It demonstrates that you've brought together all the myriad aspects of rhetoric together in one cohesive, synthesized form. Look over the requirements of a Rhetorical Analysis–all the things you've spent time reviewing and critiquing each other's works. Now, it's your turn. You need to do all the things you've studied in theory up to now.

This project comes in many different forms, depending on the school you attend and the teacher in charge of the Thesis Project. For some schools, it's a graduation requirement; for others, simply a long paper at the end of their rhetoric year. It's up to your teacher to decide how much emphasis to place on this project, but we recommend that you begin at the outset of your senior year. Here, what we will describe is the one we have employed for many years and has proven successful in multiple schools. However, variations to this style will certainly occur.

Topic

Pick a historical, social, economical, governmental, scientific, biblical, rhetorical, or literary topic to research. At most classical schools, this will cover the modern era (your teacher may direct you otherwise) and must be relevant to the current day: any topic that you have the desire and interest to explore further and argue more in-depth. For example, you can choose a person who significantly impacted the world (NOT a biography), a religion or worldview that has developed, a battle or war, a technological advancement, a theory of philosophy or government and its effects, or myriad other topics.

Pick a topic about which you could argue a thesis from a biblical worldview. That means it cannot be "just the facts." It must be something on which you could argue a point. This must apply a biblical worldview, taking it further than simply agreeing or disagreeing with a subject. As with any thesis-driven essay, you must point toward something significant. See the "Suggested Thesis Project Topics" document provided by the director of the thesis project.

This is not a report or a biography. This is to be a thesis paper, in which you propose a thesis—an argument for or against something, looking at the significance of it, discussing its progress, and stating a resolution—and then you must support it using research-based evidence (primarily secondary research).

You will begin with a Research Question: something that you will investigate the answer to. After researching this information, you will formulate an answer to it in the form of a Thesis Statement. Take a look at this document from the Modern Language Association with good pointers on how to put together a good Research Question.

Please consult with any of your teachers (as well as parents, mentors, pastors, etc) in order to glean the best input for your potential topic.

Requirements

Length

18-20 pages (6,000-7,000 words), not including the Title or Works Cited pages. It must have a thesis supported throughout with quotes and examples, though this is primarily your work.

Grading

You will be given two grades for the "Semi-Final, Nearly-Perfect" (SFNP–see Drafts, below) draft: 100 points for content and 100 points for technical. Your final Thesis Defense will take place at the end of the year.

Content requirements:

You must provide a quote for each point you make in the paper (rule of thumb: 1 quote per body paragraph, minimum). Quotes must be properly credited with in-text citations (NOT footnotes). See the MLA Handbook (or Purdue's Online Writing Lab–OWL–) for help. The amount of quotes contained in your paper cannot exceed 30% of your paper.

Thesis Proposal Speeches

At the beginning of the year, you will narrow your thesis topics to no more than 3. You will then give a speech (your teacher should supply the guidelines for the speech) which will explain the significance of your topic and how you propose to explore it and relate it to your audience. You must prove that it is a defendable, discussable, controversial topic, not simply a research paper.

Resources

A minimum of fifteen sources are required. Your Thesis Project Director will talk with you about the proper methodology for good research, as well as the best way to find resources online. Wikipedia and forum sites may not be quoted or cited within your paper. Go to your local library for research help–your librarian wants to help you with this!

Notes

As a part of the guided research process, each student will complete and submit 75 notes minimum, spread across four deadlines. The format of note cards will be reviewed in class and must be followed in order for the student to receive full marks.

The outline must contain

Thesis statement, Works Cited page, a thorough outline of the order of the paper, with support incorporated into the text.

Plagiarism

In short: plagiarism is any use of a resource in an attempt to make it seem like your own. This includes paraphrasing without a citation, quoting without a citation, or copying and pasting without quotation marks or a citation. Plagiarism results in a zero for that assignment. It is a non-negotiable consequence. Multiple instances of plagiarism may have other consequences, in many cases as severe as expulsion. Please see the *MLA Handbook's* discussion on Academic Dishonesty online.

Additional considerations

This paper must conform to the *MLA Handbook* in every respect. See the examples and details contained there (and on OWL Purdue online) about citations, works cited, quotes, and more.

There are quite a few due dates for this entire project (below). Keep up with them. Ask for help if you need it. Things will snowball if you keep it to yourself. Your teacher's job is to get you through this, but if you don't ask questions, he cannot know if there's a problem!

Drafts

Semi-final-nearly-perfect (SFNP) draft

This is the First Draft of your Thesis Paper. We call it this because the term "rough draft" has a negative connotation. If you were to turn in a "rough draft," should it be rough or poorly written? Therefore, we want the paper you turn in to be nearly perfect in every way—as good as you can make it before we see it. Thus, we call it the SFNP.

Final draft

The Second and (hopefully) Final Draft is due approximately two weeks after you get the graded SFNP returned from your teacher. In other words, if we return your paper on the 1st week of the month, your final draft is due the 3rd. If your SFNP is very rough, we will return it and ask for a second SFNP. It will be due two weeks after we return it to you.

Grading of Rhetoric II Written Thesis

Refer to Lesson Six for a description of a Thesis statement. This project is to be worked on all year, and students will be given deadlines at the beginning of the school year. Below are some reminders of the grading criteria, used by the teacher, for our Thesis Project. Keep in mind that your teacher may require more stringent criteria than we list here. The Essay Checklist is in Appendix IV.

Watch out for:

- Chatty tone, first person (I/me/my/we, the purpose of this paper is to…) second person (you, your), slang or familiar jargon, contractions
- Agreement in past tense/present tense, singular/plural verbs and people
- Quotes that are too long to be included as part of a paragraph
- Information that needs text note but does not have one

Unacceptable in the rough draft:

- Missing pieces: page numbers, bibliography, introduction, conclusion, title page
- More than ten errors per page (on average)
- Too many pages/too few pages
- Unreferenced passages or pieces of vital information (statistics, quotes, etc.)
- More than 30% of the paper in quotes

If a paper is unacceptable in too many areas, it might be necessary to write a second rough draft.

Thesis Oral Presentation

In the spring, once they have learned speaking techniques, students will be ready to present their Thesis to an audience. The audience will consist of parents, fellow students, and other teachers. If in a school, post a schedule of speeches and their topics and invite teachers to bring their classes in to watch. This is an important time for younger students to see what is expected of rhetoric students. (We tell younger students "This is what you GET to do when you are in rhetoric!")

Formal dress (jacket and tie for men, dress for ladies) is required. Each speech is to last 15 minutes, with 5 minutes at the end for questions from the audience. Students are kept to a strict schedule so that all can go smoothly. (Speech times are every 45-50 minutes: 20 minutes for speech plus 20 minutes of questions, with a 5-10 minute break in between.) Your teacher should prepare time cards ahead of time to hold up at 5-minute intervals, and then each minute during the last 5 minutes. At the end of 20 minutes, stand up and say thank you, and the speech is over. The speaker is graded, among other things, according to whether he has met the time requirement (not gone above or below).

Ahead of time students are given a copy of the Oral Presentation judging sheet (following page) so they can see what is expected of them. Two grades are earned: content (organization of speech) and delivery (technical presentation). Audio-visual accompaniment is allowed if it does not take up more than 1-2 minutes of the speech. An easel and an overhead projector, or slide show (via PowerPoint or other presentation programs) are permitted. Any slide show or other video or computer program must be worked out ahead of time so there is no "snag" just as you are ready to present your speech.

Rhetoric 2 Project Oral Presentation

<u>Length</u>: 15-17 minutes

Your oral presentation may not be a simple reading of your paper. This project accompanies your paper and would cause someone interested to read your paper. It explains your paper and why you decided to research that topic.

<u>Presentation aids</u>: Charts, graphs, photos, posters, slideshows are all acceptable forms of presentation aids (as your School or Teacher allows).

Structure:

1. Introduction: my topic, why I chose my topic, and my thesis statement (may include a discussion of how you arrived at your thesis statement; what made it easy or difficult, etc.). (About 3-5 minutes.)
2. The body of your subject: research, facts, interesting situations about the subject. Develop your subject here. (This is the bulk of the length of your speech.) (About 12-15 minutes.)
3. Conclusion. (About 1-2 minutes.)
4. Questions from the audience/panel. (15-20 minutes)
5. Grading will be done based on your preparation, your presentation (see below), the organization of the speech, whether you aroused interest in your audience, and any visual aids.

Presentation includes your physical appearance and delivery of the speech:

1. Were you dressed appropriately for a formal speech? (Shirt, tie, nice pants for men, dress for women.)
2. Did you stand straight and firm behind the lectern (not sway, slouch or otherwise appear that you don't know how to stand in front of an audience)?
3. Were you loud enough?
4. Did you enunciate your words well?
5. Did you speak too fast for human understanding?
6. Did you address the audience or did you speak to the floor or lectern?
7. Did you read from a paper in front of your face or was a large majority of your speech from memory (very familiar to you)?

Questions from audience:

You must answer the questions by facing the questioner and speaking loudly. Be as brief and clear as possible. If you do not know the answer, say so.

Lesson Twenty-Seven

Additional Worldview-focused Assignments

Worldviews also largely determine people's opinions on matters of ethics and politics. What a person thinks about abortion, euthanasia, same-sex relationships, environmental ethics, economic policy, public education, and so on will depend on his underlying worldview more than anything else. (James Anderson, Ligonier Ministries, Ligonier.org)

In short, Naturalism is the belief that the natural world as we know and experience it is all that exists. To put this in religious terms, we could say that Naturalism teaches that ultimate truth does not depend on supernatural experiences, supernatural beings or divine revelation; instead it can be derived from the natural world. Perhaps Carl Sagan expressed this most clearly in his Cosmos series which he prefaced with the statement "The universe is all that is or ever was or ever will be." Naturalism is a belief that is firmly embedded in our society. The field of science wants nothing to do with a Creator or a universe that has been intelligently designed. (Tim Challies, Challies.com)

At some time during their upper-high-school years, these topics may prove useful for whole units (one or two weeks long), depending on what you're studying in History and/or Apologetics. We have seen some teachers launch their 12th grade school year with a unit on "Why I Am/Why I Am Not" because their Apologetics teacher will be starting off the year with doctrine. Or a teacher will end the 11th grade year with Civil Rights, because perhaps the 11th grade year ends with late 19th/early 20th-century American history.

Some of these discourses have also been used in earlier lessons, but we have supplied additional discussion points for the purpose of this lesson.

The discourses and discussion questions can be found in *AFE*, with more focused questions in the Teacher Manual.[138]

"Why I Am/Why I Am Not" discourses:
- William Morris: "Why I Am a Socialist"
- Bertrand Russell: "Why I Am Not a Christian"*
- Ravi Zacharias: "Why I Am Not an Atheist"* –(This is currently only on video)
- C.S. Lewis: "Why I Am Not a Pacifist"* –This can be found in a collection of his essays in a book called *The Weight of Glory*.

---

[138] NOTE: Several of these discourses are not in the public domain and permission to reprint may not be as easy for us to obtain. However, they are easily accessed on the Internet. **They are noted with an asterisk *.** In that case, you can still find those discussion questions in *AFE* under the authors' names.

Feminism discourses:

- "I Have the Heart and Stomach of a King" by Queen Elizabeth I
- "The Destructive Male" by Elizabeth Cady Stanton
- "Whatever You Have Done Unto the Least of These, You Have Done Unto Me" by Mother Teresa
- "Ain't I a Woman?" by Sojourner Truth
- "Votes for Women" by Mark Twain
- "On Women's Right to Vote" by Susan B. Anthony
- "Today's Feminist Quandary" by Mark Earley

Civil Rights discourses:

- Frederick Douglass: "I Hear the Mournful Wail of Millions"
- William Lloyd Garrison: "For Immediate Abolition"
- Lyndon B. Johnson: "We Shall Overcome"
- Robert Kennedy: "On the Assassination of Martin Luther King Jr."
- Martin Luther King Jr.: "I Have a Dream"
- Martin Luther King Jr.: "Letter from Birmingham Jail"
- Malcolm X: "The Ballot or the Bullet"*

Presidential Inaugural Addresses:

- Vaclav Havel: "A Contaminated Moral Environment"
- Thomas Jefferson: "Let Us Unite"
- John F. Kennedy: "A New Generation of Americans"
- Abraham Lincoln: "With Malice Toward None"
- Barack Obama: "Remaking America"
- Ronald Reagan: "A New Beginning"
- Franklin Delano Roosevelt: "Fear Itself"

Appendix I

Works Cited

Anderson, James. "What is a Worldview?" *Ligonier Ministries*. www.ligonier.org/blog/what-worldview/Accessed 30 January 2018.

Aristotle. *Metaphysics*. Penguin Classics, 1999.

---. *Physics*. Loeb Classical Library. Harvard UP, 1957.

---. *The Rhetoric*. Harvard UP, 1926.

Aurelius, Marcus Antoninus. *The Meditations*. Oxford UP, 1998.

Austen, Jane. *Pride and Prejudice*. Penguin, 2002.

The Bible. English Standard Version. Concordia Publishing House, 2009.

The Bible. New American Standard Version, The Lockman Foundation, 1995.

The Bible. New International Version, International Bible Society, 1984.

The Bible. New King James Version. Thomas Nelson, Inc., 1982.

Blair, Hugh. *Lectures on Rhetoric and Belles Lettres*. Bibliolife, 2009.

Brown, Dan. *The Lost Symbol*. Anchor, 2012.

Campbell, George, *The Philosophy of Rhetoric*. Harper, 1885.

Challies, Tim. *Challies.*. www.challies.com/. Accessed 30 January 2018.

Cherry, Richard L., Robert J. Conley, and Bernard A. Hirsch, editors. *The Essay: Structure and Purpose*. Houghton Mifflin Company, 1975.

Chomsky, Noam. *Media Control*. Seven Stories Press, 2002.

Cicero. *Ad Herennium*. Translated by Harry Caplan, Loeb-Harvard UP, 1989.

---. *Against Catiline. Persius Digital Library,*

www.perseus.tufts.edu/hopper/text?doc=Perseus:text:1999.02.0019:text=Catil.:speech=1:ch

apter=1. Accessed 30 January 2018.

---. *De Inventione, Book I.* Loeb-Harvard UP, 1949.

---. *Ad Herennium.* Loeb Classical Library. Harvard University Press, 1954.

---. *De Inventione.* Loeb Classical Library. Harvard University Press, 1949.

---. *De Oratore, Book I.* Loeb Classical Library. Harvard University Press, 1942.

Clark, Adam. *Commentary on the Bible.* Baker Book House, 1967.

Conrad, Joseph. *Heart of Darkness.* Penguin, 2007.

Corbett, Edward P.J. *Classical Rhetoric for the Modern Student.* Oxford University Press, 4th Edition,

1999.

Crowley, Sharon and Debra Hawhee. *Classical Rhetoric for the Contemporary Student.* Allyn & Bacon,

1999.

Dean, John W. *Warren G. Harding: The American Presidents Series.* Macmillan, 2004.

Dickens, Charles. *A Tale of Two Cities.* Bantam Classics, 1984.

Ewbank, Henry Lee. *Discussion and Debate.* F.S. Crofts & Co., 1946.

Flew, Anthony. *Thinking About Thinking.* Fontana Press, 1989.

Frawley, James, director. *The Muppet Movie.* Henson Associates, 1979.

Gardner, Rachelle. "What is Writer's Voice?" *Rachelle Gardner,* 30 July 2010,

rachellegardner.com/what-is-writers-voice/. Accessed 30 January 2018.

Golden, James, and Edward P.J. Corbett, editors. *The Rhetoric of Blair, Campbell, and Whately.* Holt,

Rinehart, and Winston, 1968.

Goodman, Richard. "The Soul of Creative Writing." *Richard Goodman,*

 www.richardgoodman.org/_font_size__3_5__the_soul_of_creative_writing__font__70029.

 htm. . Accessed 30 January 2018.

Heilbrun, Margaret. *Inventing the Skyline: The Architecture of Cass Gilbert.* Columbia UP, 2000.

Heinlein, Robert A. *Revolt in 2100.* Spectrum Literary Agency, 2013.

Hemingway, Ernest. "Big Two-Hearted River." *The Short Stories of Ernest Hemingway.* Scribner, 2017.

Hill, David J. *The Elements of Rhetoric and Composition.* Sheldon and Company, 1886.

Hogins, James Burl, and Robert E. Yarber, editors. *Reading Writing and Rhetoric.* Science Research

 Associates, Inc., 1976.

Hurston, Zora Neale. *Their Eyes Were Watching God.* Harper Collins, 2009.

Jackson, Peter, director. *The Hobbit: An Unexpected Journey.* Warner Brothers, 2012.

John of Salisbury. Translated by Daniel D. McGarry. *The Metalogicon of John of Salisbury: A Twelfth-*

 Century Defense of the Verbal and Logical Arts of the Trivium. Paul Dry Books, 2005.

Kennedy, George A. *Aristotle On Rhetoric: A Theory of Civic Discourse.* Oxford University Press, 1991.

Kennedy, George A. *Classical Rhetoric and its Christian and Secular Tradition.* 2nd ed., The University of

 North Carolina Press, 1999.

King, Martin Luther Jr. "Letter from a Birmingham Jail." *The Martin Luther King, Jr. Research and*

 Education Institute. Stanford U, 16 Apr. 1963,

 okra.stanford.edu/transcription/document_images/undecided/630416-019.pdf. . Accessed

 30 January 2018.

Koren, Leonard. *Arranging Things.* Stone Bridge Press, 2003.

Lee, Harper. *To Kill a Mockingbird.* Warner Books, 1960.

Locke, John. *An Essay Concerning Human Understanding.* Oxford UP, 1979.

Lucas, George, director. *Star Wars Episode I: Phantom Menace*. Twentieth Century Fox, 1999.

Lucas, George, director. *Star Wars Episode II: Attack of the Clones*. Twentieth Century Fox, 2002.

MacArthur, Brian, editor. *Historic Speeches*. Penguin Books, 1995.

Milton, John. *Paradise Lost*. Penguin Classics, 2003.

Murray, Lindley. *Murray's English Grammar*. Simms & McIntyre, 1830.

Murrow, Edward R. "Murrow on Churchill" *International Churchill Society*,
    https://www.winstonchurchill.org/publications/finest-hour/finest-hour-144/thisis-london-ed-murrows-
    churchill-experience-an-anglo-american-friendship/. Accessed 30 January 2018.

Nance, James. *Intermediate Logic*. Canon Press, 2002.

---. *Introductory Logic*. Canon Press, 2002.

Orwell, George. *1984*. Signet, 1981.

Pearcey, Nancy. *Saving Leonardo*. B&H Books, 2010.

Perronet, Edward. "All Hail the Power." http://www.pdhymns.com/pdh_main_A.htm. Accessed
    30 January 2018.

Pessoa, Fernando. *The Book of Disquiet*. Penguin, 2002.

Plato. *Phaedrus*. Penguin Classics, 2005.

Quintilian. *Institutes of Oratory*. Loeb Classical Library. Harvard UP, 1980.

Rau, Andy. "Ten Tips for Memorizing Bible Verses." *Bible Gateway*,. 13 Mar. 2013,
    https://www.biblegateway.com/blog/2013/03/ten-tips-for-memorizing-bible-verses/.
    Accessed 30 January 2018.

Rowling, J.K. *Harry Potter and The Deathly Hallows*. Bloomsbury Publishing, 2011.

Shakespeare, William. *The Complete Works*. Viking, 1969.

Shelley, Mary. *Frankenstein*. Dover Publications, 1994.

Swift, Jonathan. *Writings on Religion and the Church. The Literature Network.* http://www.online-
literature.com/swift/religion-church-vol-one/. Accessed 30 January 2018.

Margaret Thatcher Foundation. www.margaretthatcher.org/. Accessed 30 January 2018.

Tolkien, J.R.R. *The Hobbit.* Ballantine, 1973.

Martin, Hugh and Ralph Blane. "The Trolley Song." *Meet Me in St. Louis.* Sony/ATV Music Publishing,
1944.

Van de Venter, Judson. "I Surrender All." http://www.pdhymns.com/pdh_main_A.htm. Accessed
30 January 2018.

Varied articles. *HistoryLearningSite.co.uk.* Accessed July 2017.

Varied authors. *GoodReads.com.* Accessed January 2018.

Various quotes. *WinstonChurchill.org.* Accessed January 2018.

Various speakers. *American Rhetoric.* www.americanrhetoric.com/. Accessed 15 July 2017.

Various speeches. *Whitehouse.gov.* Accessed 30 January 2018.

Watson, Richard A. and John S. Tuckey. *The Devil's Race-Track: Mark Twain's "Great Dark" Writings,
The Best from Which Was the Dream? and Fables of Man.* University of California Press, 2005.

Weaver, Richard. *The Ethics of Reason.* Echo Point Books & Media, 2015.

Will, George F. *One Man's America.* Crown Forum, 2009.

Regarding Progymnasmata:

Kennedy, George A. *Classical Rhetoric and its Christian and Secular Tradition.* 2nd ed., The University of
North Carolina Press, 1999.

Appendix II

Miscellaneous Assignments

The authors' love of great discourses extends beyond the assignments that are specific to these lessons. Here you will find more assignments for students who want to go deeper.

Assignment Appendix.1

Analyze Ronald Reagan's First Inaugural Address, called "A New Beginning," found in *AFE*.

Assignment Appendix.2

Analyze Alexander Solzhenitsyn's "A World Split Apart." This discourse, not in the public domain, can be found here (or search elsewhere on line): http://harvardmagazine.com/sites/default/files/1978_Alexander_Solzhenitsyn.pdf . This is one of our favorite discourses, for its eloquence and lines of argument, by a courageous and eloquent individual. Written before the collapse of the Soviet Union, he accurately assesses the philosophy of a failing system, but his evaluation of the West is surprisingly prophetic as well.

Assignment Appendix.3

Essay topic: Is love solely an emotion, or is it more? John Piper in his video series *The Blazing Center* (Desiring God Productions, 2005) discusses the subject of love. He relates a class discussion in which the proposition was presented that love cannot be an emotion because it is a commandment by God in the Bible. Discuss this in 2-3 pages. Use scripture and definition, and either agree or disagree. This may become a class discussion.

Assignment Appendix.4

Take a look at the definition that has changed over time: submission. The Son submits to the Father, and that's a good thing when we speak of the Trinity. Wives should submit to their husbands, and that's a bad thing when we speak to men and women of the 21st century. Why? What's the difference? What should submission be? What does it really mean? And what do you suppose God wants when He says "submit"? Why is one a positive term and the other a negative? Discuss in a 750-1000 word essay.

Made in United States
Troutdale, OR
07/25/2023